HOD⁻ ⁻'IVERSITY
LIBR~... - FT. MYERS

FACILITATING MULTICULTURAL GROUPS

A PRACTICAL GUIDE

D0861535

CHRISTINE HOGAN

**KOGAN
PAGE**

London and Philadelphia

To Steve, my husband and best friend,
thanks for all our discussions, your patient proofreading,
your advice, humour and IT wizardry

Publisher's note
Every possible effort has been made to ensure that the information contained in this book is accurate at the time of going to press, and the publishers and authors cannot accept responsibility for any errors or omissions, however caused. No responsibility for loss or damage occasioned to any person acting, or refraining from action, as a result of the material in this publication can be accepted by the editor, the publisher or the author.

First published in Great Britain and the United States in 2007 by Kogan Page Limited

Apart from any fair dealing for the purposes of research or private study, or criticism or review, as permitted under the Copyright, Designs and Patents Act 1988, this publication may only be reproduced, stored or transmitted, in any form or by any means, with the prior permission in writing of the publishers, or in the case of reprographic reproduction in accordance with the terms and licences issued by the CLA. Enquiries concerning reproduction outside these terms should be sent to the publishers at the undermentioned addresses:

120 Pentonville Road
London N1 9JN
United Kingdom
www.kogan-page.co.uk

525 South 4th Street, #241
Philadelphia PA 19147
USA

© Christine Hogan, 2007

The right of Christine Hogan to be identified as the author of this work has been asserted by her in accordance with the Copyright, Designs and Patents Act 1988.

ISBN-10 0 7494 4492 4
ISBN-13 978 0 7494 4492 1

British Library Cataloguing-in-Publication Data

A CIP record for this book is available from the British Library.

Library of Congress Cataloging-in-Publication Data

Hogan, Christine (Christine Frances)
    Facilitating multicultural groups : a practical guide / Christine Hogan.
        p. cm.
    ISBN-13: 978-0-7494-4492-1
    ISBN-10: 0-7494-4492-4
    1. Group facilitation. 2. Multiculturalism. 3. Cross-cultural orientation. 4. Intercultural communication. I. Title.
    HM751.H634 2007
    305.8001'4–dc22

                                                                        2006100525

Typeset by JS Typesetting Ltd, Porthcawl, Mid Glamorgan
Printed and bound in Great Britain by Bell & Bain, Glasgow

Contents

About the author

Dr Christine Hogan is a development consultant, facilitator and author with extensive consultancy experience in Australia and Asia focusing on personal, organizational and community development. She is committed to helping people to learn how to facilitate and to enhancing innovations in facilitation through reflective practice, networking and research.

She has worked and facilitated workshops in Bhutan, Lao PDR, Nepal, Mongolia, Malaysia, South Africa, England and North America as well as with diverse migrant and indigenous groups in Australia.

Christine is the author of the companion volumes: *Practical Facilitation: A toolkit of techniques* and *Understanding Facilitation: Theory and principles* (both published by Kogan Page). She has also written *Facilitating Empowerment: A handbook for facilitators, trainers and individuals* (Kogan Page) and *Facilitating Learning: Practical strategies for college and university* (Eruditions, Melbourne).

For 13 years she taught as a Senior Lecturer in Human Resources Development at Curtin University in Perth, Western Australia, where she is now an Adjunct Associate Professor in the Centre for Research and Graduate Studies.

In her spare time, Christine plays English traditional folk music in the 'Band of Hope and Glory', and paints on silk under the name of 'Isadora' after Isadora Duncan, the famous educational innovator and dancer. She is also a keen world traveller.

Christine would welcome feedback and dialogue about ideas in this book. You can find out more about her work on her website www.hogans.id.au or contact her on group@hogans.id.au

Acknowledgements

My deep thanks to my long-term friends and mentors Katrin Wilson, John Wilson and Gill Baxter for the hours of thought-provoking and fun-filled discussions.

Many other people from around the world have made contributions to this book: workshop participants and students, authors, scholars, friends and facilitators through their stories, advice, feedback and support. These include Dr Asma Abdullah, Anna Alderson, Colin Beasley, Beven Bessan, Carol Borovic, Aphay Bouakham, Nina Boydell, Gilbert Brenson-Lazán, Alison Bullock, Abigayle Carmody, Professor Fatima Alvarez Castillo, Dr Shobhana Chakrabarti, Khamsavath Chanthavysouk, Khamtanh Chanty, Frans Cilliers, Chris Corrigan, John Croft, Patricia de Boer, Russell Deal, Susan Ferguson, Hedi Hasbullah, Oren Ginzburg, Tamar Gordon, Laura Hsu, Leighton Jay, Colma Keating, Kevin Kettle, Dr Outhaki Khamphoui, Dr Tim Leah, Marie Martin, Tracy Martin, Gaynor Mitchell, Rod Mitchell, Tim Muirhead, Nilar Myaing, Lucia Nass, Peter Newsum, Margo O'Byrne, Rod Ogilvie, Vasintha Pather, Azim Pawanchik, Lawrence Philbrook, Mary Power, Deb Pyatt, Linzi Rabinowitz, Theresa Ratnam, William Rifkin, Martin Ringer, Dr Nelia Salazar, Libby Saul, Bill Savage, Dr Sandy Schuman, Dr Peter Shepherd, Vivienne Teo, Dr Wajuppa Tossa, Dorothy Wardale, Richard West, Terence Wong and the late Christine Jacobs and Professor Peter Frost. My apologies if I have omitted anyone.

Regarding the publishing process, my thanks to Charlotte Atyeo, editor and the staff at Kogan Page. Also thanks to Philip Mudd who edited my previous three books for Kogan Page and continued his support and friendship during my journey with this book.

Abbreviations

ABCD	asset-based community development
AIDS	Acquired Immune Deficiency Syndrome
ARV	anti-retroviral drug treatment for AIDS patients
ASEAN	Association of South-East Asian Nations dedicated to economic and political cooperation including Cambodia, Brunei, Indonesia, Lao PDR, Malaysia, Myanmar, Philippines, Thailand, Vietnam
ASEF	Asia Europe Foundation
ATOM	Australian Teachers of Media association
CEDAW	Convention on the Elimination of all forms of Discrimination Against Women
CRC	Convention on the Rights of the Child
DIP	deliberative inclusive processes
EQ	emotional intelligence
FGD	focused group discussion
GAD	gender and development
GDP	gross domestic product
GP	general practitioner, doctor
GIS	geographic information systems
GNH	gross national happiness
HIV	Human Immunodeficiency Virus
IAF	International Association of Facilitators
IAL	international auxiliary language, ie visual communication
ICA	Institute of Cultural Affairs (see ORID process)
IGO	inter-government organization
IKS	indigenous knowledge systems
INGO	international government organization
LGBT	lesbian, gay, bisexual and transgender
M&E	monitoring and evaluation
MBI	Mapping, bridging and integrating (model)
MDGs	millennium development goals
MOU	memorandum of understanding
MSC	most significant change technique (story collection and evaluation)

NGO	non-government organization
ORID	objective questions, reflective (feelings) questions, interpretive questions and decision questions, ie a 'focused discussion'
PME	participatory monitoring and evaluation
PMI	pluses, minuses and interesting points
PRA	previously participatory rural appraisal, now participatory reflection and action
RRA	rapid rural appraisal
RES	Re-entry syndrome or return culture shock
SC stories	significant change stories
SME	small to medium-sized enterprises
STD	sexually transmitted disease
STI	sexually transmitted infections
TB	tuberculosis
TOR	terms of reference
TRC	Truth and Reconciliation Commission
UN	United Nations
WID	Women In Development

Introduction

All people are the same ... it's only their habits that are so different!

Confucius

The purpose of this book is to assist facilitators to prepare, facilitate and evaluate workshops where participants come from a diversity of cultural backgrounds and/or cultures different from those of the facilitator.

This is not a recipe book. Nor is it a simplistic list of dos and don'ts. I have produced a mix of ideas, processes, frameworks and models based on experience, research and facilitators' stories. I have explained processes step by step so that facilitators may picture stages like the scenes in a film. Readers, however, will need to adapt these strategies to their own facilitation styles and contexts. The book provides definitions, useful quotations, references and electronic resources so that you can follow up on specific areas of interest. In addition, there are further Appendices, illustrations and photos on my website: www.hogans.id.au

To some extent all groups are multicultural; it is a question of degree. People have moved around the world for exploration, trade, conquest and travel since time immemorial, and will continue to do so. On the top level of classification we all have the universal traits of a human being. At middle levels of classification we can be divided into groups according to nationality, ethnicity, DNA, genes, language groups, blood groups, values and behaviours acquired through the teaching and programming of our culture or society. At the lowest level of classification each of us is unique.

There are probably as many definitions of culture as there are writers in this field. The common characteristics of culture described by social scientists and anthropologists include: culture is a set of values, beliefs and assumptions that influence our thoughts, behaviours and traditions; culture is learnt; cultural boundaries are not clear since many of us are hybrids of many different or blended cultures through family background, studying, living, migrating and travelling abroad; we all have multiple identities; we belong to different groups, every group has a different culture (family, team, organization, etc), and no group has only one culture (source: e-mail from Gilbert Brenson-Lazán); cultural ways of being also vary over time and context.

Participants from different cultures have different perspectives on life and internalized modes of interaction. These assumptions are implicit and often taken for granted, much like the air we breathe. But we cannot see the air, so in how many ways can we make air condense into mist or ice so that we can observe and study it? Similarly with culture, in how many different ways can facilitators help people to observe and then describe, draw and map their cultures as a basis for greater understanding? In this book many different processes are described, including card sorts, role play and drawings.

Reasons for writing

This is my fifth book about facilitation and it has been the most challenging and exciting to research and write. Facilitators are being called upon to work in international and cross-cultural arenas more than ever before, to help groups work across and within national boundaries to coordinate plans for governance, education and community development and the management of pandemics such as HIV/AIDS and disaster relief after wars, droughts, floods and earthquakes. Additionally, they work for regional governance and public participation in the management of cross-border cooperation to stop human trafficking. Scenario planning is being used by facilitators on a country-wide basis, for instance in South Africa.

Target readers

Facilitators who are successful in their own culture might experience difficulties when working with groups from other cultures because they will need to be more attuned and able to adapt their strategies and processes to new cultural settings.

This work provides a practical, down-to-earth approach for facilitators needing to enhance their skills with clients, customers, counterparts or partners from other countries; with immigrants, overseas students and foreign employees; and with the local workforce for those living and working abroad.

There are many different readers who may find this book useful, including facilitators, consultants, managers and development and relief workers who:

- work with culturally diverse and indigenous groups in their own countries;

- travel overseas and wish to prepare and sensitize themselves to the people they will be working with (ie to find out what they don't know they don't know);
- are requested to facilitate workshops to enable members of culturally diverse teams to be more aware of each other's cultures and develop bridges to enhance communication and effectiveness of their work.

It is also targeted at:

- facilitation and management students who find a gap in the facilitation literature on cultural issues;
- lecturers and teachers who are working in culturally diverse classrooms and who are facilitating workshops on cross-cultural communication and understanding.

Facilitation values and attitudes

Facilitation is a growing profession and has its own values, such as participation, equity, empowerment, having a voice and the right to speak out. We need to be aware that these values may be counter-culture, inappropriate or even dangerous in some cultural contexts. We need to work with and learn from local facilitators and cultural advisers about their successes, innovations and traditional processes. We cannot assume that our methods are better than those that already exist.

Why do we need to value diversity?

Koichi Matsuura (Office of Regional Advisor for Culture in Asia and the Pacific, 2005) commented that cultural diversity is a living and thus renewable treasure that must be perceived not as unchanging heritage, but as a process guaranteeing the survival of humanity. The Universal Declaration on Cultural Diversity was adopted unanimously in a most unusual context in the wake of the events of 11 September 2001. It reaffirmed the conviction that intercultural dialogue is the best guarantee of peace. It cited cultural diversity as the 'common heritage of humanity', as necessary for humankind as biodiversity is for nature.

Why do we need to understand culture?

> Cultural diversity is as necessary for humankind as biodiversity is for nature.
>
> UNESCO (www.unescobkk.org/index.php?id=2513)

Our experiences in the initial part of the 21st century illustrate that we need much better levels of cultural awareness and sensitivity at social, educational, community, professional, economic, environmental and political levels. Currently the news is full of misunderstandings by people of all ages, cultural and educational backgrounds and levels. The actions of some governments and some religious fundamentalists of all denominations illustrate the narrowness and dangers of polarized thinking.

Ethnic struggles, mass migrations of refugees, globalization and the potential greying of cultures are all of major concern. Cultural differences may lead to misunderstandings, and misunderstandings may lead to conflict, low morale, and lack of productivity in community, work and national and international settings.

History has shown us that cultural diversity can be a fruitful source of innovation and adaptation. The travellers along the great trade routes via land and sea led to the exchange of learning and ideas. Globalization is not a recent phenomenon. It has been going on for centuries, and as a result we know that diversity can bring colour, creativity and variety to our lives, communities and organizations. We also know that globalization can bring about a greying of cultural diversity and domination by some cultures over others, economically, socially and politically.

Current struggles

Currently our democracies appear to be in trouble. At the time of writing (2005–06) there is a feeling of distrust towards politicians, the armed forces, large corporations and the media, and with good reason, since politicians stigmatize whole regions and armed forces have at times shown extreme disrespect for cultural norms. Corporate interests frequently override local interests and there has been a lack of balanced and informed media reporting.

There is a need to retool democracy to establish processes and systems which genuinely encourage community involvement in decision making and which can be developed to fit different cultural contexts. And there is no one best way of 'doing democracy'; indeed 'democracy is a set of values that points you in a particular direction ... democracy is a work in progress' (J and K Wilson, personal communication, 2006). The innovations in community engagement and participatory processes illustrate the important role that facilitators are playing in this regard all over the world (Chambers, 2005; Gastil and Levine, 2005). There is a need to reinvent our democratic processes so that community voices are heard, and I believe the facilitation profession is taking, and will continue to take, an active part in this.

Cultural influences on facilitation from around the world

Participation is not new. The Nobel prize winner Amartya Sen (2005) credits the Mogul emperor Akbar in the 16th century with the promotion of public participation in decision-making government through discussion and religious tolerance. While Catholic Europe was undoing the devastating actions of the Inquisition, Akbar set up perhaps one of the earliest known multi-religious discussion groups in his palace in Fatehpur Sikri in India. He even designed his buildings to stimulate inquiry and dialogue. The room where these discussions took place, called the 'diwan-i-khas', still exists. At the centre was a round platform, where Akbar would sit. From it four walkways branched out to four smaller platforms where representatives of Hindus, Muslims, Christians, Jains, Jews, Parsees and atheists came together to talk about their similarities and differences and how they could live together. Akbar's message of unity through diversity needs to be heeded more than ever. He demonstrated that tolerance and open public debate are universal traditions as deeply rooted in the East as in the West (Dalrymple, 2005).

Many other traditions have influenced facilitation:

- ancient stories and myths from indigenous sources around the world and from Sufi, Zen and Chinese traditions which have influenced storytelling;
- wisdom circles; talking circles and talking sticks from First Nations of America to enhance and equalize participation and speaking from the heart;
- different uses of silence as used in Quaker meetings;
- restorative justice processes which have their roots in the peace-making processes and healing circles of North American indigenous peoples, the Maori *marae* justice systems, South African traditional systems and Celtic Brehon Laws (Consedine, 1995; Strang and Braithwaite, 2001);
- bottom-up identification of issues and projects based on village fairs of England which inspired the Search Conference process (Emery, 1976), and the idea of the African marketplace in Open Space (Owen, 1992);
- meditation strategies from Buddhist and Hindu practice which have inspired Mind Movies (Hopson and Skally, 1986) and Mind Stilling Processes (Chakraborty, 1995).

Words, phrases, generalizations

How can a fish describe water?

The terms 'culture', 'Asian', 'Africa', 'Western', 'national culture' and 'others' are over-simplistic and could lead to huge generalizations and assumptions. Rather than argue on the usefulness or otherwise of these terms it is better to focus on their function as directive terms to focus our attention. We need some words to give us a starting point to talk and think. However, they are not good as specific definitions of groups, as they may lead to stereotypes (both positive and negative). Some argue that there is no such thing as a national or dominant culture, since most countries now contain so many different cultural and indigenous groups. A more specific definition is required for analytic discussion.

Use of case stories

I would like to thank all the facilitators from around the world who have contributed suggestions, ideas and processes for this book. Some have entrusted me with their 'learning stories' of successes, innovations and mistakes for this book so that we can all learn from them. Where possible I have noted stories, returned them to the tellers and asked them to fine-tune their meaning. Some facilitators wanted to be named, others not. I have tried to be true to the wishes of each storyteller. Each story is like a parable and teaches us. We can reflect on different ways of re-enacting them as if we had been an actor in them in our own cultural contexts. I have offered some suggestions to provoke thinking. I know readers will take their own learning from these stories, which could be either similar to or different from mine.

Location of examples and stories

While writing this book, I have drawn on research findings from across the world and from my experiences, work and colleagues in Lao PDR, Bhutan, Malaysia, Myanmar, Cambodia, the United Kingdom, Sabah, South Africa, Thailand, Nepal, Hong Kong, Mongolia and Australia (in work with indigenous and multicultural groups). I encourage readers to see beyond the country context and to transfer or adapt the learning from the cited examples to your own workshop and cultural contexts.

I present this as 'work in progress' to engender further discussion, as I have found that Lao Tse was right: 'The more one travels, the less one knows.' The more I learn, the more I realize there is to learn.

Web-based pictures and additional data

I have observed many vibrant and interesting things happening in culturally diverse groups. In order to keep the size and price of this publication as low as possible I have placed photos and extra materials on my website to expand the text. See references to refer you to my website www.hogans.id.au and click on 'Facilitating multicultural groups'.

Cultural background of the author

Without doubt this book bears the imprint of my own cultural background and biases. I was born and raised in North London, England, in a middle-class family. My parents encouraged me to travel, learn and mix with people of other cultures. As a child I always had a passion for geography and pored over books depicting people from other countries.

I have spent most of my working life in Australia, with extended periods in Nepal, Hong Kong, Lao PDR and Bhutan. I now have dual citizenship and as a result jokingly tell people when I introduce myself, 'I'm a "Possie"': that is, 'I'm half Pom [a slang word for English] and half Aussie.' I found through my own experience that you have to move out of your own culture in order to learn about it.

Reference to previous books

From time to time through this book, to minimize repetition, I make reference to topics and processes covered in my previous publications. At other times, I have repeated short explanations of terms and models where necessary to enhance the flow of ideas. In some cases my thoughts and opinions have changed and expanded as my learning has increased; such is the joy of life and learning.

Feedback

If you would like to discuss or give any suggestions and feedback regarding this book, please email me on: groups@hogans.id.au

Happy facilitating!

1

Preparations with clients

Introduction

Working with a minority group even within one's own community may feel like a temporary voyage into another country. This chapter focuses on preparations, negotiations and planning before a facilitator prepares to cross a threshold into a new culture at some level: national, community or organizational, locally or overseas. It includes:

- preparation research: client types and contexts, knowing your own culture and the participants' cultural values and background, and facilitation values;
- a generic cultural competencies framework: language, cultural windows, negotiations, integrity and ethics, marketing;
- what to take with you if working overseas;
- arrival strategies: watching, getting to know 'the others', questioning;
- incorporation of local facilitation techniques and cultural interpreters;
- diversity checklist for workshop design;
- getting to know and contracting with local facilitators and local counterparts;
- planning workshop openings and endings;
- endings and evaluation.

Preparation research

Client types and contexts

Facilitators and clients do not operate in a cultural vacuum. All parties are inextricably linked to different cultural contexts, wider communities and national and international contexts. Figure 1.1 illustrates the many layers of clients. Wherever possible, facilitators should try to integrate aspects of the local traditional and cultural heritage into their practice. Facilitators

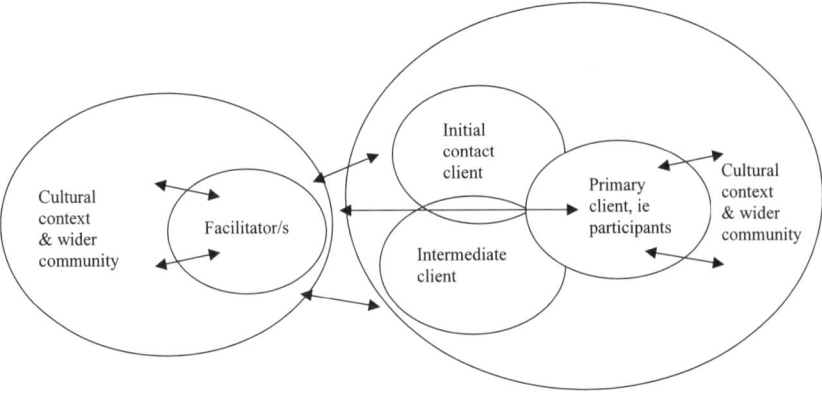

Figure 1.1   Client types and contexts

Source: adapted from Schein (1987) and Schwarz (2002).

also need to be as fully informed as possible of areas where the local traditional and cultural heritage is opposite to the values of facilitation. In such instances there may be a need to assess whether facilitated workshops are the best way of approaching local issues.

Knowing your own cultural values

Before going to work in unfamiliar countries or with people from other cultures you need to know your own cultural values and how they can be described. (See the cultural mapping exercises in Chapter 4.)

Researching the cultural context

It is important to find out about the context of where you will be working and who you will be working with. This sounds obvious, but it can be quite time-consuming, and it is time well spent. No culture is homogeneous. There is a huge amount of diversity between and within countries, for instance in customs, values, religion, ethnicity, politics, socioeconomic circumstances and gender issues, to name just a few areas.

Facilitation values and attitudes

Facilitation is a growing profession and has its own values, such as participation, equity, empowerment, having a voice and the right to speak out. We need to be aware that these values may be counter-culture, inappropriate or even dangerous in some cultural contexts. We also need to find out and utilize local processes and facilitators. We cannot assume that our methods are better than those that already exist.

Researching the background of participants

People have multiple identities: they wear many hats and labels depending on the groups they belong to. No matter how much research you do beforehand, be prepared for surprises. Many of the books written on culture are written by Western authors and through Western eyes, which might distort important characteristics and lead to assumptions and stereotypes.

It is useful to approach everyone as an individual first, and to construct your own theory, little by little, of what makes people from different cultures the way they are, beginning with information synthesized from reading, films and documentaries, and continuing as you interact with people from the culture (Hooker, 2003).

Here are some notes I made on an overseas project:

- Sit down informally and get to know and interview key people about their work (ie the story so far). Make a mental note (or tabulate in a journal) where they were born, educated, family details, past work experiences, achievements and difficulties to get a feel for the 'whole person'.
- Meet with stakeholders, ie the local and overseas team leaders and team members, to ensure they know what is in your brief. What are their priorities? Do they agree on this? What are your initial thoughts? What ground rules can there be to help you work together? How often should you meet to share ideas?
- Is there a whiteboard where you can put up your main movements/ plans so you can see where you can help one another?
- Check local power groups. Do they understand that you are there to support them too?
- Get a list of main stakeholders, ie names and positions, titles, and if possible job descriptions (both formal and what people actually do on the job).

Generic cultural competencies framework

Choi and Mihaela (1995) developed a framework of four cultural competencies (Figure 1.2) which are useful to apply at this stage.

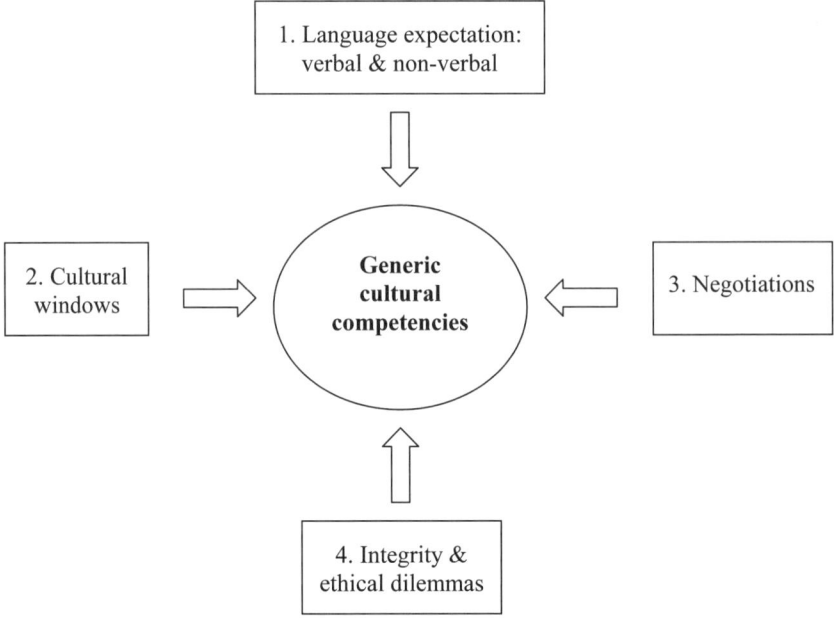

Figure 1.2   Generic cultural competencies framework

Source: adapted from Choi and Mihaela (1995).

1   Language expectations

Discussions on language abilities are important from the beginning. Language expectations relate not only to the mechanics and technicalities of a language, but also to when and how a language should be used. What are the language expectations and competencies of the participants? Should a minimum level of language proficiency be described in workshop advertising? For equity issues, will interpreters be needed? Or if this is not possible, is it viable on the day to suggest that some participants may like to sit in pairs so one can translate for the other? This may have implications on seating arrangements, as it is less distracting for everyone if these participants sit at the back.

Even though English may be regarded as the international language of business, diplomacy and research, how it is used locally may be very different. In a workshop it may be the 'language of power'. If a facilitator suggests that participants may like to discuss issues in their own language, will this be taken as an insult? Some people from parts of Asia and Africa regard English with pride as their first language.

Terms that describe cultural groups

The terms that are considered acceptable descriptors of different cultural groups change over the years and may even be in contention within groups. The word 'native' is acceptable in some countries, for example among Native Americans, but not in others. In Australia the term 'native' was once used even in legislation, but it is no longer acceptable: now the terms 'indigenous Australian' and 'Aboriginal people' are used. The word 'Aboriginal' is an adjective (the noun is Aborigine), and offence may be caused by people who refer to 'Aboriginals' rather than 'Aboriginal people'. In some countries, the word 'minority group' may offend. So 'When it doubt, check it out.'

Learning local words

It is useful to learn some local words. Lonely Planet publishes pocket-sized phrase books. In most countries it is appreciated when outsiders attempt to learn some words and are prepared to try basic greetings. It also helps to learn about local language structures (see Chapter 9).

2   Cultural windows

Cultural windows are opportunities to become part of the local environment and gain trust and empathy with local people, in a time-efficient way. This includes a willingness to engage in local customs, sports, entertainment and national pastimes. It also includes the ability to acquire and appreciate local information which may be useful (Choi and Mihaela, 1995). Some methods are more effective than others. There are four main aspects.

The ability to survive and 'get by' and 'jump in quickly'

When we arrived in Ulaan Baatar, Mongolia a couple of days ahead of schedule in the early evening, it was minus 30 degrees and dark. At the airport we received a quick invitation. The participants in the course we were to facilitate had just finished their English module, and were going to a restaurant and disco to celebrate. They invited us to join them. So our ice breaker was to celebrate successes, and we danced with each and every participant. A useful motto is 'Say "yes" to invitations' (although in some countries you may need to investigate the purpose of the invite and who will be there!).

Being prepared to 'have a go' and join in local dances, for example attempting to learn the delicate hand gestures used in the *lamvong*, the national dance in Lao PDR, gains kudos. Joining in singing with locals or singing a song from your own country is an advantage. I have found it worth paying for extra luggage to take musical instruments on longer working trips.

Being able to relate to or converse about topics of local interest and/or importance

A search on the web and look at the local newspapers before departure helps. In Kuala Lumpur, I took in the local paper in to class every day as a discussion starter at lunchtime. Sport is a great international unifier. Football and the World Cup are widely discussed. Cricket is universally popular, especially in India, and so are archery in Bhutan and golf in Japan.

Being able to acquire local information quickly for use in workshops

Networking is the skill to acquire locally important social, business and political information. It is important that you know which issues are not acceptable for open discussion in workshops. These are not always apparent from research in guidebooks beforehand.

Being adaptable and flexible

Patience is needed, plus an ability to work and cope with problems such as inefficient computers, slow and intermittent e-mail and web access, phone and transport and difficult weather conditions. Being adaptable to 'last minute changes in plan' is another issue.

One potential problem is 'social drinking'. In Muslim countries, drinking alcohol may insult your colleagues or be against the law. In other countries such as China, Japan and Lao PDR, brandy and skolling is part of the building of camaraderie, especially amongst males. I met some male European consultants in Lao PDR who made it known at work that they were teetotallers, as they found it was impossible to have just one drink at social occasions. A Lao female friend, on field visits, told villagers that she was pregnant and therefore could not drink the local spirits!

3   Negotiations

There are different styles of negotiation across cultures (Fisher and Brown, 1989; Adler, 1997). It is important to find out as much as possible beforehand, as any changes to contracts may be difficult later on. What is and what is not included is important, so consider for example per diems, accommodation and/or allowances, travel during a project, hire and/or use of vehicles after hours, medical and personal effects insurance cover, and income tax at home and at the destination.

4   Integrity and ethical dilemmas

If you want your clients to respect you, you need to respect them.

David Cox, health worker, Kununurra

Ethical dilemmas can occur at any level and at any time, in any culture including your own. In *Participation: The new tyranny?* Bill Cooke and Uma Kothari (2001) focus on the unjust and illegitimate exercise of power, and participatory practices that reinforce rather than overthrow existing inequalities. Some questions to ask yourself include:

● Are you being asked to work as a facilitator merely to 'rubber stamp' policies that are already planned?
● Does the organization you are going to work for 'walk its talk'? For instance, is the organization involved in proselytizing indirectly even though it says it is not?
● What should you do when the 'local culture' is oppressive to certain people?
● What should you do when local knowledge or practices are detrimental to the health and well-being of participants?
● Will there be gender equity? Will women feel free to talk?
● What should you do if you are invited to dine with authority figures who you understand oppress the local population? If you decline, the local organizers may be in trouble.

Accountability

Accountability affects everything that facilitators and development consultants do. Participants usually accept 'upward accountability' (to the donors or funding agencies) but not always 'downwards accountability' (to the local people).

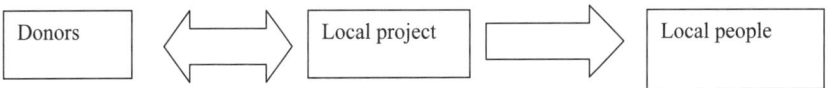

Kevin Kettle commented (in discussions with the author, 2006) that 'We are very blunt in workshops about the fact that our money comes with accountability hooks attached. This means:

● accountability upwards and downwards;
● gender-sensitive usage of funds;
● inclusive participation: that is, if it is put down on paper that women and/or particular groups are to attend meetings, we will check it out.'

5   Marketing

The terms used to advertise workshops may need to be adapted according to the cultures you are working in. It may be necessary to neutralize certain terms that are potentially threatening, or non-translatable. For example, the word 'empowerment' may not exist in some languages and may need to be expressed as 'being heard and taking action'.

Cultural intelligence

> At the heart of cultural intelligence is your motivation to learn about 'the other'.
>
> Anon.

The development of 'cultural intelligence' requires that we balance our head, heart and body when managing new or uncomfortable cross-cultural situations (see Table 1.1). The term was first coined by Chris Earley in 2002. It was chosen to resonate with Daniel Goleman's (1996) 'emotional intelligence' (EQ), but the comparison is apt because both involve high levels of self-awareness, as well as an ability to connect with and understand others. Cultural intelligence can and should be developed 'on the ground' wherever possible, living in the country and socializing with people from other cultural groups by participating in community activities and ceremonies, eating local foods, learning about local stories, songs and dances.

The *cognitive component* refers to learning about the history, politics, religion, climate, geography and living conditions of the country/culture.

The *motivational component* deals with the desire to have 'cultural awareness' of your own culture and the enthusiasm to understand the culture of others: in other words, 'cultural sensitivity' in a non-judgemental way. It helps if you try to learn a few basic words of a language.

Table 1.1 Three facets of cultural intelligence

1. Head	Cognition Learning	The skills needed to think about and gather information about new and/or different worlds. The ability to develop patterns from cultural cues. Knowledge to understand cross-cultural interactions. Mindfulness to observe and interpret situations.
2. Heart	Motivation Demeanour	The desire to adapt to other cultures and ability to engage with 'others'. You are motivated to learn about their culture and you are well meaning towards the 'other'.
3. Body	Behaviour Actions	The capability to act by combining your thoughts and feelings. You can observe, interpret and use body language. You can adapt your body language to the situation.

Source: Earley and Ang (2003).

The *behavioural component* requires that we adapt our body language to the situation. For example, some ethnic groups might need you to talk more softly, be more gentle and be comfortable with long silences in certain situations.

There must be congruence in all three of the above. The most important is the heart. If you show others that you are genuinely interested in their culture, they will usually excuse any small mistakes and teach you (if you show that you are willing to learn).

What to take with you if working overseas

Take pictures from home

It is useful to put pictures of family, friends, home and surrounding towns and countryside on your laptop and to take some photos in your wallet.

STORY: SOME PICTURES MAY OFFEND

I noticed one Australian who arrived in Lao had left his laptop open on his desk in an open-plan office. I was most alarmed at seeing his screen saver which included a mix of scantily clad 'girly' pictures. It was his first visit to Lao and I knew he came from a male-dominated work environment at home. When I chatted to him about it he replied, 'Oh, I'll just put the lid down when I've finished.' He forgot and so I had to raise the subject again. He just didn't seem to understand the offence that this could cause, and of course this would then have reflected badly on all the expatriates working on the project.

Take music

I have invested in a variety of world music CDs which I use in workshops. Often music from the country you are visiting may be obtainable locally. If you plan to play music at a workshop I recommend that you use or borrow a good CD player. Playing music through a computer does not provide appropriate sound quality.

Small gifts

Check the norms for gift giving beforehand. A gift for office staff of a large box of chocolates of a make that is not available locally is always appreciated. In collective societies, these are usually meticulously shared out equally.

Clothing

Ask 'What is suitable clothing?' Dress communicates so many things. Often in Asia formality of clothing indicates respect for others and the occasion. It is often necessary to take formal clothing and suits for special functions. So dress respectfully. In rural areas, overly formal dress may be intimidating.

Long or elbow-length sleeves on shirts are better than bare arms for men and women. For women it is important to adhere to local dress codes of modesty. Clingy and artificial fabrics may be inappropriate and hot. Skirts usually should cover the knees. In some cultures it is not acceptable for women to wear trousers; in others it is the tradition, as with the *shalwar kameez*, a tunic and trousers worn in India, Nepal, Pakistan and Bangladesh, which is very comfortable wear for workshops. Shorts may offend. I always buy and wear some local clothing, and have always found that it has been appreciated.

Check activities. If you want everyone to dress informally this often happens after the first day. If female participants and facilitators wear traditional dress, such as long straight *lungis, sins, sarongs* or *saris* it may restrict their movement, so give at least a day's notice if you want participants to wear casual clothing for an activity that is different from the norms they are used to.

Customizing materials

In many countries where English is a second language, the speakers are often far better at writing and reading than speaking and listening, hence the need for excellent and clear use by facilitators of simple oral and written English and clear visuals. Check the content, and vocabulary. Simplify phraseology and structures, shorten sentences, remove arcane language and preferably use the active voice. Include a list of terms and explanations. Short paragraphs with plenty of white space are easiest to read (Radloff and Murphy, 1992). Do not use anything smaller than 12 pt font size. Check visuals, anecdotes and metaphors. Check cartoons as some might be hard to understand cross-culturally or could even offend. For more information about the customization of materials across multinational companies, see Kim (1999).

What to check if going overseas

Do not make assumptions. Check on the availability of resources locally. What are power supplies like? Are there frequent power cuts and/or surges? Are stabilizers available? Are workshop materials such as flipchart paper, Blu-Tac, masking tape and large felt pens available on a continuous basis? Check whether there is a budget locally for photocopying and/or whether paper is available. In one country we requested college timetables, but there was neither paper nor ink for the photocopier.

It is useful to be as independent as possible from the start. Some basics include a power board (which will hold four local plugs), multiway adaptor, rechargeable batteries and charger, and electric mosquito repellent. Take photocopies of passport main pages, extra passport-sized photos, a list of bank card and other numbers, and phone numbers to call if vital items are lost or stolen.

Arrival strategies

If it can go wrong, it often does, and in a big way. When we arrived in Thimphu in Bhutan, for instance, our luggage was nowhere to be seen. The most important thing is to keep calm. In most Asian countries foreigners who show exasperation and/or anger lose face, and in some places they are deemed to be behaving like children.

Finding your way around

On short assignments of a few days or weeks, I often try to arrive at a weekend, a couple of days in advance, so I can walk around and get the feel of a place before going to my new workplace. When I was unsure what to expect, I have even paid to undertake a reconnaissance trip. This proved to be well worthwhile as when I finally arrived I was greeted as a returnee. I also try to return after projects for holidays or on stopovers. Locals appreciate this since they see such a trail of short-term expatriates. We should not underestimate the importance of 'those who come back'.

Watch others

Always watch how people act around you. For information on 'multi-cultural manners' and etiquette on a country-by-country basis see Dresser (1996) and Appendix 6 on my website, www.hogans.id.au. The Kuperard 'Culture Shock' series of guides can be rather simplistic, so I always take them in to show local counterparts. This is a useful focus for discussion (and sometimes great hilarity).

You don't know what you don't know

> The more one travels the less one knows.
>
> Lao Tse

On arrival there are so many things you don't know and that you don't know you don't know, and as a result, you don't know what questions to ask. An adaptation of the Johari window is useful here: see Figure 1.3.

Present state: Before communicating and participatory workshops

	What clients know	What clients do not know
What facilitators know	**Shared knowledge** Everybody knows	**Learning required** Facilitators know Clients do not know (Blind spot: there are new things for clients to learn, but they often don't know what they don't know and don't know what questions to ask.)
What facilitators do not know	**Learning required** Clients know Facilitators do not know (Blind spot: there are new things for facilitators to learn, but they often don't know what they don't know and don't know what questions to ask.)	**Shared ignorance** Nobody knows

Desired state: After communicating and participatory workshops

	What clients know	What clients do not know
What facilitators know	**Shared knowledge** Everybody knows	**Learning required** Facilitators know Clients do not know (Blind spot: there are new things for clients to learn, but they often don't know what they don't know and don't know what questions to ask.)
What facilitators do not know	**Learning required** Clients know Facilitators do not know (Blind spot: there are new things for facilitators to learn, but they often don't know what they don't know and don't know what questions to ask.)	**Shared ignorance** Nobody knows

Figure 1.3   The Johari window for facilitators

Source: adapted from Luft and Ingham (1984).

The original Johari window is a model of communication and perception developed by Joseph Luft and Harry Ingham (1984). Shared knowledge refers to things everybody knows about a culture or issues. But there are 'new things to learn'. There are 'blind spots' for both facilitators and clients: that is, there are things they don't know they don't know, and as a result they don't always know what questions to ask.

Getting to know colleagues

> A desk is a dangerous place from which to watch the world.
>
> John le Carré

In one Dutch INGO (international non-government agency), as part of my induction, appointments were made for me to sit with each colleague so he or she could explain to me his/her job role. It was a useful time to start building relationships on a one-to-one level, so I found out about families and interests as well as job roles. It is time when you can ask local cultural advisers about 'unspoken rules' of behaviour, but it may be hard for locals to think of examples, as unspoken rules of behaviour are tacit for them. Another way, after trust is built, is to ask for stories of previous outsiders and visitors who have inadvertently shown cultural indiscretions.

This approach was useful to a degree (though information overload was a problem, so I kept copious notes). However, it did not give me a cultural induction. Also many of the local counterparts/advisers had worked for so long with international development workers that they had become acculturalized to this environment, and when I asked for local 'dos and don'ts' they were not sure. I kept a detailed daily computer journal of information, questions, dilemmas, assumptions, hints and hunches. I keep lists of abbreviations and new terms and local vocabulary.

Use of questions

Questions can be levers to open up conversation and indicate that you are interested in local people and customs, but some questions may appear somewhat accusatory. For instance, the use of 'why' may lead to resentment, when you ask 'Why do you do things this way?' Often people do not know why they do something, they have just always done things 'that way'. We all carry out certain cultural rituals without thinking. Even when questions are asked, elders may say 'I don't know' or 'I cannot say', perhaps because some local knowledge is the province of respected elders or is kept solely by males or females. (See Strachan, 2006.)

'Safe' questions

John and Katrin Wilson, anthropologists who worked with diverse indigenous groups in Australia, developed a series of 'safe questions' to use when getting to know the local situation. They used 'safe' questions first, as a preliminary study to learn what to focus on later. However, these were only used after days and sometimes weeks of living with and/ or being seen by groups. At first it is best to 'sit on your hands and just "be"', and that is not easy for many Westerners who feel it is better to do something rather than nothing, and whose terms of reference (TORs) have a huge list of activities to be achieved yesterday.

It is useful to focus on the place rather than the individual. Consider the following questions:

- What is it like to live here?
- What are people talking about at the moment?
- What is xxx like as a place to bring up children?
- What is xxx like as a place to work?
- What is xxx like as a place to shop?
- What is xxx like as a place to retire?

These questions give local people a chance to choose what they wish to divulge to an outsider. John Wilson told me, 'I was tempted to ask "What is it like to die here?" But didn't. However, for some who were in "their country" no matter how isolated it might feel to outsiders, they felt they were home and certainly not isolated as they are just where they want to be (or eventually die).'

Frameworks

Development workers and facilitators should build on assumptions that they do not know the problems, answers and what to do. But they do know processes to build on the resources of and within people.

For example, one development worker listened to women in small villages who were subjected to domestic violence by drunken husbands. The police never arrived, stood by helpless, or sided with the men. Instead of offering solutions (or a workshop), the development worker asked, 'What is the best strategy you use?' By active and empathic listening, facilitators can enable people to tell stories from different angles the best way they can, and develop a framework of key issues and key ideas.

The women in this case decided that if they made a commotion by banging their pots, others would come running. On one occasion they tied a drunken husband to a tree, so he could not harm anyone. They gave him water and waited until he sobered up. These small groups often have no names, but they do have some collective power and have creatively developed new ways of dealing with old realities. They don't have to depend on the police. In the long term the public shaming also had an impact and the beatings became less frequent (Tony, 2005).

The term 'facilitator'

The term 'facilitator' is only a quarter of a century old in the 'West'. In many countries if you stand in front of a group it is because you have something to offer: your knowledge, skills and/or experience. A facilitator offers process knowledge and skills, and yet these may not be fully understood. Many managers in the west do not understand fully either.

Discussions with power holders

On arrival, I usually spend some time discussing the project, what the local people really see as my role, and what I see I can contribute. Local staff may or may not have been directly involved in writing the TOR, so I find it is important to clarify both their and my perceptions. It may be necessary to renegotiate the ToR with the funding agency and team leader. It is important to ask questions and sit back and listen intently. Then generate realistic work plans and time lines, especially where participation is involved.

Meeting key stakeholders

Who are the key stakeholders? It is vital to know this prior to commencing work, in order to build trust and credibility. Obtaining maps of organizational structures and roles is useful (if they are available), but you need to discover the informal as well as formal power holders. (It takes a long time to determine who the real power holders behind the scenes are, and in some cases you will never truly know.) It is also useful to map the key stakeholders (see Chapter 4).

Report writing

In the early stages, find out what reporting methods are required, for what audiences (such as local government departments or funding agencies), in what format and how frequently. Is it better to take a participatory approach so that there is shared responsibility for what is written? Sometimes locals will be wary of sharing the responsibility, or they may prefer an outsider to state things they feel unable to say. How can you ensure your reports will not end up on a shelf somewhere?

Abbreviations and acronyms

Keep a pocketbook and note down abbreviations and acronyms as you hear them. Then add them to a computer list and they can be used in later report writing.

Use of local facilitation techniques and facilitators

Facilitators from outside need to be aware that the group or society into which they are entering may well have existing local facilitators and respected wise people *and* participatory methods, structures and procedures. We need to ask what processes are already being used and by whom, and in what contexts these can be applied.

For example, anthropologists John and Katrin Wilson described to me an Aboriginal mining and pastoral community in the Pilbarra in the north-west of Western Australia, which had been formed by strikers who left the pastoral stations in 1946. This community had by 1959 established sophisticated communal problem solving and methods of facilitation using group meetings. Facilitators who were recognized as having both the specific skills and the authority needed ran these special group meetings. This pattern of problem solving had been adapted and applied in the emergent community. It derived from long-held traditional means of settling disputes amongst gatherings of diverse groups attending important large regional sacred ceremonies, when inter-group harmony was a prerequisite for success, but residual tensions were otherwise a possibility. Before starting, however, these facilitators would hold a secular ceremony in order to 'clear the space'.

Cultural interpreters

Look for local people recommended by others as 'cultural interpreters': people who have in-depth knowledge of, or have lived in, two or more relevant cultures, who can work in close harmony and with mutual trust with a facilitator. They may have an important role as cultural mentors before, during or after a workshop or interaction. They may act as cultural go-betweens to improve communication and understanding.

These people can often tell you about faux pas to avoid. It is important to have more than one cultural interpreter, as not everyone knows every-thing about a culture. There are so many cultures within cultures. Also be careful of stirring up jealousies between different factions, as you may appear to be favouring one group over another. Be aware too that not all information you are given is of equal value. Some informants may try to curry favour either by telling you what they think you want to hear, or by going beyond what they know and extrapolating. In some cases they may even make things up so that they can appear knowledgeable or 'in the know'.

When considering trying out new behaviours, Brislin (2000) suggests four useful questions to ask yourself:

- Are you familiar with this behaviour? Do you need to practise at home or in a workshop before you leave?

- Do you know why you should adopt this behaviour? An example is the need for participants to speak out in a Western-style workshop and/or classroom, to establish their presence in a group and with the facilitator/teacher.
- What is your comfort level with the new procedure? As a facilitator you may need to become used to long 'opening ceremonies' at workshops. Can you accept these as times to relax, centre yourself, observe participants and go over the day ahead in your mind?
- Are substitute behaviours available and/or preferable? Some behaviour may be ethically difficult, for instance the giving of large presents rather than token gifts. In Bhutan, bowing low towards regional leaders (*lympos*) was obligatory for locals and foreigners, but foreigners were briefed, 'Do not bow too low; otherwise people might think you are trying to be more Bhutanese than the Bhutanese!'

Having fun

When I travel overseas I pay to transport my musical instruments. Music is a fantastic door opener. Likewise at home: after my visit to Mongolia, we had 30 Mongolian students come to our home in Perth. We organized the entertainment to go 'two-way': the Mongolians performed a song or dance, then the Australians showed them something from their own culture. This form of mutual exchange is great fun. We were absolutely stunned when our Mongolian guests started by dancing the Macarena!

It doesn't matter if you can't play an instrument, but it is useful to have some sort of activity to do at a party: a magic trick, a song, preferably with a chorus that everyone can join in (take words with you), a poem or a story.

Making friends and getting help from local people

Everywhere I have visited I have been greeted warmly in the workplace by the majority of people I have met. It is important not to forget that 'the locals' see consultants come and go at regular intervals. In addition they are often committed to extended family, religious and community obligations after hours. So you have to be careful not to overuse the hospitality of your hosts, as they often will not say 'No' to inconvenient requests.

Diversity checklist for workshop design

The cultural composition of a group is only one aspect of diversity. The checklist below contains questions for facilitators to think about when planning, facilitating and evaluating workshops with regard to the gender, race, age, disability, sexual orientation *and* cultural background of participants.

Of course the best learning is achieved if you create your own lens based on local needs. However, this needs to be accomplished by asking 'others' around you what needs to be taken into consideration, as we are all culturally biased and all have our blind spots to the cultural views of others.

This is an awareness-raising tool. It is not necessary to assess all of these points, but it is useful to be aware that they exist, and to check them through from time to time as a reminder of issues that may need attention. It is useful to remember too that 'No *one* facilitative process or technique will work in all cultures or with all groups' (e-mail from Gilbert Brenson-Lazán, 2003).

DIVERSITY CHECKLIST FOR WORKSHOP DESIGN

Adapted from a handout from the Teaching and Learning Committee (1999) and the UNESCO Cultural Diversity Programming Lens (see below).

1   Workshop design

Logistics

- Who should be invited? For community-based workshops, have you checked who are the informal as well as the formal leaders, power holders and those who do not possess power, but whose voices need to be heard?
- Is there a balanced representation from local, regional and national levels: government, NGOs, business, volunteers?
- Will some participants (such as the unwaged, volunteers, the poor) need to be sponsored?
- How will the workshop be announced and promoted? Will a mix of communication channels and media be used?
- Is the venue safe? Are there escape stairs and fire exits? Is access clear?
- Is the shape of the room appropriate?
- Is adequate time allowed for interactive discussions?
- Has someone been allocated to collate disaggregated data (by culture, religion, age, sex and ethnicity) before, during and at the end of the workshop?

Access and inclusion of all

- Is the location accessible by public transport?
- Is there provision for wheelchairs?
- Is there a crèche?
- Is the location conducive to the participants (for instance, street kids probably will not come to a town hall in the upmarket centre of town)?
- Is it necessary to have a pre-workshop session for a group that may feel intimidated in the wider group? For instance, young people may hesitate to speak in front of elders: how can intergenerational dialogue be promoted?

- How can dialogue between peoples of different cultures be promoted?

Promoting cultural heritage, goods and services

- Is there an opportunity to showcase local crafts, performing arts, stories and videos?
- Is there an opportunity to make cultural visits locally?

Dates

- Check workshop dates and religious calendars. For example, religious festivals such as Ramadan, when Muslim participants are fasting from food and drinks, may have an impact on attendance and/or energy levels. See the diversity calendars available in hard copy or electronic format, for example:
  - City Nations Diversity Calendar (Australian based): www.citynations.com
  - Diversity Calendar: Honoring Differences (US based): www.diversitycalendar.com/
  - Multicultural Calendar (US based): www.tcm.com/calendar/
- Check the extended holiday dates. For example, New Year celebrations in some cultures cover many days, as people take holidays at that time to travel to see relations.
- Have you allowed for a longer lunch break if your workshop falls on a Friday if you have Muslim participants?
- Check prayer times as it is useful to have community meetings after prayers in many cultures when everyone is together.
- Check forthcoming sports final dates, for instance a football cup final.

Getting advice

- Check the metaphors and/or teaching stories you will use. Attributes of animals vary across cultures. For example, if you use an exercise in which you ask individuals to identify with certain animals, remember that dogs and pigs are regarded as unclean in Jewish and Muslim societies, and as food in many parts of China. Dogs are regarded as pets and working animals in many Western societies. Cows are regarded as holy by Hindus. A white elephant is considered very positively in Thailand and Lao PDR, but in many Western societies, white elephants refer to knick-knacks of little or no value that nobody wants.
- Seek assistance in workshop design from facilitators or cultural advisers who are knowledgeable about the culture/s you will be working with.

Getting to know participants beforehand

- Contact participants in advance (perhaps by e-mail, if available) to ascertain cultural and dietary needs and/or concerns.
- Check the ratio of men to women among participants (and facilitators).
- Check the representation of ethnic minority groups and indigenous peoples.
- Consider the participants' cultural background, learning, thinking and communication styles, age range, health and disability status, values and past experiences.

- Check English-language proficiency and/or dialect: will interpreters be needed? If 'yes' you will need to double the amount of workshop time.
- Include opportunities for a positive engagement with people from other cultures, practices and life expectations.

Workshop materials

- Check the design and layout of print materials for clarity and readability.
- Include handouts and readings which are relevant to the participants and reflect a diversity of perspectives, situations and examples.
- Check the visuals to ensure they are inclusive: that is, they include examples of people from the different ethnic groups in the workshops (Röhr-Rouendaal, 2006).

Activities

- Think about warm-up activities. Is physical touch involved? For some groups, touching and/or close proximity to members of the opposite sex might be embarrassing, so you may wish to use single-sex groups for some activities. Or if you wish to form a whole circle, ask women to be on one side and men on the other. Where the two groups meet, ensure you have women who do not mind being next to men they have not met before.
- Think about ground rules that will include all groups – for example, 'Your comfort in the workshop is important, so please make your needs known' – and invite people to discuss ways in which they may value differences as well as similarities.
- Prepare multisensory learning activities. Concentrating on verbal modes can be tiring for those whose first language is not the one used in the workshop.
- Cater to a range of learning styles and left- and right-brain activities by mixing group processes (such as different turn-taking procedures), communication modes (verbal, written, picture, story), and size of groups (such as pairs, triads, up to a maximum of seven people) (Gardenswartz *et al*, 2003).
- Check role plays for cultural suitability. For instance, a role play where a team member challenges the ideas of the team leader, which is acceptable in one culture, might be totally unsuitable for use in a culture where indirect communication is the norm.

2   Content

- Instead of automatically introducing models and definitions from outside the culture, build in time at the beginning to ask participants, 'What does this 'xxx' mean and involve in your culture?' (Use the triggers of the letters of the alphabet if this helps: see 'A–Z process' in Hogan, 1999.) Ask for local metaphors.
- Acknowledge diversity of knowledge and experience of your participants.
- Help participants to 'map' (explain) their different perspectives using visual techniques such as concept maps, drawings and PRA visual techniques using sand, coloured powder, clay and/or sticks.
- Ensure terms and words used are clarified and reviewed during the workshop. Be very careful of the use of esoteric terms and phases. Terms can mean very

different things in different cultures. The same problem applies to different corporate cultures or working cultures.

- Use examples/case studies/stories that are free of negative stereotypes or assumptions.
- Use participants' examples and/or stories, and prepared case studies as a basis for discussion. (See comparison of these in Chapter 5.)
- Examine the implications of diversity as part of the organizational issues being examined.
- Encourage participants to recognize and understand different ways of knowing and perceiving the world.
- If you are using standard development frameworks from outside, it is useful to add in the question, 'In how many different ways can "culture" be built into "project cycles" (in project management) and "log frames" (in planning contexts)?' A shorthand code could be developed, for instance an additional column for culture or numbered asterisks.

3   Facilitation

- Negotiate and invite discussion on ground rules generated by participants. If they suggest 'Treat everyone with respect', ask them to describe behaviours that illustrate 'respect' and 'rudeness' in their cultures.
- Encourage participants to get to know and listen deeply to each other.
- You may need to raise the awareness of participants who use negative or potentially offensive stereotypes or assumptions.
- What are appropriate or desired dress codes for the workshop? Have participants been advised?
- What are the attitudes of participants to sitting on the floor? Some groups are more at ease sitting on mats on the floor, whereas others regard the floor as unclean or unsuitable because of their clothing and/or status. Some older people or people with back trouble may find the floor uncomfortable.
- Provide opportunities for members of different cultural groups to explore their differing perceptions of the goals of the workshop, the processes to achieve them and the ground rules.
- Provide participants with learning opportunities to stimulate different learning styles (such as activist, reflector, theorist, pragmatist (Honey and Mumford, 1986, 1992), and visual, verbal and tactile styles).
- Encourage participants to use their backgrounds and experiences as learning tools.
- Encourage participants to think from one another's perspectives, using role-reversal techniques.
- Speak in plain English, with short simple sentences. Explain acronyms and avoid using arcane language or colloquialisms.
- Use simple humour, and avoid puns and jokes that are culturally specific or difficult to explain.
- Actively discourage language or behaviour that is racist, sexist or homophobic.
- Actively watch and listen for any cross-cultural issues that may be influencing group dynamics, communication and learning.
- Be prepared to let go of the expert, power role. In other words, 'Let go of the stick' (Chambers, 2005).

4   Evaluation

- Provide participants with opportunities to give you feedback early on in a workshop regarding your pace, volume, use of language and degree of clarity of explanations. (See Chapter 9.)
- Provide participants with a range of different anonymous and informal feedback mechanisms.
- Provide participants with the opportunity for one or a group of representatives to act as 'messenger' to give you informal verbal feedback.
- Does the evaluation form ask for disaggregated information so that you can analyse whether all cultural needs and expectations have been met?

5   Follow-up

- Ensure that ideas and knowledge generated in workshops are given back to groups and villagers in some form so that information may be retrieved at a later date for recall and/or updating. In this way people can be kept accountable for delivering what they promise.
- In non-literate societies provide tape recordings.
- Do final report recommendations reflect the cultural diversity issues raised in the workshop?

This is not an exhaustive list, but it illustrates the sorts of things that are useful in terms of learning about the cultural practices and preferences of the people you will be working with. Be prepared for surprises.

The 'Cultural Diversity Programming Lens: General framework' developed by UNESCO gives checklists for organizing conferences, museums, exhibitions, cultural events, revitalizing languages, folklore and music, and is downloadable from www.unescobkk.org/fileadmin/user_upload/culture/Cultural_lens/CDPL_Toolkit-August_Workshop.pdf

> No tool is a panacea. No tool is guaranteed to be always successful.
>
> Deal and Masman (2003)

Getting to know and contracting with co-facilitators

It is now common to work with co-facilitators and interpreters from other cultures. Marie Martin in her PhD thesis defined co-facilitation as follows (the italics are her emphases):

> Co-facilitation is a *dynamic* working relationship focused on the task of facilitating a group, *involving strong, self-reliant individuals* who *share a commitment* to each other, the task of co-facilitation and the profession. Co-facilitators *develop and implement processes for working together*, as well

as processes for working with the group, in order to help the group achieve identified outcomes in a professional way that is *greater than the sum of the energies of all of the individuals involved.*

(Martin, 2003: 388)

Co-facilitation is time-hungry. It is important to invest time in getting to know each other as well as possible beforehand, as individuals, cultural advisors and facilitators, and to spend time on process communication during a workshop. A laissez-faire attitude and 'hoping for the best' may work, but if it does not, there might be many problems for everyone. There may be a big difference between the facilitators' 'espoused theories' versus 'theories in use' (Schön, 1983). So what are your values regarding facilitation, and what are the other facilitators' values?

As with any group, co-facilitators go through stages of development as they get to know one another. There are many degrees of closeness of co-facilitators. When facilitators are new to working together they often 'do their bit' and then swap roles. Some interact almost like brother and sister or husband and wife. They can sense what the other is going to do, or if the other needs help, and interweave their inputs.

When co-facilitators are working together for the first time, a checklist gives them permission to ask the questions that they might feel embarrassed to ask. Some focus questions might also provoke anticipation of things they had not thought of.

Desired outcomes

- What do you hope will come out of the workshop for participants, facilitators, and the community?
- What do we all need to do to achieve this?

Cultural experiences

- What do you bring as an individual to the workshop: for instance your cultural heritage/s, cross-cultural facilitation and cultural translation experiences?
- What cultural knowledge, stories and myths do you bring to the group?

Facilitation style/s

- What are your favourite ways of working with groups? (Some facilitators like to pre-plan what they do, others like to improvise.)
- What help do you want from the others, and how can you signal when you need help?

Formative evaluation

- When shall we meet each day to catch up on events and re-plan the next day?
- What do we know/not know about the participants?
- How can we maximize our learning from each other?

Maximizing the 'co-ness': having more than one facilitator

- How can we make the most out of having more than one facilitator? (It may be useful to have a co-facilitator watching the participation rates of the dominant cultural group and minority groups, males and females, younger and older participants, people of high and low status, and so on.)
- How can we bring one another into the discourse?

Trouble shooting

A very important discussion is to 'catastrophize': to ask 'What types of things could go wrong?' (For example, there might be a cultural faux pas or cultural clash between participants, or between participants and a facilitator.) So ask, 'What could we do?' 'Who should intervene?' If there are many facilitators it may be that everyone looks to everyone else to act.

Prior preparation by local counterparts

Donor groups often have little understanding of the work and time involved for their local counterparts. For example, in Lao PDR to organize a one-day workshop involving government officials took an enormous amount of time, work, letter writing and delivery, phone calls and so on. Then approval would not come perhaps until the day before. At times it was very stressful for everyone involved.

Planning workshop openings

I have heard it said that the impressions made in the first few minutes of a workshop, conference or interview can set the tone for the whole session. So it is well worth investing time and effort in this session, even if it only lasts a short time. It is essential to check who will open the session, how to choose the person and who will brief the person.

'Welcome to country'

As part of the reconciliation movement in Australia, official openings at big events now start with a 'Welcome to country' by a local indigenous elder, and an acknowledgement to the traditional land owners. The 'Welcome to country' must be conducted by a recognized elder or other appropriate person within the area.

Each indigenous elder or representative who gives a 'Welcome to country' has his or her individual way of presenting it. Sometimes it is in the form of the individual's own story: his or her life as an indigenous person and relationship to his/her family and the local area. In Western Australia, one workshop was opened by a welcome from a local Maori dance group. The local indigenous participants were understandably highly offended. The facilitator tried to smooth and excuse rather than admit and apologize for the cultural faux pas, and the situation was exacerbated as a result.

Acknowledgement of the original land custodians by a non-indigenous person

In a common form of welcome to small workshops in Australia, a facilitator or other session-opener acknowledges the original land custodians, along the lines of 'I acknowledge the original custodians of this land.' It is important to find out and include the name of the specific local indigenous community or communities before the event.

Openings in hierarchical societies

Very formal opening ceremonies in many cultures are an entrenched part of the local government, business and development culture. In some countries this ceremony not only has organizational significance (as a way of giving honour to the people of high status, the organizers, the guests and participants), it also has spiritual importance.

There is often an official top table (with a large printed banner behind on the wall) and often participants sit in formal rows to listen to opening welcoming speeches. To omit these formalities would devalue the workshop in the eyes of everyone: the participants, the managers in other parts of the organization, and government officials. It is also highly likely that senior staff might be insulted.

Often straight after the opening ceremony there is an early morning tea and coffee break, which is a wonderful ice breaker, as what is more natural than greeting people with hospitality and a warm drink and a snack? This time may also be used to rearrange furniture to a less formal workshop setting.

Ending rituals and celebration

It is useful to find out what kind of endings and farewells are usually adopted by the different cultures you are working with. In some cultures less importance is given to closing ceremonies than opening ceremonies. Choosing an appropriate ending to a workshop is important, as an ending influences how participants feel about themselves, co-participants, the facilitator/s and the topic. The ending may also impact on their motivation and confidence to put ideas into practice (or not), and strategies to re-enter their work places and home and community lives. (See the chapters on 'Endings' and 'Evaluation' in Hogan, 2003.)

Water lilies: commitment to team and individual goals

This exercise was described by Tracy Martin, a development worker in Cambodia, as a memorable ritual for the end of a workshop. Water lilies have significance in Asia as they are so beautiful and grow out of muddy lakes. The lotus flower (blossom) is a water lily with its roots in the mud. It features frequently in Buddhist imagery, symbolizing that enlightenment (the flower) can be achieved in the midst of human suffering (the mud beneath the water) and that nothing lasts forever. In China, the characters for a swamp (*Xing wu zhi tan*) mean 'awakening', and have a primeval sense of life coming out of the ocean and lilies from the mud.

Stages

- Prepare cut-out lilies (about 110 mm in diameter) beforehand using a variety of different coloured papers (see Figure 1.4).

Figure 1.4   A template for water lillies (reproduced at half size).

- Find a suitable large glass, plastic or porcelain bowl.
- Ask each participant to write one commitment to the team (or whatever is the goal of the exercise).
- Each person folds this written commitment in the petals of the water lily and sets it afloat on the water.
- As the papers get wet, the petals unfold and everyone can read each other's statements.

Formative evaluation

In an ideal world there is open dialogue and feedback between the whole group of participants and facilitators from the beginning. However, in reality participants do not always tell you everything, especially near the beginning of a workshop.

Dialogue between facilitators and participants

I have found it difficult to obtain open and in-depth feedback from daily questionnaires, especially in cultures that value indirect communication. In an extended workshop or course, it really does help to tap into participant feedback early on. I observed a very useful process at a workshop in Paro in Bhutan. The facilitators conducted a short written formative evaluation and then offered four free beers, one for each Bhutanese participant who would join with them for some extra time at the end of each day to discuss the process of the workshop. This meant that Bhutanese participants could read the feedback sheets, interpret some of the comments, and elaborate on and discuss in depth with the facilitators the way that issues were dealt with during the day. The facilitators were not in a vacuum. The four Bhutanese participants were then invited to summarize the feedback and resulting changes to the programme the next day.

Ask the group each evening to select between two and four participants to join the facilitators during their debriefing discussion. Ask the participants to speak first. One 'round robin' to respond to the question 'What went well?' gets the dialogue going for everyone. Other rounds could include questions like 'What was unclear?' and 'What could be improved for tomorrow?' I have seen this process work well in Bhutan and Malaysia. However, facilitators should not get defensive if participants give them feedback they do not wish to hear.

It is useful to have written feedback from everyone as well, as the feedback from a few representatives may not be representative of the whole group.

My preference is for facilitators to receive information the same evening, as they can then jointly discuss adjustments or even major changes to the workshop process, as required, and think about strategies overnight.

Participants make formative evaluation presentations

On a workshop lasting a few days, keep conversations open, as some cross-cultural issues may be simmering. It is useful to ask groups of participants to meet each evening and prepare an evaluation of the day, which they then present first thing next morning. Divide up the participants into groups randomly so people meet with people they have not been sitting with each day. You could for instance designate red, blue, green and white groups. On Monday evening, the red group meets and presents the next day; on Tuesday the blue group, and so on (Kettle *et al*, 2005). If there are five days (that is, four mornings), ask each group to use a different process to feed back information: for example a PowerPoint presentation, role play, song, metaphors, poems, news broadcasts or using the letters of the alphabet A–Z as triggers (see Chapter 2).

The only drawback with this process is apparent when a major issue comes up. The facilitators have to be:

- able to listen closely to feedback without becoming defensive;
- at ease with uncertainty;
- able and willing to renegotiate the programme day if necessary.

ORID process for formative evaluation of previous day

There is a tendency for some groups to merely summarize the previous day's timetable, reporting for example, 'First we did this, next we did that.' It is therefore helpful to brief participants by asking them to complete the experiential learning cycle (Kolb, 1984) with emphasis on questioning as in the ORID focused conversation process (Spencer, 1989; Stanfield, 1997; see Figure 1.5). Both are described in Hogan (2003). Of course experiential learning is like a washing machine and the stages are not always separate or sequential at all, but it is a useful framework.

The goal is to develop a shared understanding of what happened yesterday and to celebrate accomplishments. (This section is adapted from Stanfield, 1997: 57.) It needs to be emphasized that not all the questions will be appropriate or needed. The four stages may also be placed on separate flipchart stands and participants divided into groups, who spend about five minutes on each and then move on.

Objective questions

- What do you remember from yesterday: key scenes, events, conversations?
- Are there any key words or expressions that you heard?
- What did the group achieve?
- Which parts were unclear?

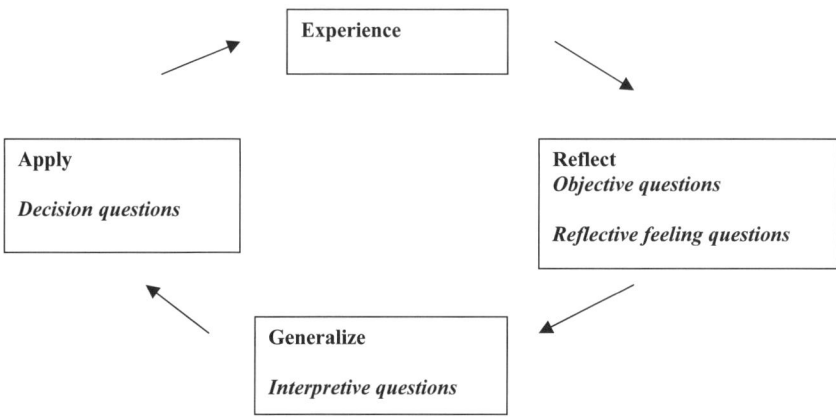

Figure 1.5 The experiential learning model and ORID stages (in italics)

Source: Kolb (1984).

Reflective (feeling) questions

- What did you enjoy yesterday?
- What was the high point/the low point?
- Where did you struggle most?
- Where did you have a new insight? How did it feel?
- What image/s might capture the emotional tone/s of the day?

Interpretive questions

- What did you learn?
- What were your key insights?

Decision questions

- What will you apply in your work, home or community life?
- What would you need to adapt to your culture?
- Is there any unfinished business that needs to be addressed today?
- What changes do you suggest for today/the rest of the course?

I observed participants in Sabah, Malaysia, creatively construct a 'News bulletin of the previous day', including headlines, news in brief, 'quotable quotes' and in-depth stories from our reporters, plus an overview of the weather (feelings) and forecast (and suggestions) for the next day.

In one workshop the first group of participants used PowerPoint very well, including photos of participants in action the previous day, and they avoided long lists of bullet points! However, if it may be useful to suggest that participants should experiment with the use different ways of presenting each day, such as PowerPoint, role play and news bulletins. Participants are amazingly creative.

Long-term evaluation

Longer-term evaluation may be necessary to measure the success of change projects.

Most significant change (MSC) technique

Author/background

The most significant change (MSC) technique is a story-telling process for participatory monitoring and evaluation. Traditional systems of measurement using predefined indicators and outputs are often not appropriate across diverse programmes which had different goals, processes, contexts and time frames. MSC was invented by Rick Davies because of the difficulties posed in monitoring and evaluating (M&E) complex and diverse participatory rural development programmes in Bangladesh. He later developed the process as part of the fieldwork for his PhD (Davies, 1998), and further developed it with Jess Hart (Davies and Hart, 2005).

The technique focuses on who did what, when and why, and the reasons the event was significant. It is a technique that needs to be used in conjunction with other M&E strategies. See the full user guide on the Australian Development Gateway website: www.developmentgateway. com.au/ or go directly to www.clearhorizon.com.au/site/papers/DD-2005-MSC_User_Guide.pdf

Advantages

Many people find it easier to think in stories than in indicators. Story-telling is a part of all cultures, so it comes naturally to people. Stories enable the description of contexts, complexities and the unexpected. The MSC technique:

- helps everyone at all levels to clarify the values of the organization or project;
- is participatory, requires no special skills and is easy to communicate across cultures: all participants can tell stories they think are important;
- encourages data collection of processes along the way, not just outcomes and outputs;
- encourages analysis as well as data collection because people have to explain why they believe a particular change story was important;
- builds the capacity of staff to analyse data and conceptualize the impact of change strategies;

- delivers a rich picture of what is happening currently and has happened in the past;
- can be used to evaluate initiatives that do not have predefined outcomes;
- keeps senior staff in touch with what is going on in the field.

Disadvantages

Stories alone in an evaluation report are not valid. They must be analysed and substantiated. The MSC technique is not suitable for programmes with easily defined and quantifiable outcomes such as medical vaccinations.

Facilitator health and well-being

Facilitation work across cultures is stimulating and challenging, but can be very demanding and tiring. Keeping a heightened sense of awareness and being ready to adapt to cultural issues makes more mental and emotional work.

I mentioned the care needed while sitting for long hours at a computer. Additionally, I take a keyboard to use with a laptop, and a computer package called 'Gym-break' which interrupts me and has programmable exercises to ensure I take regular stretch breaks.

When working overseas I take Swiss 'Micropur' tablets to ensure that the local water functions as safe drinking (and teeth washing) water (to minimize plastic waste bottles). I also take a basic first aid kit as there is nothing worse than feeling ill, trying to find a chemist and then not being able to read or recognize labels on drugs. (See the list of health and other insurance on my website: www.hogans.id.au)

For further information, see 'On-going learning and maintenance', chapter 17 of Hogan (2003), and the Lonely Planet 'Healthy Travel Series' and website: www.lonelyplanet.com/health/predeparture.htm

See also *Working Abroad: The complete guide to overseas employment* (Reuvid, 2006).

2

Workshop delivery

Introduction

This chapter covers a variety of strategies and processes in workshop delivery including:

- claiming the workshop space and being prepared;
- introductions, clarifying roles, contracting, creating cultural and physical safety;
- enhancing respect for each other, culture and the environment;
- warm-ups, energizers, room maintenance and gaining attention;
- strategies to encourage networking and provoke thinking;
- ways of getting attention;
- processes to explore understanding of concepts;
- processes to explore multiple realities and perceptions;
- assumptions about individuals, content, processes, questioning, understanding;
- linking parts of the workshop together;
- group formation;
- transference of learning;
- adapting processes to different cultural contexts;
- stop–start role play.

Claiming the workshop space

> The environment is the third teacher.
>
> Loris Malaguzzi, Reggio Emilia, Italy

The ambiance of workshop rooms and surrounds varies enormously. An invitation to all to take something personal to the workshop (such as flowers or a cloth) can help to 'make the space our own'. Claiming and decorating the space can be a useful practical warm-up activity. However, if there are socioeconomic differences in the resources of participants this may not be appropriate, or it may be necessary to set limits. I keep a box of bright materials and sarongs which I take to a workshop to hang up or drape over unused equipment.

Being prepared

Arriving early and having everything prepared enables you to greet and meet participants informally, and you can pick up important information. The 'wisdom of being prepared' suggests that it is important early on to tune in to 'throwaway' or initial comments from participants, such as 'I'm only here because my wife/organization made me come' (source: discussion with Gill Baxter, 2006). Facilitators can pick up on issues or resistance early on, and if necessary confront people indirectly, perhaps by saying, 'I prefer that participants come voluntarily to workshops. I understand that some of you may have been told to come. That could make things difficult for you. What could be done to enable you to make the most out of our time together?'

Introductions

Facilitator/s

> There is a thin line between arrogance and confidence.
>
> Lead International (2004: 62)

Participants are often curious about the facilitator(s) and want to know about their accomplishments. It is often expected and also useful to have a senior local person to introduce you. Brief him or her carefully first, and in that way you will not be made to sound arrogant by listing your own achievements. Include information about your family and interests.

It may be necessary to reinforce the difference between a 'presenter', 'trainer' and 'facilitator', as many participants experience 'workshop culture shock' if they are accustomed to being taught in a didactic way.

Participants

One of the accepted norms at the beginning of workshops is for facilitators to ask all those present to introduce themselves. Not only does this give everyone an opportunity to have his or her voice heard by the group, in that room space, it also helps to establish 'who we are'. People who have been regular workshop attendees have been acculturated into these norms.

(Imagine what it is like for those who have not attended a workshop before and who do not know what is going on.)

Our sense of 'self' has unlimited potential, but what we divulge is also bounded by everyday cultural and organizational norms. Think about the emphasis and context to which people from different cultural groups instinctively respond. In some cultures it is the norm to announce one's rank and achievements with pride; in others one should be modest. Some cultures focus on birthplace and family links, others on individual work achievements. Should the facilitator invite the highest-ranking person to start as a mark of respect? If that person is used to talking for a long time, how can the facilitator ensure that he/she does not set the norm for long verbose introductions? It would be rude to interrupt. It may be prudent to talk to him/her beforehand to elicit cooperation in managing the time.

Cultural differences in describing the self: individualistic versus collective

In a recent workshop in which general practitioner doctors were being trained in methods to communicate and interact more effectively with indigenous patients, an Aboriginal facilitator opened the workshop by inviting them to introduce themselves the Aboriginal way: that is, by describing their 'country' (their place of origin: city, town or rural area) and then their family: their parents and siblings. By the end of the introductions everyone had a feel for who was in the room and their context. It was also a useful experience for the GPs, as they knew then how to introduce themselves when meeting indigenous patients and health care workers.

This format works well in groups that are composed of participants from collective cultures, or where you want participants from more individualistic cultures to appreciate alternative ways of introduction. People from individualistic cultures tend to introduce their self, what they do and their accomplishments.

It is useful to ask people to ask everyone 'What do you do?' as often this is not apparent from the person's job title. Many cultures like to know people's context, and a question such as 'Where are you from?' gives an opportunity for everyone to tell a little about his/her culture and ethnic group.

Timing of introductions

I noted in workshops with co-facilitators in Myanmar that introductions to the whole group were left until after morning tea. Kevin Kettle commented, 'This happened by mistake in one workshop. We forgot to do the introductions, but we noted that doing them a little later made it easier and more relaxed for everyone' (Kettle *et al*, 2005).

Introducing one another

There is a rather over-used introduction activity conducted in pairs, whereby participants have to introduce their partner to the group. Personally I find this warm-up nerve-racking in case I describe my partner wrongly. Also the other participants look at the speaker, not the person about whom he or she is speaking, so it does little to help everyone remember names.

Group clusters

With what cultural group do you most identify? In a workshop I ask participants to define and go to groups they identified in turn. The more common groupings include:

- the types of organizations they come from, such as NGOs, INGOs, government, volunteers, private, inter-government agencies (IGAs);
- their fields of work, such as arts, formal education, community education, business;
- professional areas or fields of study, such as business, health sciences, social sciences, agriculture, science, technology, engineering, geology, surveying;
- culture of birth;
- numbers of languages spoken;
- number of times they have left their own countries to travel overseas.

These associations are paramount in our lives, and often participants want to problem solve and interact with others in these groups.

The question 'What do you actually do?' is useful, as often this is not apparent from the person's job title. It may be that university lecturers researching subjects like 'environmental issues' or 'poverty' have much in common with participants from NGOs. In this case there may be a strong case to form 'interest groups' to enable people from different types of organizations to mix.

Clarifying individual roles

Facilitator roles

The term 'facilitation' is relatively new in the English language, and in many languages there is no directly equivalent term. Stakeholders, clients and participants from diverse cultures have different perceptions about the roles of facilitators, facilitation processes and desirable behavioural norms in workshops (Verghese, 2003). So I find it useful to state my roles clearly at the beginning and invite clarification questions.

Assumptions about the roles of facilitators and participants

In Asia, if a person has been invited to be 'in front of a group', there are immediate assumptions about by participants that this person:

- has status in order to be speaking to them;
- has a body of knowledge to impart to them;
- has experience they can learn from;
- deserves their respect;
- will have planned a list of objectives that must be achieved in the time available.

If the person is from overseas, there may be some covert feelings of resentment towards an outsider: people ask themselves 'Who is the person, and what does he/she have to offer us?'

If the person standing up is a 'facilitator', he/she might assume that the participants:

- have a wealth of knowledge;
- have local and cultural experience;
- will want to share their stories, and as a result might have to adapt the content of the planned session, or delete some parts of it.

In order to 'bridge' these assumptions, it may be necessary to clarify role/s beforehand, and to take time to present some information rather than purely facilitate. See the stages of the 'transitional learning model' (James, 2000, also described in Hogan, 2003). (See also the assumptions in Chapter 7 on 'Facilitating difference'.)

Didactic versus experiential learning

People on the whole enjoy experiential work provided they feel safe and the activities are perceived as worthwhile. However, some participants have a problem picking out the main ideas from a discussion. You may need to 'build a bridge' (see Chapter 4) and take a more formal approach to debriefing, for example by summarizing key discussion points on flipchart paper.

Contracting participants' needs and responsibilities

Contracting regarding expectations is now an established part of facilitation work, and helps facilitators to refine information regarding participants' real needs (as opposed to those espoused by intermediate clients).

Expectations

I often ask participants in pairs to interview one another by asking each other 'What do you want to get out of the workshop?' to check whether the workshop marketing has given correct or misleading information regarding the scope of the workshop.

In collating these expectations, it helps if the facilitator asks for one item per person in a 'round robin' until all ideas have been expressed (emphasizing that if an item has been requested, people do not need to repeat it). However, there are often some suggestions that are either too big or too esoteric to be covered in the workshop. It is best if the facilitator does not immediately tell a person in front of the group 'We cannot cover this', but waits until all items have been listed. Then, it is helpful to clarify if some 'expectations' are beyond the scope of the workshop and available time. In this way the person who requested an item that is not to be covered does not 'lose face', as the items listed have been depersonalized.

It is useful to keep these items on display and to refer to them during the workshop, tick them off as they are achieved, add items if necessary and analyse the extent to which other objectives have been met at the end.

Responsibilities for contributing to the workshop

'What can you *contribute* to the workshop?' This question balances out responsibilities for contributing and learning. The participants are not to be passive recipients: to make the workshop 'work' they need to be active contributors too. This question generates many of the same issues as are often generated by the question to establish ground rules, 'How can we get the most out of our time together?'

I also add that everyone has the right to say 'no' to participation, and to simply observe an activity if he or she prefers. For many participants this choice is very freeing.

Cultural attitudes to technology

Technology is making a big impact on our lives and the way we interact. We are still developing protocols of behaviours regarding how we use (and abuse) technology in meetings and workshops. In many countries mobile phones are a status symbol, and for someone to be phoned during a workshop implies that he or she is important and indispensable. In one Asian country, before a workshop I visited the highest power holder to seek his support to ask participants to turn off phones at the beginning, with the exception of anyone expecting an urgent call. It worked.

Digital cameras are very useful for facilitators and participants alike to record ideas from flipcharts or poignant parts of role plays. It may be necessary to discuss permission to take photos – when, where and who takes them – as this can be distracting.

Creating physical safety

A facilitator is responsible for finding out evacuation procedures before booking a venue. When checking out a venue, find out about the emergency exits. Are there any? If 'yes', are they accessible? What are the emergency procedures and where are the emergency meeting areas? It is a good idea to walk down escape staircases to the ground floor to check they are not blocked or locked. Give participants safety information at the beginning of a workshop, and make sure that safety exits are not blocked by boxes or equipment during the workshop.

Creating cultural safety

The reason that a facilitator is brought into a group is that there is some element of 'difference' that requires process assistance. Current facilitator jargon talks about creating a 'safe space'. Is this really possible?

Cultural safety is defined as:

> An environment that is safe for people; where there is no assault, challenge or denial of their identity, of who they are and what they need. It is about shared respect, shared meaning, shared knowledge and experience, of learning, living and working together with dignity, and truly listening.

> (Williams, 2002)

It is now accepted practice for facilitators to invite participants to generate and agree upon 'ground rules' at the beginning of workshops. This is useful, but some participants may become a bit like robots, and list issues such as 'listen to one another', 'be open to new ideas' and 'be respectful' without really realizing what these desirable codes of behaviour mean and how they can properly be maintained. So a facilitator may need to ask 'What behaviours illustrate respect?'

A different style of questioning may provoke deeper thought. One approach is to say 'The focus of the workshop is ... In how many different ways can we ensure that we create a space and time for everyone to speak and be heard so that you can explore different perceptions of cultures and so on?'

There may inevitably be some discomfort. You need to engender trust and cultural safety without compromising the participants' ability to say the 'unsaid'. It is no use if all the participants are so 'politically correct' that they do not admit to their inner stereotypes and assumptions. It may be risky and messy at times!

Participants often generate the need for:

● respect;
● tolerance;
● trust and confidentiality: a code of silence on certain issues.

Another useful question is 'Who is responsible for keeping participants to these ground rules?' The more that participants learn to take on these roles (in a cooperative mode, or sharing power with the facilitators), the better (see Chapter 3), as participants can learn to notice and intervene appropriately when behaviours may not engender cultural safety.

It is worth noting that something that feels 'safe' for one person may not feel 'safe' for another. It is a balancing act like a see-saw (see Figure 2.1). In some regimes, it may be necessary to remind participants indirectly of boundaries, for example: 'Can you give examples that you feel happy to share in this context today?'

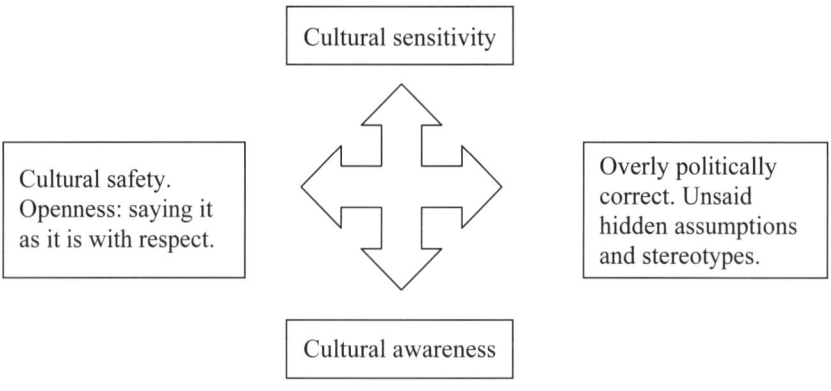

Figure 2.1   Balancing the variables

Learning about the assumptions and values of peoples from other cultures can feel uncomfortable, as the values and assumptions of participants are challenged. Facilitators need to be able to build trust and sequence activities carefully. Participants need to be invited to think and stretch a little outside their 'comfort zone' gradually.

Enhancing respect

The behaviours that indicate 'respect' are different in different cultures, so it may be necessary to ask participants to describe what they mean by respect in their cultures early on, to prevent misunderstandings.

Individuals, institutions and countries may inflict feelings of humiliation, 'the nuclear bomb of emotions', according to Evelin Gerda Lindner (2006). The repercussions of past hurt and put-downs may impinge on the sensibilities and reactions of some participants and cultural groups.

Respect for people

> People everywhere need to know they are being treated as people of account.
>
> Dr John Von Sturmer

Everyone has the right to be treated with 'respect'. But what does this really mean, and are the behavioural manifestations of 'respect' different in different cultures? Respect can be interpreted and achieved in a number of different ways, so when generating ground rules we need to ask participants 'What does respect mean to you? What can you see when people are treating you with respect?' Some look at me in puzzlement. Sometimes a concept is best defined by what it is not, for example, 'What behaviours do you observe when you feel that people are not showing you respect?'

MYTH: THE MYSTIC'S GIFT

A community which had once been thriving and vibrant had fallen on bad times. Indeed it was dying, as only five people were left. A mystic used to come to meditate every year in the nearby woods, so the community leader visited the mystic and asked for advice. The mystic said, 'I don't know what it is, but the spirit has gone out of your people. It's the same in my town. Almost no one comes together any more.' And they sat quietly and wept together. When the mystic came to leave, the leader asked for advice on how to save the dying community. 'No, I'm sorry,' the mystic said. 'I have no advice to give you, but I'm sure the answer is in one of you.'

The others asked the leader what the mystic had advised, and all he could reply was that the answer was in one of them. They all reflected on the mystic's words. How could he have meant one of them could lead them out of this mess? Sandra was hard to get along with but she was almost always right about things. Philip was too shy to be a leader, but he was there when people needed him. Maybe the mystic meant me, each person wondered. Surely not – but suppose I'm the answer? As they all thought about this, the five elderly people started to treat each other with respect, just in case one of them would become the community's saviour.

People who came to visit the beautiful forest began to sense something very compelling about the small hamlet. Visitors returned with their friends to picnic, play and meditate with the inhabitants, because the place felt good. Younger people came too and enjoyed their stay. One asked if he could join the community, then another did, then another. So within a few years the community was thriving once again, thanks to the mystic's gift: a vibrant centre of light and hope in the community and a sense of respect.

Adapted from M Scott Peck, *The Different Drum* (1990)

Respect for seniors

In many cultures elders are highly respected and as a result accorded more 'talking time'. At times this is a difficult dilemma for a facilitator who may need to move things on because of time. If a senior, older person is speaking for a long time and repetitiously, I behave very innocently. 'I am really interested. Perhaps if you have time later at lunch you could tell me more on this.' Later I make a point of contacting the person to hear more stories.

Valuing the worth of everyone's insights and contributions

When there is a minority of participants in a workshop with a different culture from the other participants (or a different workplace culture), it is important for the facilitator to validate their potential different perceptions of the world. This may be achieved by inviting them to contribute, and giving them the role of cultural advisors, for example 'Can you tell us how this would be defined in ...?' or 'Can you tell us how you approach this in ...?' Of course there is a fine dividing line between bringing people into a dialogue and embarrassing them by bringing attention to their difference. Newcomers to a country often, though not always, want to fit in at all costs. First and second-generation migrants may not know how things are done in their motherland 'now' but only have a hazy idea of the past. Migrants may be going through some emotional turmoil as they struggle with their sense of identity and 'who they are'. So we need to be sensitive: see Figure 2.2.

Respect for the facilitator

In some cultures, facilitators start from a position of respect because of their role, which is sometimes linked to that of teachers. But respect also

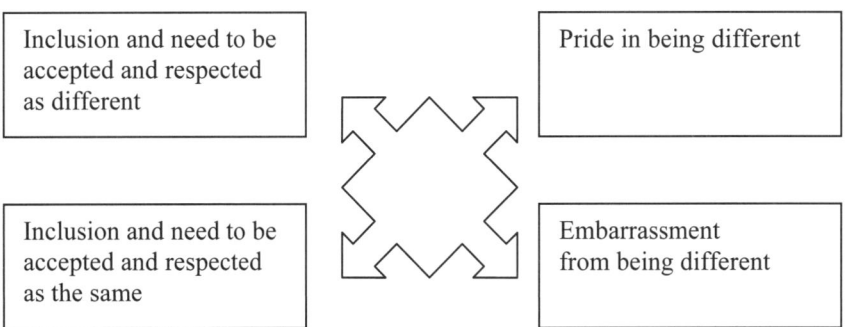

Figure 2.2   Choices and dilemmas

has to be earned. There are some behaviours to show respect that are only superficial, and underneath you still have to *earn* a deeper kind of respect.

However, facilitators from a different cultural group can also be challenged openly, when a participant storms against the facilitator being in 'their' group. I heard one story in South Africa where a facilitator was challenged by a Zulu chief. 'Why are you here? You are a woman, you do not even speak Zulu properly and you are wearing trousers!' This challenge would certainly need some careful unpacking and signal the need for careful introductions. It is worth noting that certain forms of dress might be perceived by a participant as disrespectful or inappropriate, and this emphasizes the need for research beforehand.

Age factor in gaining credibility as a facilitator

Does the age of a facilitator have an impact on the perception and behaviour of the participants? A young facilitator may be challenged by participants of similar age or those who are older (especially in hierarchical societies).

STORY: GREY HAIR HELPS IN SOME CULTURAL CONTEXTS LIKE EAST TIMOR

I think my grey hair helps me along a little. The Timorese culture has strong respect for elders. Fifty per cent of the population is under 16. Few participants are older. So mostly I'm working a lot with young people. I have always felt a mutual liking and respect. Some of them call me *Avo Feto* (grandmother). In one group they call me 'Super Mum'. Being able to develop easy relationships is very helpful.

Carol Borovic, Anglo-Australian facilitator working in East Timor

---

Respect for culture

Facilitators must 'walk their talk', and need to show an open attitude and intention to learn about the local culture via their words, actions and non-actions. Participants perceive very quickly whether the facilitator is authentically interested in and respectful of cultural differences.

Respect for the environment

Sarkissian and Walsh (2000) suggest that 'Nature' should be on the agenda when planning workshops and that 'how' facilitators do their work reflects their values. Some suggestions include:

- Ensure that the workshop venue is close to public transport.
- Provide participants with public transport details.
- Invite participants to share vehicles wherever possible.
- Print handouts on both sides of the paper.
- Use recyclable paper wherever possible.
- Collect paper at the end and use the backs of spare printed sheets.
- Produce reports on recycled paper printed on both sides.
- Use washable crockery rather than disposable cups, plates and utensils (ask everyone to being their own and be responsible for reusing and cleaning their own dishes).
- If plastic name badges are used, provide boxes to collect them for reuse at the end.
- Use whiteboards instead of flipchart paper wherever possible.
- Give half-used sheets of flipchart paper to local primary schools.

It is important, however, not to sacrifice clarity. That is, writing on flipcharts needs to be big enough for everyone to read, and fonts in handouts should not be less than 12 pt.

Warm-up activities

Warm-up activities are not generalizable to all groups and cultures. I find it useful to ask participants about the warm-ups they use or have experienced. I also watch activities when I am overseas, knowing that I am seeing through my own cultural spectacles.

Songs and activities

In Thailand, I witnessed a very beautiful opening to a workshop by Dr Wajuppa Tossa. She invited everyone to sit for a moment to recall all the different teachers in their lives. Then she and her colleagues chanted in

Thai. I experienced it as a very moving moment of reflection and gratitude to my wonderful teachers, mentors and friends, living and dead. Later, I asked her what the words meant. She replied 'It is a famous chant, it starts with honouring the greatest teacher of all, Lord Buddha, and then other teachers but I did not sing it in English in case some people from other religions might be offended.' I thought she showed great cultural sensitivity.

Morning songs with percussion worked very well in many Asian countries with middle-level government workers/managers.

Cultural bingo

This activity is based on the work of Kohls and Knight (1994). It may be used to gather information on the knowledge and prior cultural experiences of participants.

Instructions

● Distribute the sheets shown as Figure 2.3 and ask participants to obtain the first name of different participants in each square in say 10 minutes.

Someone from a different culture to your own. Name that culture.	Someone who is wearing something of cultural significance. Name what it is and its meaning.	Someone who can speak two or more languages other than English. Name them.
Someone who has left his/her home country more than five times.	Someone who ate rice for breakfast.	Someone who has left his/her home country for the first time.
Someone who has acted as a language interpreter.	Someone who comes from an intercultural family. Find out what groups the person belongs to.	Someone who has something interesting to say about their culture. What is that?

Figure 2.3   Cultural bingo handout

- It is important that the facilitator asks participants to find out about the person rather than just gain information and a name and quickly move on.
- There is a prize for the first to fill the sheet in correctly (a bag of sweets to share is a good idea, especially in collective societies).

What have we got in common?

In Ulaan Bataar in Mongolia, I was asked to work with local academics to help them learn facilitation and interactive group processes. I drew a map of Mongolia and a map of Australia side by side. We started with the question 'What have we got in common?' – our countries – and then focused on a list of our academic roles from Radloff and Murphy (1992). As we found similarities with our lives and problems I sensed some 'bonding' taking place regarding funding issues, class sizes, contact hours (although our so-called problems were minuscule compared with theirs). We then explored 'What are our differences?'

Even simple warm-up activities may cause offence

Watch the body language in warm-up activities. We have to be careful if we are lulled into a sense of security because we have used an activity many times. Close proximity, touching, holding hands and/or pointing may cause embarrassment for some.

Learning basic words in the other languages of group members

Inviting participants to teach one another basic greetings in their mother tongues works well and tips the balance in favour of non-English speakers. See the 'Colourful flags' project described in Hogan (2003) or website: www.class.csupomona.edu/colorfulflags/index.html

Energizers

Energizers are exercises designed to enable participants to move, laugh and inhale more oxygen, leading to increased energy and alertness.

Thunder

One participant from Zambia demonstrated rain making: rub palms for wind; tap fingers on palm for heavier rain; pause clap for thunder, pause clap for thunder, pause clap for thunder.

Laughter yoga

What soap is to the body, laughter is to the soul.

Yiddish proverb

In the late 20th century, Dr Madan Kataria, a Hindu doctor in Mumbai, started laughter therapy methods (*hasya yoga*) and founded laughter clubs in India (Kataria 1999a, 1999b). They combine laughter with yoga breathing exercises.

Laughter is a universal language. However, if the facilitator is self-conscious, the participants might also be. So if you are not sure it might be best to try this out on some friends first. Here are some examples. It is easy to think of others. Let participants choose to be part of this or observe.

Steps

In my opinion it is always best to let participants choose to participate or watch or join in when and if they feel ready.

1. Clap in rhythm, 1–2, 1–2–3 at the same time chanting 'Ho-ho, Ha-ha-ha'. (When you demonstrate do not take yourself too seriously, experiment with sounds and then the participants will take your lead.)
2. Take in deep breaths through the nose and exhale through the mouth.
3. Participants greet at least four or five people in turn and laugh on shaking hands or greeting in Indian style (*Namaste*).
4. Repeat 2 and 3.
5. Hold an imaginary cell phone, imagine someone is saying something funny, and laugh with laughing gestures.
4. Repeat 2 and 3.

For more information see the following websites: www.humorproject. com, www.up.givegain.com and www.laughteryoga.org

Room maintenance

Whose responsibility is it to keep workshop spaces clean and uncluttered? In most Western facilitation literature it is described as the facilitator's job to monitor the space during a workshop (Owen, 1992). In some cultures this is regarded as the cleaners' job to remove coffee cups and so on. In one Asian country I was advised by a male *not* to clean up coffee cups as I would lose face in front of male participants.

Strategies to encourage networking

Participants often say in their evaluations that the best part is the breaks! That is the chance to network and exchange ideas, issues and problem-solving methods with others from similar and different fields.

Open Space

Facilitators can enhance networking in many ways, for example by including an 'Open Space' section in the workshop programme. This process has now been used successfully across the world and with culturally mixed groups (Owen, 1992, 1995, 1997; Owen and Stadler, 1999). It is hard to market the Open Space idea, so I have found it most useful to introduce all participants to Open Space in the first morning of a conference (Hogan, 2003).

Making wall space

Simple wall charts can also enable people to meet up and/or share their expertise.

Name of participant	Area of interest	Would like to meet *Other participants add their names*

Please list useful resources below	
Internet resources	Other resources

Figure 2.4   Flipcharts to encourage networking

Making evening space

In the evenings, voluntary 'Show times' are a great way to relax together to view documentaries, DVDs and videos brought by participants about their work.

Barn-raising process

The name 'barn raising' comes from the cooperative process of putting up barns for newly weds by collective societies like the Amish in North

America. Just before a couple get married the whole community sets aside one day to build a barn for them. There is division of labour: some people chop wood, others saw, finish the frame; others cook, run errands and so on. Similar activities occur in different parts of the world, showing the power of mutual, ongoing cooperation and trust. In Australia, a suitable name might be 'shed building' in urban or rural cooperative situations.

In our context, 'barn raising' is a process initially developed by Barbara Sher in *Wishcraft* (1979) to help people to network in order to change or find jobs. I added problem-posing and solution-giving stages. In what other ways could you adapt or use this process?

Purpose/rationale

This process can be used to:

- support and encourage networking between group members to gain information and/or resources or to get rid of resources;
- engage the group in problem solving.

Time

It is useful to set a time limit on each person's issue (use a kitchen timer). You can continue until energy is dissipated.

Strategy 1 Networking stages:

1. State the ground rules:
   a. Individuals are invited to take turns to state their needs/requests as specifically as possible, for example 'I'm looking for training resources on ...', 'I want to get hold of a video on ... and I don't know where to look' or 'I want to give away, sell or swap ...'
   b. Agree on a time limit for each person's request – say, three minutes.
   c. Appoint a time keeper.
2. Everyone thinks.
3. The rest of the participants make quick suggestions. This is not an opportunity to give a long explanation. What are needed are comments like 'I've got materials on ... Let's chat at the break' and 'Why don't you give the state reference library a call?'
4. The person who requested help quickly writes down ideas and/or asks clarifying questions where necessary.
5. The facilitator keeps the pace going.

Strategy 2 Problem-posing/questioning stages:

Invite one participant at a time to describe to the group one problem or issue with people, situations or organizations (or whatever is the focus of the group, such as dealing with difficult behaviour).

State the changed ground rules:

- The group must listen carefully to the problem-poser.
- The problem-poser needs to try to keep an open mind.
- If a participant tells a story of an event, he/she may need reminding to use pseudonyms to protect people who are not present but are known by the group.
- Group members may need to be reminded about confidentiality.
- Any participant may ask clarifying questions.
- Participants should only ask questions, *not* pose solutions, so that the problem-poser tries to solve his/her own problems.
- Questions like: 'Have you tried …?' are not allowed as they are solutions in disguise.

Strategy 3   Solution-giving stages

I only use this stage as a last resort. State the changed ground rules:
- Everyone must listen carefully to the problem-poser.
- Individuals may offer suggestions/strategies and so on.
- The facilitator may need to summarize options and lead a discussion about the potential advantages and disadvantages of each suggestion where appropriate.
- The person who poses the problem must keep an open mind and listen rather than immediately rejecting an idea.

If the issue being discussed relates to interpersonal issues, it may be useful to role play different suggestions and/or strategies. Be careful to give volunteer role players pseudonyms so it is clear to the group that they are acting out of their normal role.

Advantages

Barn raising is a useful process to develop mutual helping within a group. It also invites individuals to 'make their needs known'. This is a very useful process to develop the values of a learning organization.

Disadvantages

The process relies on the group members having trust in one another. In some cultures admitting to having a problem may be perceived as weakness. Some problems may be considered by some as inappropriate for an open forum (for example power issues, gender issues).

Strategies to provoke thinking

Use of quotations

Published quotes

Leaving quotations around the walls can often make a point without labouring it. For example, in a workshop for doctors on indigenous health in Australia, we displayed charts indicating the abysmal health statistics for indigenous people. The point was illustrated without the facilitators saying anything. We also displayed a powerful poem entitled 'Speaking out' by Pastor Niemoeller (a victim of the Nazis) to encourage doctors to take a more proactive role in Aboriginal health in their community. I noticed a few of them copied it into their notebooks (see my website, www.hogans.id.au).

Participants' quotable quotes

Participants sometimes make the most beautiful and inspired comments, yet so often these get lost. It is useful to have a co-facilitator or a participant to listen out for these and put them on a card for display. Examples include 'Empowerment means learning to illuminate the choices available.' and 'If you always do the same thing, nothing will change.'

Processes to explore understanding of concepts

Body sculptures

It is useful to introduce a group body sculpture exercise as a warm-up. This requires small groups (in some societies it is best to ask women and men to form separate groups) to make a tableau of their perception of a concept and to illustrate it as if they are a still sculpture in a museum. Then they explain their interpretation to the group. The facilitator can take a photo on a digital camera or sketch it and its meaning on a flipchart, and then compare with another sculpture made by the same group at the end to show changes in understanding by inviting each group to explain how their interpretations of a concept has changed.

The same technique can be adapted by asking participants to draw their perceptions, before and after.

Exploring meaning of 'culture' through definitions

One way to engage people actively is to ask them to explore current definitions of a concept.

Purpose

This exercise was developed to enable participants to:

- develop a deep understanding of the concept of 'culture';
- come to an understanding that there is no one 'best' definition (what is important is that members of a work team and/or community need to know what each other means by certain words and concepts: Kettle and Saul, 2004).

Stages

1. Divide participants into small groups of a maximum of five people.
2. Distribute eight definitions of 'culture' minus their source (as this may bias perceptions), each on a separate card to each group (see Figure 2.5).
3. Ask each group to discuss the definitions, and note what they do and don't like about each one. (Note that definition number 8 includes gender-specific language on purpose to see if participants react to it and to stimulate discussion.)
4. Ask the participants to select the 'best' definition and to alter it to improve it (if necessary).
5. Ask each group to write their own definition, if they are not completely happy with those provided.
6. Ask each group to select a representative to report back to the whole workshop.

Note that some participants who are used to didactic teaching may find this exercise a little uncomfortable and expect facilitators to sum up by giving the 'best' definition.

In one workshop comprising Malaysian, Filipino and Indonesian participants, they selected words from the quotations they 'liked', such as 'rich', 'complex', 'dynamic', 'living', 'stories', 'organic', 'unconsciously' and 'evolving'. They also identified words they disliked, such as 'man', as it was not gender-sensitive, and 'simple', as culture was anything but simple. What was interesting is that all six groups developed their own preferred definition. However, in the debrief some participants still expected to be given the 'best definition' by the facilitators, as that is what they were used to in their formal education setting.

Exploring meaning through drawings

See Chapter 6.

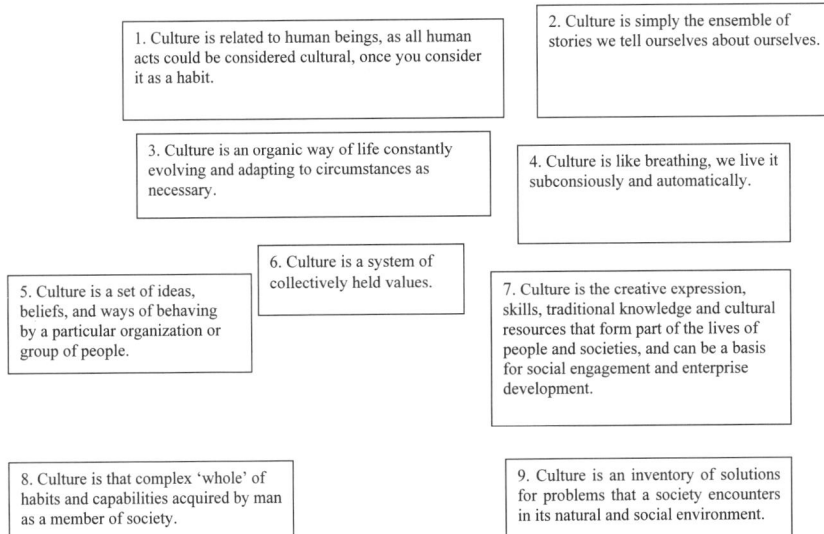

Figure 2.5 Examples of quotations given to participants to discuss

Processes to explore multiple realities and perception

Perceptions, generalizations and assumptions

We all make assumptions. They are a fact of life. This was really driven home to me by a development worker in Asia who visited teachers who had been on a course about 'participant-centred learning'. The teachers had all returned to their classrooms and introduced 'group work'. When the development worker visited the school later, she observed a group of teachers chatting happily outside their classrooms. The children inside were in small groups chatting too, but with few if any directives. In other words the teachers had not fully understood what the concept of 'group work' meant, and the need for teachers to be visible, walk around, monitor, encourage questions and so on. Both sides had deficiencies in their understanding. Partly it may have been due to semantics: after all the students *were* in groups.

Sometimes it is important to learn people's levels of perception of reality, by asking questions such as: 'What does education mean to you?' 'Can you describe a meaningful learning experience?' 'What were the components of that experience?' 'In how many different ways do you learn?' 'What do you learn when you talk to one another in small groups?' 'Are you concerned that students/participants will talk about something else? If "yes", how can you design activities to ensure they stay on task?' 'Why might it be useful to teach students/participants how to discuss issues in small groups?' 'How can you manage the noise?'

See the work of Epstein (1999) and Kotler, Roberto and Lee (2002) on 'social marketing' techniques to stimulate behaviour change.

Heightening awareness of perceptions and assumptions using cultural objects

In this exercise, the facilitator passes around a number of unusual objects or pictures of unusual scenes from different cultures to the participants to identify. This strategy illustrates how quickly we jump to conclusions about things we know nothing about.

The DIE model is designed to stop us jumping to conclusions when we see new things (Wendt,1984):

Describe	what you see
Interpret	the evidence
Evaluate	your decision

I would add 'When in doubt, ask', and check responses with more than one person. It is easy for facilitators to gather examples that might include:

- an Aboriginal message stick or musical click sticks;
- a Jewish *mezuzah* (container nailed to a doorpost containing a parchment with words from the Torah);
- a small metal earpick or wax remover spoon (available in markets in Asia);
- sticky rice baskets from Lao PDR.
- Khipus, Peruvian Inca knotted cards for accounting and recording events.

See processes in Chapter 7: Raising awareness of assumptions and stereotypes.

Heightening awareness of perceptions and assumptions of outsiders and insiders

In workshops with people from different cultures, a story can raise awareness of how 'insiders' and 'outsiders' perceive the same environment and their own needs and wants totally differently. The story of the 'Millionaire and the boat' (source unknown) is an example of one way to lighten the seriousness of workshops and jolt thinking about the value differences which underpin our perceptions of development, happiness, career and life aspirations.

STORY: THE MILLIONAIRE AND THE BOAT

A millionaire had just arrived at a tropical island in his whale-sized white yacht. He walked along a jetty and met a local fisherman. The two men sat staring out across the turquoise sea, chatting calmly about this and that.

The visitor asked the fisherman about his life. The fisherman gladly obliged and described his simple existence, a few hours of fishing in the morning and how he loved to sit and chat with friends, doze or gaze out to sea under the palm trees in the heat of the afternoon. He pointed proudly to a rather old flaking boat moored in the harbour.

The millionaire was not impressed, and said, 'If you take your boat out twice a day, instead of once, you could make a profit and gradually you could build up enough money to get a loan from the bank, and then you could buy another boat, then get another loan, and then get a fleet. Then you will be able to be like me and go off for vacations on a yacht to an island like this.'

The puzzled fisherman looked at him, shook his head in bewilderment, and replied, 'But I'm already here.'

This story is wonderful for illustrating the different cultural values of 'being' and 'doing' described in Chapter 4.

Heightening awareness of perceptions and assumptions about individuals

We all make assumptions about people we see and meet, often because of age (either 'they might be too young to know anything about ...' or 'they might be too old to be able to do ...' I saw the following exercise demonstrated at the beginning of an organizational behaviour teaching conference in the United States some years ago. The conference organizers asked the 350 delegates to arrange themselves down the stepped lecture theatre according to age, with the oldest at the top and youngest at the front. I and my colleagues from Australia sat dumbfounded as this seemed totally inappropriate. However, we noticed the senior Chinese delegates quite happily climbing the stairs to the top and most important place. Then the organizers stopped the exercise and asked those who had moved to return to their seats. They invited us to discuss the different cultural approaches to age. Indeed they had started the exercise to provoke us to think about what is suitable and what is not suitable in culturally diverse groups.

I witnessed the same exercise used by other facilitators in Myanmar; older women were particularly embarrassed and said so at lunchtime. We cannot assume that in cultures where older people are more respected that people still do not feel reluctant and or compromised by an exercise where they feel group pressure to divulge their ages (Heslop, 2002). So personally I do not use this exercise. As a result of this experience, I often warn facilitation students not to use this exercise in case some people might feel embarrassed. See 'Ladder of assumptions or inference' in Chapter 7.

Creative visualization or 'mind movies'

Creative visualizations or 'mind movies' are guided meditations led by the facilitator to focus the attention of participants on a topic (past, present, future; real or imaginary): for specific instructions see Hogan (2000: 129–30).

I was facilitating a workshop entitled 'Managing transitions to your home country' for mature postgraduate international students. We were at the stage of thinking about issues of returning to previous workplaces. I invited participants to visualize walking into their office, saying 'Close your eyes. Let's think about your life on your return.' Some participants from Papua New Guinea looked alarmed, and said, 'Are you trying to hypnotize us?' So now I always give options along the lines 'We are going to do a visualization exercise. It requires your focused concentration. You might like to close your eyes, or stare at the carpet or the wall.' I had made a process assumption that to close eyes in a group was all right for everyone. It is not.

Assumptions

Assumptions about questions and understanding

> He who asks is a fool for five minutes, but he who does not ask remains a fool forever.
>
> Chinese proverb

Somehow the facilitator needs to find out ways of giving participants confidence to communicate when they do not understand. The request 'Ask if you do not understand' is not always heeded, as in as many cultures this can mean loss of face. The question 'Do you understand?' is unlikely to get a genuine response. It is useful to remember that in many cultures:

> There are 1,000 ways of saying 'yes', and 999 mean 'no'.

In some cultures, questions are discouraged by controlling teaching systems. So as facilitators we need to be mindful of our participants and the dynamics of their schooling. Their lack of questioning may not mean that they do not have questions, but be the result of their having developed very practical survival tactics.

Bhutan was heavily influenced by the Indian didactic education system (which in turn was moulded by six to seven generations subjected to the British colonial system). A local work colleague, let's call her Sonam, who was very outgoing, was keen to learn about facilitation. As I was mentoring her, I asked her what some of the terms that she was using meant. She admitted she had not understood them when another Bhutanese colleague had briefed her. I asked why she did not ask for an explanation at the time. Her first response was 'Oh, he was very busy', but then she added, 'At school we were taught that it was so insulting to the teacher to ask questions. It was our job to understand and if we didn't it was our fault.' I asked Sonam what she did if she did not understand something. 'Oh, I just buried it.' She had obviously developed a way of coping with the stress of not understanding.

Without questions we become moribund.

Kaplan (2002)

In many cultures asking a question may mean loss of face not only for the student but also for the teacher (as it implies he/she may not have explained something properly).

Content assumptions

'Content assumptions' are those that deal with data, concepts and facts, such as roles, status, contracts and governance functions. Some things to take into consideration are noted below.

Cultural bias of facilitation

- Be aware that all facilitation strategies contain a cultural imprint, whether implicit or explicit. Facilitation is not value-free, nor are facilitation processes.
- In some cultures, participation of people from all levels is neither wanted nor valued, and as a result, a workshop may not be the most appropriate way of gathering ideas. A better choice might be shuttle diplomacy: that is, talking with individuals separately or in groups of people from similar levels.
- Note the danger that group facilitation techniques may submerge individual differences (or those of minority groups). You are likely to need strategies to overcome this (such as brain writing – see chapter 10 of Hogan, 2003). The non-conformist or divergent view may throw up some really interesting aspects of an issue. Paradox is often important in itself! Paradoxes or seemingly absurd or contradictory statements are often important, and help participants to think about ideas from different angles.

- The choice of processes and techniques needs to be compatible with the aims of the workshop and the cultures and context of the participants.
- Avoid stereotyping and generalizations: for example, that an individual represents a culture, that all age groups have the same cultural values, and that city and rural dwellers have the same values.

Realize cross-cultural facilitation is messy and confusing at times

- Be curious. Ask questions. Investigate differences in perceptions and understandings.
- Be aware that sometimes you, the facilitator, do not know what questions need to be asked.
- Be aware that sometimes participants do not know what questions to ask. Their culture may have suppressed questioning and the learning of questioning skills as a result.
- Participants may not know what they don't know, and what they need to know.
- Facilitators may not know what they don't know, and what they need to know.
- Be aware that some questions may cause offence, so you may need to preface them with 'I'm not sure if I should ask this question …' and wait for a response.
- Use your mind, body and spirit to integrate what is happening. When judging begins, learning stops (Richard West, personal communication, 2003).
- Be sensitive to possible differences as well as to similarities.
- Actively listen with empathy and set the scene to encourage participants to do the same. A key facilitation skill is to 'facilitate learning'.

Develop strategies to manage when you are out of your comfort zone

- Be comfortable (or develop strategies to be comfortable) with silence.
- Be comfortable (or develop strategies to be comfortable) with everyone talking and showing emotion at once as happens in some Hispanic cultures.
- Establish comfortable contexts for interaction.
- Develop a high tolerance for ambiguity. Be flexible and open.
- Look for ways of building bridges with two-way and multi-way interactions. Better still, encourage participants to identify bridges.
- Look for examples of music from different cultures, and play music that represents different cultures represented in your workshop. Invite participants to sing their songs, and teach them to others.
- Do not swear.

- It is important to involve participants in evaluation of the processes used as well as feedback on the overall success factors of the workshop.

Learn about other cultures in a variety of ways

- Learn about your own culture, and its 'cultural values' (see Chapter 4).
- Show genuine interest in learning about other cultures;
- Watch movies like: *Babel*; *Ten Canoes*; *Rabit-Proof Fence*; *Yasmin*; *Bend it like Beckham*; *Japanese Story*; *Farewell My Concubine*; *Madam Sowatka*; *The Joy Luck Club*; *Mississippi Masala*; *The Wedding Banquet*; *Wild Swans*; *Iron and Silk*; *My Beautiful Laundrette*; *The Scent of the Green Papaya*; *Gung Ho*; *A Tale of O*; *Blue Eyes/Brown Eyes*; *Himalaya*; *The Other Final*; *Travellers and Magicians*; *Bride and Prejudice*; *Amandla!*; *Ae Fond Kiss*; *Suzie Gold*; *Spring, Summer, Autumn, Winter, Spring*; *Yesterday*; *Live and Become* and *Sons for the Return Home*.
- Read books on diversity issues including, biographies and autobiographies.
- Collect folk tales from around the world; they can teach us so much.
- Step out of your own 'space' in your own community and participate in multicultural events and celebrations.
- Develop friendships with people from other cultures.
- Discover the truth and wisdom in every culture, and concentrate on acknowledging and understanding specific behaviours rather than judging them (Gibert Brenson-Lazán, personal communication, 2003).

Time assumptions

Flexible process versus tight timekeeping

A common value held in facilitation circles is to be flexible according to the needs of the group members. However, in cultures where facilitation is new, being flexible and changing the agenda may appear unorganized to some who see the facilitator as an authority figure. 'I tell them I will be flexible in timing according to the energies of the group, and have breaks when they need them', Lucia Nass commented to me.

Some participants may still be seeing you as a 'teacher', therefore if some objectives are not met because of how you facilitated, they may feel disappointed. It's a dilemma! There are different cultural attitudes to 'completing' objectives. In facilitation 'culture' we expect some groups to finish everything quickly, while others may not finish. Sometimes we want to give participants an introduction to a process, trusting that they will learn it quickly and may use it later.

Process assumptions in indigenous communities

The following story illustrates the many ways in which we as facilitators make assumptions, especially when we have much loved, tried and tested processes which we then transfer to different situations.

STORY: IT'S NOT YOUR FAULT YOU ARE WHITEFELLAS

My co-facilitator and I went to Warburton (a very remote small community of about 150 people) in the remote east of Western Australia (WA) to conduct a workshop. We had been employed to work with the teaching assistants to help them understand the concept of 'learning outcomes' as enunciated in the WA Curriculum Framework. All the assistants were Aboriginal women.

We had already been informed that the Standard Australian English literacy levels of the women were not high, and that their own experience of school meant that they required that children listen, sit still and write. Flexible teaching strategies, active and experiential activities that the teachers were endeavouring to use with the children were often overtaken by the teaching assistants' desire for the children to get things right and 'learn'. In part, our job was to help the assistants understand that schooling in WA was changing, and that their children would still learn in the new ways, perhaps even more effectively than they did when they were in school.

We prepared a series of activities for the women to do: storytelling, drawing, writing, creating with playdough and some physical activities designed to focus on number and measurement. The last of these was based on one of our favourite 'tried and tested' activities. We asked the women to line up alphabetically by the initial of their first name. The women completed this task easily. We asked them to line up again in order of height. They just stood and looked at us, totally bewildered. 'You know,' we tried to explain, 'some of you are taller or shorter than the others.' Again total confusion and now, some giggling as we stood the women back to back and asked others who was taller or shorter and slowly created the line.

Having not yet worked out the problem, we decided we would ask them to line up again in order of shoe size. This time, while there was understanding of what was required, the whole process was just ridiculous and, though they completed the task, there was a great deal of laughter and much animated conversation in their Aboriginal language.

For the rest of the day, the women worked together, conversed excitedly, participated in everything and there was much laughter, both with us and at us. The next morning, all of the women returned to complete the workshop: a sign, we knew, that we had done something right. They were all pretty adept too at naming the outcomes that were being demonstrated in the tasks we did.

At the end of the workshop, we played another favourite game of ours, Knots, where people hold hands across the circle and untie the knot without letting go of hands. There was enthusiastic participation in this game, and the task was achieved very quickly with four and five people. Then the women suggested that we try to play the game with everyone, us included. Thirteen women then tried to disentangle themselves over about 15 minutes. These women were tenacious. They were going to solve this problem! My head was in someone's armpit, my co-facilitator had to lean on my head to step over someone's arm, I seemed to spend a lot of time on my knees. All of these positions were noted and there was great hilarity with it all.

In talking about the workshop later, with the women themselves, with the principal of the school and with an Aboriginal friend, we realized how ludicrous some of the tasks had been. The notions of height and size were totally immaterial to these women. They were accepted for who and what they were, tall or short, big feet or small feet. These were things that were unchangeable and unnoteable. They do not use numerical measures in their culture. Their 'comparisons' would have been their links: where they were from ('their country') and who they were related to ('their extended family').

The notion of playing a game to learn to solve a problem was also unbelievable to them. There were so many real-life problems facing these women, the idea that you would need to create something was just fanciful. So much of our schooling is like this, unrelated to the lives of the people in places like this community where daily living is a struggle, living in two worlds is challenging and finding one's future is difficult. Each of the tasks we did could have been more appropriate to the context and culture. There were bowls to be made of clay, there were lines to be woven and knotted, there were stories to be told, drawn and painted, there were whitefella ways to fathom and work with.

Yet nothing we did that day resulted in anger, confrontation or isolation, and the women achieved what was desired, at least by us and the principal who had engaged us. Like any of our non-Aboriginal groups, the physical activities were obviously enjoyed and appreciated, and helped transform thinking.

Our understanding of working cross-culturally increased astronomically – and could not have without this experience. We are still grateful to the kindness of those women, for indulging two *wadjelas* (white people) and accepting the absurdity of the tasks we set in good spirit. As our Aboriginal friend explained, 'You can't help it. It isn't your fault that you are whitefellas. You just don't know any better.'

Marie Martin and Anna Alderson, Anglo-Australian,
facilitators in Perth, Western Australia

Silence

In many indigenous cultures, silence is a normal way to greet newcomers. Many are wary of outsiders coming in and out of their communities. When there is ambiguity about a person's role and/or motives, silence is the best option while you weigh up a new person. On the other hand many outsiders try to engage in small talk as a way of finding out about the 'other'. (See Chapter 9 for an in-depth discussion on silence.)

Linking the parts of a workshop

Speed/pace of workshop

The transitions and links between workshop sessions are most important, especially when some individuals are participating in their second or third language. Before proceeding to the next stage it is important to ask participants whether they are ready to continue forward. Unfortunately we cannot assume that everyone is at the same level of understanding, as those who are confused often feel embarrassed to say so. At times, some participants need to be helped to see an overview of a long workshop as whole, and the transitions and links between sections.

During a workshop it is vital to help participants to link the relevant sections together. There are many strategies to help with this.

Stages

1. A table of contents in words can be linked to a mindscape picture representing the learning event.
2. Presenting a daily summary could be a bit dull; however, a fun way to do this is with two facilitators. I drew in advance symbols to summarize the previous day's events (see Figure 2.6). My co-facilitator Libby explained verbally, I pointed to the symbols and at the same time mimed some of the activities and the participants clapped!

Figure 2.6   Using pictures and words

Participants' summarizing

See under formative evaluation (Chapter 1).

A–Z summary process

Invite participants to summarize key words from the day.

Stages

1. Prepare some flipcharts with letters of the alphabet down the left-hand side.
2. Pin up around the room.
3. Divide the participants into small groups and allow them to move around the room, reading and adding to points made by other facilitators.
4. Alternatively, ask participants to do the same task alone in their notebooks and then pool their ideas.

(Idea from Thinley Dorgi; heritage: Bhutanese, a facilitator in Thimphu, Bhutan.)

Getting to the heart of the matter and attitudinal change

> 'What do you feel about this?' Rather than 'What do you think?'
>
> Gill Baxter, counsellor, Perth, Western Australia

If you concentrate on theory, participants can 'stay in their heads'. Issues are kept 'out there' as someone else's problem. That is why I do not use simulations now, as learning transfer is so much more difficult to achieve.

To get any movement of ideas and shifts in opinions, it is important to try to keep things on an interpersonal level. If you ask, 'What do you feel about this?', participants often answer, 'I feel that ...', which is synonymous with 'I think'. So a useful facilitation strategy is to ask participants to fill in an adjective, for example 'I feel xxx.' It's useful even to give them a sample of adjectives, and they often correct the facilitator. See the page of 'feeling' words in Hogan (2003, 86), and the item on Feelings cards in Chapter 6 on Visuals.

Group formation

In culturally diverse groups there is a tendency for some Westerners to dominate verbally. This may be subconscious, partly since Westerners are taught to 'say something', and 'anything', while many people from other cultures are taught to listen as a sign of respect and give others the opportunity to speak first. There also may be a tendency for some expatriates to talk in a paternalistic way, believing in universalism (that their way is best and is transferable to all situations) (see Figure 2.7). Likewise in some groups who have lived under colonial rule, participants may give unwarranted respect and deference to expatriates and may also play the part of the less experienced even though they have a wealth of local knowledge.

Depending on the nature and goals of the workshop, it often pays to put the expatriates together in groups and the locals in other groups. Invite the local groups to give feedback first.

Paired discussions

At the beginning of the discussions, and at appropriate places throughout a workshop, paired discussions are useful since everyone has an opportunity to say aloud what is on his/her mind. Frequently, people will feel safer in a one-on-one interaction than in a large group (depending of course on who they are paired with). It is useful to equalize the time divided between the two participants to talk and to listen. Tell participants that one person will talk while the other listens; the listener does not interrupt or ask questions. The facilitator keeps time and lets participants know when to switch from speaker to listener.

Communication patterns

It is useful if you observe the ways in which you interact with participants and the ways in which groups of participants interact. In transactional analysis terms, the patterns shown in Figure 2.7 may arise between some more dominant expatriates and locals who may take on a more subservient role.

What if they don't understand?

Even with written instructions, clarifying questions from participants, and responses, participants still sometimes misunderstand the intent of a facilitative question. A facilitator cannot say 'You've got it wrong' as responsibility for understanding is a two-way responsibility. Indeed, sometimes when participants interpret something their way, novel ideas develop and it is the responsibility of facilitators to respond to 'where the participants are at' and the serendipity of the moment.

Key

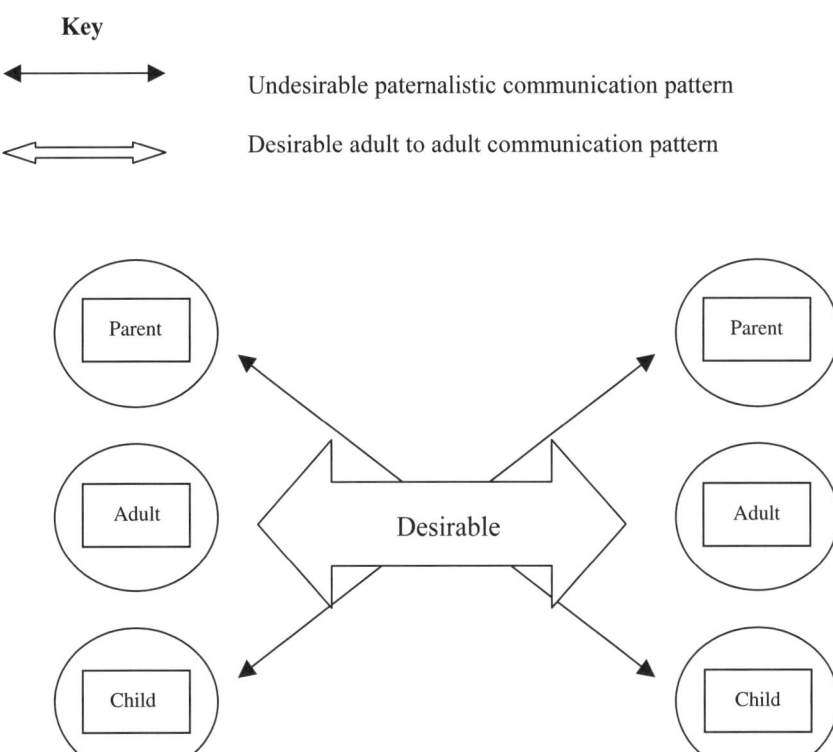

Undesirable paternalistic communication pattern

Desirable adult to adult communication pattern

Figure 2.7 Possible styles of interaction

Transference of learning

Do participatory workshops really make a difference? Do things change afterwards? The transfer of learning and ideas back to the home, workplace or community is a key issue. The following list was compiled in conjunction with Norizan Haj Azizan (a Malaysian facilitator) and Eileen McCaffrey (an Australian facilitator). I have picked out the elements that most relate to cross-cultural situations.

Facilitators/trainers

Transference of learning is maximized if facilitators/trainers:

- conduct needs analysis and tailor the workshop to the specific needs and educational levels of participants;
- create an environment of cultural safety;
- check language needs of participants and make adaptations (to verbal and written language) where necessary (such as sitting a participant with a translator/helper if necessary);
- invite participants to tell their own cultural stories;
- adapt the processes to the cultural needs of participants;
- ensure that learning is 'locally problem based' rather than only 'show and tell';
- encourage participants to give examples and stories from their own culture, work and community perspectives.

Participants

Transference of learning is maximized if participants:

- feel valued and are treated with respect by the facilitator and other participants;
- are asked to discuss with colleagues and/or managers what they need to learn before and after the workshop;
- are given time at a workshop to practise new skills and devise action plans to implement on their return to work;
- can see personal value/purpose in learning rather than seeing the workshop as a perk or prestigious day out;
- understand and have been informed by management why they have to attend the selected training programmes, and what is required or expected from them upon completion of the training (when they return to the workplace) if the course is compulsory;
- are asked to summarize learning or facilitate a workshop for colleagues on their return (if they know they have to do this in advance, this may be discussed and planned for at the workshop).

Managers

Transference of learning is maximized if managers:

- attend workshops with their staff wherever possible so everyone learns new terms together;
- attend skills workshops without their staff watching them and vice versa in some hierarchical societies (depends on the workshop topic);
- support new initiatives such as bridge-building strategies to help maximize cultural differences (see Chapter 4);

- encourage staff to conduct workshops on their return to transfer knowledge and skills to colleagues (if you have to teach something, you have to learn it first);
- cover the work of participants so participants can focus their energies totally on the workshop;
- can see value to the team/organization in participants attending training;
- provide opportunities for participants to apply learning in their jobs.

Motivating participants to read outside a workshop

It is always difficult to get participants to read materials before a workshop or overnight. In culturally diverse groups or if you are working through interpreters, it speeds up communication if participants have had a chance to read and think beforehand.

An incentive is often needed, especially in cultures where reading is not widespread because of the lack of books. Sometimes advance reading for participants is useful, and gives participants a chance to think through ideas to be discussed in the workshop. In Lao PDR, I distributed yellow highlighter pens to participants attending a one-month programme. I thought it would be useful to give reading overnight and ask everyone to highlight the main points. Again my 'assumption antennae' were not switched on. I noticed that many read, but they had not learnt the skill to identify 'key words'. So I changed hats from facilitator to teacher momentarily, and taught them how to pick out key words. Soon everyone used the highlighters to good effect. The use of highlighter pens enabled me to see whether participants had completed their overnight reading at a glance and what concepts they deem important.

Another method is the 'jigsaw process'. For example, in a group of 16 people, ask participants to form four groups of four people by designating them as A,B,C,D, A,B,C,D and so on. All the As read the first quarter of a document, all the Bs the next quarter and so on. Then the next day 'expert groups' form to discuss the content of each quarter of the document. They have to summarize main points to the others, develop discussion questions and so on.

Another strategy is to make time for reading at the workshop. The problem is of course there is then no gestation or 'sleep time' to think about ideas and formulate responses. Also participants have varied reading and comprehension speeds.

Adapting processes to different cultural contexts

Many of these processes we have never seen before.

Government worker

I have found it helps if participants learn to apply the processes we use in workshops in their own cultural contexts. It sometimes helps if they give their own names to a process which makes sense to them in their culture. However, there is a dilemma here in that if they are later talking to other facilitators or reading the facilitation literature, two names may be confusing.

Round robin process

The term 'round robin' in English is quite obscure, as it comes from the sporting field. In Lao, participants renamed it the 'Beer Lao process' because socially you hand out one glass of Beer Lao to each person in turn. After they had named it, the process was never forgotten and they used it in their group work.

Snowball process

Also in Lao, participants changed the name 'Snowball process' to 'Sticky rice process' because they roll sticky rice in their hand to make a bigger and bigger portion before eating it. Each participant thinks for a few moments alone (useful in multicultural situations), then two participants join up; then they form groups of four people to discuss and pull out main ideas. The process is used to maximize participation, to generate questions or answers. In very hierarchical societies, it may be useful to ensure that groups snowball with people of similar rank, or separate workshops are conducted with people from different levels.

Acts of god process

I heard that facilitators in Indonesia and Malaysia renamed the 'Acts of god' process originally written by Bob Dick in Queensland (Dick, 1984; Hogan, 2003) as *force majeure* or major force. Even though the term in English relates to a phrase used in the insurance industry, it is not worth upsetting participants who may think the name of their god is being used inappropriately. Even the term *'force majeure'* can mean under duress in other settings.

Search conference

The search conference process was developed in the UK by Australians Fred Emery and Eric Trist. They suggested inviting representative participants from every level of the organization. In other words they were working in cultures where they assumed that mixed groups from different levels in the hierarchy can and will converse easily. In hierarchical societies this may not be the case. However, there are some options in such situations:

● Seat participants of equal rank together.
● Conduct separate workshop with participants from different levels and then pool the information.

Stop–start role play

In some cultures role play is received warmly; in others, participants are more wary. Stop–start drama is a type of role play where all participants have the equivalent of a 'pause control' for a television. A short role play can take place, but then anyone can call out 'stop' and take over and demonstrate another approach.

> I use 'stop–start drama'. It worked so well in Ghana at all levels, so I even did it the first afternoon in a workshop and the participants then carried on all week and kept saying 'Stop – show us!' In Bhutan the same method was more difficult as the higher officials in Thimphu [the capital] were less playful in their approach to learning, even though they said they used this approach in their workshops with villagers.
>
> Lucia Nass, Heritage Dutch (personal comment, 2005)

Stop–start drama process

Stop–start drama is a very useful problem-solving technique to enable everyone to analyse a problem and try out possible solutions.

Stages

The main stages are:

● Investigate how role play has been received in the past. Decide whether to use, adapt or reject the past method.
● Identify a problem.
● Ask participants in pairs to discuss the problem, and with the whole group reframe the problem if necessary.
● Ask participants in pairs to discuss how they could act out the issue.
● Invite volunteers to demonstrate some possible solutions.

- Call 'Stop' and discuss what happened.
- Invite other pairs to describe a different strategy.
- If participants go into discussion, say, 'That's an interesting idea. Can you show us?'

Debrief

Useful debriefing facilitation questions include:

- What did you see, hear, feel?
- Does this problem happen in every family/community?
- Would this solution work?
- What other solutions can you demonstrate?
- What new problems might occur if you did ...?
- How can these be overcome? Show us.

Application of stop–start drama in Ghana

Lucia Nass described a story in Ghana where women were not making use of water from a newly established, safe borehole. Because they were over-worked they went to the stream, which was closer but not clean, and they did not have to queue. At a community health meeting the issue was raised and then acted out using 'stop–start drama'. At the end of the meeting participants said they saw the problem more clearly, and as a result some men now fetch water (Nass, 1998: 52–53).

Application of stop–start drama in an Asian country

In one Asian country, the workshop space was limited to the one metre wide corridor between the front desks and the whiteboard. However, we still managed to use this space for role plays, for example on communicating with villagers with empathy, and on the five stages of dealing with complaints.

First, the concept of 'customer service' was an issue as it had been introduced from outside. The concept of the general public being regarded as 'customers' or 'clients' to be served did not exist, and the entrenched attitude was that the general public should be grateful for anything done by government officials at all levels. Second, stories of poor customer service within the project were discussed. Some I introduced as 'Gossip I heard which may be incorrect', or I asked participants for their stories.

Participants responded enthusiastically to analysing role plays illustrating 'undesirable' and 'desirable' behaviours. Role plays gave participants the opportunity to observe and discuss alternative ways for handling disputes. At times 'role reversal' was used so that behaviour towards women could be reproduced towards men. For example, 'A female villager who visited a government office was dismissed, without her issue being heard, for not wearing the traditional long wrap-over skirt worn by women.' The story was enacted, showing the resulting frustration, hurt and inconvenience to the woman, plus her passing on the story to fellow villagers. Then the role play was repeated to show how she should have been helped. The saga further unfolded to illustrate a man being dismissed from a government office for inappropriate dress, which drew long discussions about differential treatment of men and women.

At the end of each 'Learning from experience' activity, participants were taught to question one another using the ORID process (see Chapter 1). The government staff were also learning how to contact villagers using a variety of media. As there was no video camera available they made a cardboard screen and role-played creatively and humorously. (There are photos to illustrate this and other ideas in this chapter on my website, www.hogans.id.au)

3

Power and empowerment in groups

Introduction

> If you have come to help me, you are wasting our time. But, if you have come because your liberation is bound up with mine, then let us work together.
>
> Lila Watson, Australian Aboriginal woman (1995)

Power, its use, abuse and issues, pervades and influences everything we do. In this chapter I develop and review various models and processes that I have found useful over the years working in culturally diverse environments. This chapter contains:

- a review of how power is shared in groups, modes of facilitation and types of facilitation;
- ladders of participation, empowerment, equity (gender issues) and political safety;
- values implicit in facilitation participation and issues in totalitarian regimes;
- uses of power and power bases;
- positive and empowering processes (appreciative inquiry, most significant change technique, asset-based community development, open space technology).

Power in groups

Power is neither good nor bad. It is not finite and it permeates everything we do. In Figure 3.1 various models and ladders of facilitation, empowerment and power are placed side by side. The levels are not meant to be read from left to right. The highest levels of people/participant power and control are at the top, but movement up and down may be fluid. My reason for including these is to give you a framework which may be applied to:

*Levels 1–2 = non-participation, levels 3–5 = degrees of tokenism, levels 6–8 = degrees of citizen power

Facilitation power modes (Heron, 1999)	Ladder of participation (Arnstein, 1969) *	Ladder of empowerment (Rocha, 1997: 34)	Ladders of equity	Ladder of political safety & permissible open & safe communication	Use of power (Chambers, 2005) and power bases (Hogan, 2000) Knowledge of sources and uses of power
Participant empowerment	*Community empowerment*	*Community empowerment*	*Equity controls* Whose values & whose goals count?	*High levels of openness OK*	1 Power within: personal power and capacity building
1 Autonomous power mode: Power is conferred, delegated to or seized by participants	8 Citizen/worker control	5 Political empowerment	Status: – uppers or lowers? – haves or have-nots?	1 Freedom of speech	
	7 Delegated power	4 Socio-political empowerment	Cultural groups: – dominant, – indigenous and – minority groups		2 Power to: get things done, achieve and use 'power with' (below)
2 Cooperative power mode Power shared between facilitator and participants	6 Partnership	3 Mediated empowerment	Cultural emphases and behaviours: – empowering – depowering practices		3 Power with: networks, alliances, trust, sharing, solidarity
	5 Placation	2 Embedded individual empowerment	Gender issues: – male – female – homosexual		
3. Hierarchical power mode: Power in hands of facilitator	4 Consultation	1 Atomistic individual empowerment	Age: – children – youth – aged		4 Power over: (control)
	3 Informing		Ability: – educational – physical – mental		
	2. Therapy			2 Guarded speech	
	1. Manipulation				
Facilitator empowerment	*Non-participation community de-empowerment*	*Individual empowerment*	Group pressure: in and out groups	*Low levels of openness & political safety*	5. Power to enhance empowerment of others

Figure 3.1 Key facilitation models: a holistic view of power

- different societal, political and organizational contexts;
- progressive stages in the relationships with clients (such as client contact, negotiating client/contractor relationships, and primary clients: that is, the participants), remembering that these groups will not be culturally homogenous;
- analysis of where you are at the beginning (where participants would like to be compared with the contextual reality), where participants should be, and where they are at the middle and end of workshops.

I give a brief overview of each model below. Each is useful when exploring questions such as 'What do I as a facilitator need to take into account based on the context of the culture and country I am working in, and the cultures I am working with?'

We need to examine the relationship of our facilitator roles to clients, participants, and levels of participation in terms of power. We need to ask ourselves who allocates the power, sets goals and timelines, and who sets the limits on the facilitator, client, contractor, participants and outcomes (personal communication from J and K Wilson, 2006).

When analysing Figure 3.1 please note:

- Higher on the ladder does not necessarily imply more desirable or better. It depends on the context. It is often desirable to work with groups through stages, such as hierarchical to autonomous.
- Different models might be more useful with different planning and decision-making contexts and processes.
- The models may be applied to different scales of cultures from national cultures through to organizations or even families.
- What is negotiable?
- What is not negotiable?
- What ethically as a facilitator and as an individual are you willing and/or able to work with?
- Where does the real power lie: that is, who are the informal as well as formal power holders?

Modes of facilitation

John Heron developed a model describing three modes or ways of using power in groups (Heron 1989, 1993, 1999), which is outlined below.

Hierarchical mode: direction

The facilitator directs the learning and group process and does things for the group. For example, he/she makes decisions about planning and objectives, interprets the meaning of key concepts, confronts resistance, manages feelings, develops structures for learning events and values participants' contributions. All these decisions are made by the facilitator.

Cooperative mode: negotiation

In the cooperative mode, power is shared between the facilitator and the group members. The facilitator works with the group and ideas are shared, processes are negotiated together.

Autonomous mode: delegation

In the autonomous mode power is shifted to the participants. 'This does not mean abdication of responsibility. It is the subtle art of creating conditions within which people can exercise full self-determination' (Heron, 1989: 17). It may occur in one of three ways. Autonomy:

- is conferred by the facilitator to the group;
- may evolve by negotiations between the facilitator and the group;
- may be seized by the group (Heron, 1999), either to good effect or perhaps to sabotage proceedings.

Ladder of participation

Empowerment in groups involves various levels of participation and power sharing. In English the word 'participation' means different things to different people.

> Participation has no final meaning. It is not a rock. It is mobile and malleable, an amoeba, a sculptor's clay, a plasticine shape as it passes from hand to hand. And perhaps that's how it should be so, and that each generation, each group, each person, should puzzle out what they think it should mean and how they can best give it expression.
>
> (Chambers, 2005: 104)

The word 'participation' implies some norms, rules and structures, and it is important to ask:

- What norms and implicit rules exist already?
- Who makes and implements these rules?
- Are there rules about emergent leadership or rotating leadership?

It is important that, as facilitators, we are very clear about which roles we agree or do not agree to undertake, such as facilitator, consultant, negotiator, mediator, researcher, go-between and trainer.

A seminal model of the levels of participation was developed by Sherry Arnstein (1969), a consultant in urban affairs, who worked with numerous US government agencies and community groups. As a result of her experience, she identified eight levels of participation, which she defined as degrees of citizen power, and depicted as the rungs of a ladder (see Figure 3.1).

A brief description of each level is necessary here, as attempts to create an empowered environment will need to include the upper levels, and so often only the lower levels are used by management yet they are still termed 'participation' and 'empowerment'.

1 Manipulation

At the manipulation level, citizens or members of private organizations merely serve to 'rubber stamp' the desires of advisory committees who educate, persuade and advise workers rather than the reverse.

2 Therapy

Power holders allow workers to 'let off steam' under the masquerade of participation. Yet their anger or frustration is not heeded.

3 Informing

Arnstein maintains that information giving is the first step towards legitimate participation, since workers at least become aware of some of their rights, responsibilities and options. As communication is only one-way, there is scope for misunderstandings. This one-way communication may be achieved through such channels as pamphlets, faxes and e-mail.

4 Consultation

If consultation takes place, the communication should be two-way in that workers' ideas and opinions are truly valued and solicited in a respectful two-way discussion. Preferably prior warning is given so that participants have a chance to think about their stance before a meeting. Consultation is fine if this level of decision making is made clear from the outset: that is, it is 'transparent' and the managers have not already made their decision before the consultation process begins.

There is a manipulative and disempowering tactic where a facilitator and/or manager appears to be consulting group members for their ideas, but the ideas are eliminated or edited out of the discussion process. They might be acknowledged verbally, but they are discreetly omitted from the flipchart, or they might be edited out later when the workshop outcomes are written up.

5   Placation

At the placation level a hand-picked few 'worthy' workers are placed on committees and begin to have some degree of influence, usually small. The power holders retain the right to judge the legitimacy of the advice. Arnstein refers to informing, consultation and placation as 'degrees of tokenism' because the ground rules allow the have-nots to advise, though the power holders retain the continuous right to decide.

6   Partnership

When partnership occurs, power is redistributed through negotiation between workers and power holders. They agree to share planning and decision-making responsibilities through such structures as joint policy boards, planning committees and mechanisms for resolving impasses.

7   Delegated power

The level of delegated power occurs when workers achieve dominant decision-making authority over a particular plan or programme, usually as a result of negotiation.

8   Citizen/worker control

Finally at this level workers are given full autonomy over an area, and are put in charge of policy making and managerial aspects of a decision, as happens in a worker cooperative.

For more information on Arnstein's model see, for example, Hogan (2002).

Participation can be interpreted differently by two people from the same culture. Different cultures perceive participation differently. When the king of Bhutan decided to delegate more power and responsibility to the *dzongkhags* (regions) in 2001, the *lympos* (regional heads) were concerned about their return home from an annual governance meeting in Thimphu, the capital, as the notion of 'participation' would be so new to villagers and they feared they would be seen as traitors to the king (Bhutan Planning Department, 2004). As facilitators, we need to find out about and utilize local or traditional methods of dialogue and face-saving ways of dealing with difference which may be better than our own (Braden and Huong, 1998). In addition, we also need to be aware of the ramifications for people and authorities who engage in new forms of dialogue. We need to be able to offer both people and authorities safe ground on which to practise and use a variety of forms of dialogue (some new, some not).

The arrival of external facilitators in communities, organizations and villages may bring expectations of grants, aid and improvements in materials and welfare. As a result facilitators have a responsibility to ensure that there is feedback, and wherever possible follow-through of any promises made by authorities.

Ladder of empowerment

> Empowerment is the opposite of manipulation.
>
> Peavey (1994: 97)

Twenty-eight years after Arnstein, Elizabeth Rocha (1997) also used the ladder metaphor to develop five levels of empowerment based on McClelland's classification of power experiences, which itself is based on the source of power and the object (or target) of power (see Table 3.1). Arnstein's model focused on community, whereas Rocha's ladder moves from individual to community levels with gradations in between.

1   Individual empowerment

This level is called 'atomistic individual empowerment' by Rocha, but I find the term 'individual empowerment' easier for participants. In this level strength is gained from within, using personal power and an internalized locus of control. It is extended by learning, coping and other skills, and aided by nurturing support from others. It is only usefully applied to one-off problems that do not require alterations to systems, structures or social relations to prevent their recurrence. The many 'self-help' books illustrate the popularity of self-improvement.

2   Embedded individual empowerment

At this level the individual is considered as embedded within a larger context: ie the social, environmental, economic and political system. The goal is to understand what is going on around you and your place in it.

We cannot assume that facilitation is always empowering. Paulo Freire (1972) wrote of the process of 'conscientization' and awareness raising about the power structures in society. Awareness of the reality, however, may be a disempowering experience, as happened with the collapse of the USSR when communications opened up and the people realized that they were far less well off than their leaders had led them to believe. Awareness raising on its own is empty without some processes to change the status quo linked to the five levels above. Freire later wrote 'One of the tasks of the progressive educator, through a serious, correct political analysis, is to unveil opportunities for hope, no matter what the obstacles may be. After all, without hope there is little we can do' (1997: 9).

Table 3.1 Five empowerment models

Empowerment models					
Dimensions →	*1. Individual*	*2. Embedded individual*	*3. Mediated*	*4. Sociopolitical*	*5. Political*
Locus intended arena of change	• individual	• individual in context	• individual and/or community	• individual, groups, communities	• community
Goal intended outcomes	• personal satisfaction • increased coping ability	• personal satisfaction • competence in negotiating daily environment	• knowledge and information for proper decision making	• individual development • expanded access to community resources	• expanded access to community services, goods and rights
Process methods used	• therapy • daily living skills • self-help	• organizational participation	• professional/client relationship	• organizational participation • collaborative grassroots activity	• political action, voting, protest • political representation
Power experience	• nurturing support	• nurturing support • direct and control self	• support • strengthen self • control by helping • moralized action	• support • strengthen self • influence, coerce others • togetherness	• influence, coerce others • assertion

Source: adapted from Rocha (1997: 35).

3   Mediated empowerment

Mediated empowerment is about how individuals or communities are helped by an expert or professional to develop necessary knowledge for decision making and action. That is, there is unequal power between the so-called expert and his or her clients. Examples are facilitated workshops on the 'empowerment cycle' and 'sources of power bases' whereby participants draw up their own action plans to be carried out after the workshop (Hogan, 2000).

4   Sociopolitical empowerment

This level is based on the work of Paulo Freire to raise the consciousness of individuals and communities, to rethink their relationships to power and power structures and to take collective action. For example, Mahatma Gandhi raised awareness of the injustices of the colonial salt taxes and led the famous 'Salt March' to the sea not only to raise awareness on the way, but also to use peaceful means to elicit political change. Also see the section 'What facilitators can do to facilitate effective empowerment of participants' later in this chapter.

5   Political empowerment

In this model, political action is taken to instigate institutional and legislative change through democratic processes to gain access to resources, for example in education, housing, health care, government benefits and loans. An example is the video produced by villagers in Vietnam (see Chapter 6 on 'Visual techniques').

Ladders of equity

Equity is an implicit value in facilitation and in many, though not all societies, groups and networks. That is, to enable equal outcomes we may need to treat participants differently (by giving extra help regarding differences in language capabilities, gender, age, physical and mental abilities, or educational levels). We need to consider carefully the attitudes towards equity in the cultures we work in, and how to manage a clash if one exists (personal communication, J and K Wilson, 2006).

Robert Chambers (2005) suggests we should ask 'Who gains, who loses?' and also we need to ask 'Who decides?' and 'Who decides who decides?' This implies a zero-sum view of power as a finite entity. Perhaps we should be asking 'Whose values and whose goals count or should count?' Chambers suggested there should be a ladder of equity, but went no further, so I have endeavoured to develop one (see Figure 3.1, above). There is no up or down staging in this ladder. Each one of these groups has a ladder of its own. There are multiple hierarchies of values and goals.

As facilitators we may need to invoke laws and regulations (if they exist), and impose or elicit structures and/or processes to ensure equity of access. Or if these do not exist, we should consider whether to accept or reject the work, and look at ways of negotiation and educating the client. If there is a values clash at the outset we need to be careful, otherwise we may end up 'facipulating' the participants (Cooke and Kothari, 2001). Facipulation refers to using facilitation techniques in a manipulating way.

Equity issues may relate to how stakeholders are identified, invited to workshops and catered for in workshops. For example:

- Uppers and lowers: uppers are people who in certain contexts are dominant or superior to lowers. Lowers are subordinate to uppers.
- Cultural groups: dominant, indigenous and minority groups.
- Cultural values and behaviours: disempowering practices (caste, dowry system, inheritance system, treatment of women, homosexuals).
- Gender: male, female, homosexual, lesbian.
- Age: children, young people, the aged.
- Ability: educational, physical, mental.
- Pressure groups, 'in' and 'out' groups.

Key concepts: equality and equity

In workshops it is important to help participants distinguish between 'equality' and 'equity'. Equity is a means of achieving equality. An equity approach recognizes that women are disadvantaged in certain areas compared with men, and includes proactive measures that take into account the differing needs of men, women, parents (and the disabled and elderly). Equality is treating everyone exactly the same.

STORY: THE STORK AND THE FOX

An easy way to illustrate the need for equity (ie, taking into account the different needs of men, women and people) is the story of the stork and the fox. Both need to eat. A stork has a long neck, a fox a short neck. So a stork cannot eat out of a shallow bowl and a fox cannot eat out of a long narrow bowl.

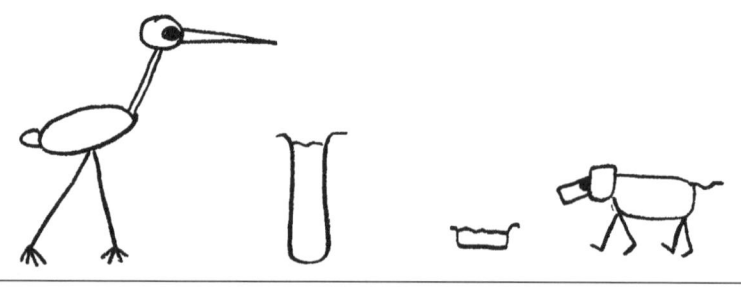

Taking gender issues into account in workshops is part of equity planning

> Women constitute half the world's population, perform nearly two-thirds of its work hours, receive one-tenth of the world's income and own less than one-hundredth of the world's property.
>
> UN report, 1980

Unfortunately the workload, income and property ownership levels of most women have not changed much in a quarter of a century. Indeed for many women the situation has become worse because of the ravages of conflict, the HIV/AIDS pandemic and the slower than ideal introduction and implementation of equal opportunity laws. Stephen Lewis, the UN Secretary-General's special envoy for HIV/AIDS in Africa, commented in *Race Against Time* that 'women and girls are an endangered species ... the Millennium Development goals are doomed unless we make gender inequality history' (Lewis, 2006: 154).

Gender roles are built into us, and as with culture, often we do not notice our own programming. So it helps both male and female facilitators occasionally to reflect on our own practice. It seems important that facilitators should be aware of the following framework (from a discussion with Rod Mitchell, 2006):

- the destructive impact of gender-blind development (from Women in Development (WID) to Gender and Development (GAD));
- the potentially destructive power of gender divisions and levels of constraints and oppression of women in different cultures (Lewis, 2006);
- how and why this happens: the context and history (Cranny-Francis *et al*, 2003);
- how gender divisions can interfere with development in all cultures;
- how gender divisions may impact on the way women (and men) act in workshops (through internalized sexism and racism);
- the need to help raise awareness of gender divisions, inequities and the impact of oppression of women in workshops in sensitive ways.
- the need to adjust group processes, and use of single-sex groups where necessary;
- the need to enhance ways for men to share power, and for some to explore more humane ways of being.

There is a need to enhance the power of women by ensuring that there are specialist groups at all levels to work for gender equity. Gender mainstreaming is not the answer.

The following list of questions and suggestions is built partly on the work of Barben and Ryter (2005), and may be used as a checklist for workshop design.

Workshop advertising

There are many channels for advertising workshops. However, ground work is important:

- Is it necessary to talk to men (the husbands, fathers and wise elders) first to discuss the reasons for including women in workshops and to illicit their support?
- Are women consulted directly regarding suitable venues, times and duration of workshops?
- Are there at least 30 per cent of female participants (anything smaller, and they will function as a minority group)?
- Is it best to have separate courses for men and for women and later joint workshops?
- How will child care and care of seniors be handled?

Workshop language and listening

Do the facilitators:

- encourage and model gender-neutral verbal and written language?
- allocate one co-facilitator to monitor male–female turn taking, interruptions, listening habits and length of inputs?

Per diems

Per diems are the daily allowances for travel and food often given at workshops in developing countries. This can be an important cash supplement, for women especially.

- How will participants be compensated for giving up their work to attend a workshop?
- Will travel expenses, food and accommodation be provided or a cash sum paid?
- Will lunches be provided en masse to save money, or cash allocated? In the West, communal lunches are often provided to give opportunities for networking. However, in poorer countries participants often prefer cash and to provide food for themselves so that they can save some money.

Workshop content

- Does the content need to be presented in different ways for men and for women, and then in a mixed-gender context?
- What examples and stories will be relevant to men, women or both?

Workshop materials

- Do the pictures prepared for workshops stereotype roles of men and women or open up alternatives: for example, pictures of sharing child care and house jobs, or pictures of girls and women engaged in community roles?

Stories

- Are there stories of local and international females who have made great achievements despite the obstacles, and become role models and heroines, like Wangari Maathai, the Kenyan environmentalist who won the Nobel Peace Prize in 2004?
- How can participants voice stories of those who inspire them?
- Are there people who can form close mentoring relationships with women, functioning more as a coach than just a role model?

Workshop and village meetings and time

- Are women consulted regarding the most suitable days, seasons, and start and finish times for workshops?
- Are men consulted regarding the most suitable days, seasons, and start and finish times for workshops?

Workshop processes

As individuals we all have many different and preferred learning styles. To generalize (dangerous territory, I realize), some men may find it difficult to talk about feelings and may be sceptical about role play. Some women shy away from open debates (preferring non-competitive dialogue) and avoid presentations. Some have been taught from a young age to show modesty or to put down their own achievements. They often 'give face' to men and their achievements by allowing men to speak out. These are enculturated behaviours rather than essential attributes of males and females.

Women may use different codes of communication, and their contributions to a discussion may be discounted by some males, only to be raised later on by a male participant. Brainstorming favours the more outgoing individuals, and in societies where women are encouraged to let men speak, it may be better for facilitators to maximize participation by using writing on cards rather than mere verbal processes (provided that literacy is not a problem).

Composition of small groups

Certain topics are best discussed in single-sex groups (such as health issues, reproduction, contraception, disability, STDs, HIV/AIDS, and issues regarding roles and responsibilities, division of labour, land, power and money). It is important to have time for men to air their views separately in a safe environment; otherwise they may cover their concerns and sabotage any changes in the status quo at a later date.

Encouraging women to participate in workshops

Lucia Nass pointed out that it is important for facilitators to know how to facilitate women's participation, and that our behaviour, no matter how well-meaning, may even lessen the inputs from women. She cited her own observations while working in Ghana in Africa (Nass. 1998: 51):

- Men and women are often seated separately. When facilitators speak, our body and eyes tend to be directed towards the men. Even though we don't mean to, this makes women feel less important, less invited to respond to what we are saying. *In meetings look at women when you talk! It makes them feel valued (in cultures where direct eye contact is a valued and polite form of communication. In some cultures looking down is a form of respect towards power figures).*
- When we ask a question men usually respond first. Only when we notice that women do not talk, do facilitators invite them also to say something. Will they dare contradict their husbands and the elders? *Ask people to discuss questions in pairs, then invite the women to talk first.*
- We personally invite the chief, village head and elders, but leave it to them to inform the women.
- We know about women's high workload, but 'forget' to meet at their convenience.
- We chose 'male' ways of meeting: formal meetings with elders at men's meeting places in which women traditionally may have little or no power.
- We let meetings go on for hours, so women have to leave before the end to cook meals or tend to children. *Informally, find out from the women when, where and for how long they like to meet. Would they prefer meetings amongst themselves first?*
- We over-praise women's contributions (for example with loud clapping when a woman has 'dared' to say something). It reconfirms their low self-esteem, because we apparently did not expect them to say something useful. *The best way to value women's contributions is to remind the meeting what the women have said if they are 'forgetting' or 'omitting' the women's contributions.*

Some aspects of participation in workshops may not seem obvious, as the following stories illustrate.

At a village meeting in a remote part of Nepal, I observed the farmers (both men and women) gathering for the first PRA meeting to map the village. A man sat down in front with his wife, and turned to her and whispered. I did not understand and asked a development worker to translate. 'Oh,' he said, 'the man said, "You can stay but don't say anything."' This incident shows how difficult (or impossible) it can be for some women to speak even if they are present. In many cultures they feel the need to give their husbands 'face', by giving them the space to talk in public.

In Myanmar, development workers commented on how hard it was at times to get conversations going with groups of sex workers. 'They only started to relax when we just chatted to them about everything in general. Sometimes we sit and have a drink with them. That loosens everyone up. Also we ask them to 'Tell us your friend's stories', so they do not have to talk about themselves directly.'

One facilitator working in Lao PDR and Thailand described how she used magic tricks with groups of child sex workers to gain their confidence with play. Later when she had gained their trust they could tell her about their lives and what they needed to do to escape their predicament.

Workshop evaluation

Check:

- Are there any significant numbers of dropouts of either men, women, young or old participants?
- Was there a difference between the evaluation completed by males and females?
- Were there any perceived changes in opinions/attitudes/behaviours of women and men during the course?
- Were there any perceived changes in opinions/attitudes/behaviours of women and men in the long term?

STORY: THE WOMEN'S WISH

The story of 'The women's wish' is told in Hogan (2000) and on my website, www.hogans.id.au

---

UN gender training tools and resources

Useful material can be found on the website www.un.org/womenwatch/ asp/user/list.asp?ParentID=10879

UN gender inequality index

The UN gender inequality index is the UN composite index measuring gender inequality in three basic dimensions of: empowerment – economic participation and decision making; political participation and decision making; power over economic resources. The index can be found on www. bahraintribune.com/ArticleDetail.asp?CategoryId=7&ArticleId=28407. How these dimensions are measured is not described.

CEDAW

See also the reports on the Convention on the Elimination of All Forms of Discrimination Agains Women (CEDAW) website, www.un.org/women watch/daw/cedaw

Institute of Development Studies, Sussex, UK (Eldis)

Eldis includes descriptions and links to over 4,500 organizations and over 15,000 full-text online documents covering development, environmental and gender issues. See www.eldis.org/wnew. You can subscribe by e-mail: eldis@ids.ac.uk or go to: www2.ids.ac.uk/bns/updates/eldis/index.cfm

Ladder of political safety, open and safe communication

The ladder of political safety, open and safe communication illustrates the degrees of safety and transparency within countries' political regimes, organizations and even within families (see Figure 3.1). Facilitators need to be aware of hidden boundaries, and work within these or take precautions, remembering that they are often temporary visitors in a culture.

I strongly believe that facilitators have a moral obligation to tread carefully when conducting workshops in totalitarian or repressive regimes. To try to suggest 'It is safe to speak out' in some organizations and countries is dangerous and unethical.

In one country in which I worked, the expatriates claimed that 'The locals are so cautious that before they open their mouths to speak, they twist their heads around 180 degrees at least to check who is in the room.' This behaviour seems eminently rational. As facilitators we need to remember that participants have to survive long after expatriate facilitators and development workers have gone home. There are often participants present whose role is to give feedback to the authorities. In many instances a useful motto is:

Stay clear of politics, sex and religion.

Here are some thought-provoking quotes from facilitators working in countries with totalitarian regimes:

> If things get too political, I hold my hands up with wrists together, as if they are cuff linked. As a facilitator you cannot say anything as you never know who might report.

> Often people blame their woes such as alcoholism on the government. So I have to jolt them out of this to make them think of their choices and options.

Observations on ladders as a metaphor

Ladders can show how much participation is about power (Chambers, 2005). It is important to remember:

- Life doesn't happen in neat sequences. There may be movement up and down, and stages may be missed.
- At times sequences help us to plan or evaluate where we are (or are not) and ideally where we want to be.
- Higher on a ladder is not necessarily better or more appropriate.
- Who gains and who loses as you 'climb ladders'? Empowerment for some may mean disempowerment for others.

At times a mindscape may be a more useful way of representing reality with all its complex pathways and choices. (See Chapter 6 on 'Visual techniques', and on the ladder of assumptions or inference on page 226.)

Values in facilitation and participation

'Facilitation' and 'participation' as concepts are based on a number of assumptions and values about:

- the perceived advantages of incorporating and consulting people so they can voice their knowledge, skills and attitudes;
- whose knowledge counts: insiders (local inhabitants) and outsiders (consultants) (Samovar and Porter, 2004: 109) or 'experts' (and who are the real experts?);
- people-led development and change processes;
- attitudes of power holders to sharing and delegating power;
- attitudes of power holders to hearing, valuing and using the ideas of those less powerful than themselves;
- attitudes of people with less power to sharing and using powers delegated to them or seized by them.

Facilitators need to be extremely sensitive to culture and context. There is a danger in encouraging people to speak out, in that in some contexts it could lead to exposing people to 'pay back'.

Uses of power and power bases

Robert Chambers (2005) talked of 'transforming power and relationships' by clarifying four types of power. I have added a fifth:

- Power within: personal power and capacity building.
- Power to: get things done, achieve and use power.
- Power with: via networks, alliances, trust, sharing, solidarity.
- Power over: (control) which may be transformed into:
- Power to enhance
  empowerment: of others.

As facilitators we may need to think about our stance on empowerment. Are we using our power to enhance empowerment? Or are we taking a top-down approach and think we hold the power to empower others? (See Figure 3.1.)

In *Facilitating Empowerment* (Hogan, 2000), I described 60 power bases or sources which were identified by participants in workshops as having helped them to feel more powerful, or power bases they had observed being used by others. These may also be useful for facilitators to observe the kinds of power being exerted by organizers, clients and participants.

What facilitators can do to enhance effective empowerment of participants

Rocha (1997) poses some useful questions for planners to think about. I have adapted and expanded on these questions and replaced the word 'planner' with 'facilitator'. These models enable facilitators to read between the lines of organizational and community change proposals, terms of reference and workshop requests to:

- See where various interventions fit into a wider framework.
- Explore the ethical issues. For example, ask who is really gaining out of this exercise?
- Evaluate the long-term sustainability of proposed interventions . For example, ask is this a short-term solution? Will it continue once the funding runs out?
- Reflect on our assumptions, particularly assumptions about empowerment. In what ways should this occur?

- How does this fit with local cultural, structural, economic and political considerations?

This then leads to more informed answers to questions such as:

- Do I want to be part of a rubber-stamping exercise that only pays lip service to participation and empowerment?
- Do I want to be part of this and work with the donor agencies and/or clients to ensure that a project is sustainable, ethical and so on?

How can we as facilitators use our power to utilize political and administrative resources to enhance the empowerment of those with less power? We cannot assume that those with less power (or for that matter those with power) are humanitarian and egalitarian.

STORY: SOME STUDENTS CALL ME THE 'EMPOWERMENT TEACHER'

Professor Fatima Alvarez Castillo of the University of the Philippines, Manila tells her students, 'It is easier to be disempowered than empowered.'

I ask the students, 'What excites you, what needs to be done?' There is always something that needs to be changed. I make them do projects that have a transformative effect. I tell them, 'To be empowered, you have to take risks.' By mid-semester I suggest they undertake some projects. One group took on McDonald's for dirty kitchens and for serving smaller and smaller servings, and changes have resulted. Another group contacted the Dean because students who arrived by car did not have to show IDs, but students on foot were always checked and discriminated against. In every case they have to research their cases, reflect, document action and outcomes, and leave the documentation of these cases in the library as a legacy to future students. They learn they can make changes if they dare to.

Power: facilitator and teacher roles

Participants often see a facilitator as a kind of teacher who should also be treated with high respect. Participants who have been raised in countries that have a didactic form of education may find the concept of facilitation hard to understand at first. This is not surprising. Indeed at one time my own family members used to ask me, 'What is it exactly that you do?' We need to be able to explain this easily and simply. Facilitation is a relatively new word in the English language. To the best of my knowledge it is only about a quarter of a century old. The word comes from the French word 'facile' meaning 'to make easy', so the core meaning is to help a group of people to learn and achieve their goals together.

Empowering processes to harness positive thinking

The concept of working with a positive approach of 'the glass is half full' rather than 'the glass is half empty' has proved to be successful across the world. Participants feel empowered when focusing on positives or reframing negatives in such a way that they can manage them. Four major approaches are:

- The appreciative inquiry process (described below).
- The most significant change (MSC) technique (see Chapter 1).
- Asset-based community development (ABCD), whereby communities are energized by focusing on their assets and mobilizing these assets to help solve problems (Kretzmann and McKnight, 1993). This is described in detail at www.communitybuilders.nsw.gov.au/getting_started/needs/abcd.html
- Open space technology, in which participants set the agenda and work on their own issues. This is outlined in Owen (1992, 1995, 1997) and Owen and Stadler (1999), and described in Hogan (2003).

Appreciative inquiry process

So often facilitators are called in to help groups solve their problems and the tendency is to focus on negatives. Indeed in terms of reference (TOR), whole regions and cultural groups are often described from a pathological point of view. I am not suggesting that people in developing areas do not have problems; however ToRs rarely mention the vibrant aspect of cultures that have managed to exist for thousands of years. These ideas on the appreciative inquiry process were adapted from the works of Lovell (e-mail 19 March 2000, plovell@wlf.com.au) and Hammond (1996).

Author/background

In the 1970s in the United States, Dr David Cooperrider challenged the traditional 'medical' approach to change of 'Look for the problem, do a diagnosis and find a solution.' David suggested that we should look for 'what works' in the group or organization we are working with, and build on that using a clear process of inquiry with an 'appreciative perspective' to it. He coined the term 'appreciative inquiry', and he and his associates developed the concept further. The process has spread rapidly through

Problem solving	Appreciative inquiry
Identification of problem 'Felt needs', 'pain' ⬇	Appreciating and valuing The best of 'What exists already' ⬇
Analysis of causes ⬇	Envisioning 'What might be' ⬇
Analysis of possible solutions ⬇	Dialoguing 'What should be' ⬇
Action planning (Treatment)	Innovating 'What will be'
Focus: Doing less of something you do not do well	**Focus:** Doing more of what works
Basic assumption: An organization is a problem to be solved	**Basic assumption:** An organization is a learning system to be embraced
Metaphor: Problems	**Metaphor:** Solutions
Methodology: Idea based	**Methodology:** Story based

Figure 3.2 Comparison between problem-solving and appreciative inquiry approaches

Source: adapted from Cooperrider and Srivastva, in Pasmore and Woodman (1987).

the development world because it is easily learnt, feels comfortable and achieves results. See Figure 3.2.

Purpose/rationale

The appreciative inquiry process encourages the building of participants into a 'learning community', whether it is a community of common or diverse interests, a geographical community, an organization or a company. It is both a theory of change and a methodology for encouraging action.

Assumptions of appreciative inquiry

The following assumptions underlie the process of appreciative inquiry, according to Hammond (1996):

- In every society, organization or group, some things work well.
- What we focus on becomes our reality.
- There are multiple realities.
- The act of asking questions of an organization or group influences the group in some way.
- Participants have more confidence to plan for the future (the unknown) when they carry forward parts of the past (the known).
- If participants carry parts of the past forward, they should be the best aspects of the past.
- The language used creates our reality. Compare your reactions to this list of words:

> Don't, problems, issues, difficulties, dysfunctional

to your reaction to these phrases:

> We do this well and let's improve this aspect.
> This really works.
> Yes!

Size of group

Groups of no more than 20 are most appropriate.

Materials

Flipchart paper, felt-tip pens, masking tape. Pens and writing paper for each participant. A large blank wall.

Venue layout

Participants sit in a semicircle facing the facilitator and flipchart containing wall minutes (participants' ideas summarized by the facilitator).

Time

Two hours minimum. The action planning stage (see stage 5) may generate the need for future workshops.

Stages

1   Paired interviews

In order to maximize participation, the facilitator invites participants to conduct 'paired interviews'. The questioner makes brief notes and is allowed to probe or ask for clarification when necessary. Questions may need to be tailored to the goals of the workshop.

Some examples of possible questions follow. These were applied to a group of facilitators who wished to improve their 'facilitation practice' by using appreciative inquiry.

> Take 20 minutes to interview a partner using the following questions as a guideline:
>
> 1. Describe your most wonderful experience/s as a facilitator, ie a high point when you felt most excited about the work you were doing. Describe the scene.
> 2. How did you feel?
> 3. What factors contributed to making it feel like a peak experience?
> 4. Who else was involved and how were they significant?
> 5. What is it about facilitation that you value?
> 6. What are your three wishes or dreams for all facilitators and the facilitation profession in general?

These questions may be adapted to an appreciative inquiry of a development team or project.

2   Generate common themes from stories

The purpose of appreciative inquiry is to uncover the 'common will' or purpose of the group, and help them to put this into practice. The facilitator invites each pair to share key words, phrases, images, common themes or quotable quotes with the whole group on a storyboard (or the facilitator can note these on a flipchart – see Table 3.2).

Table 3.2   Ways of describing common themes

Key words	*Phrases*	*Images*	*Common themes*	*Quotable quotes*
●	●	●	●	●
●	●	●	●	●
●	●	●	●	●

By establishing a list, the group discovers what elements made it possible to provide 'exciting, memorable, effective facilitation'.

3   Develop provocative propositions from the themes

1. Find examples of the best facilitation achievements (from the paired interviews).
2. Determine what circumstances made the best facilitation experiences possible (in detail).

3. Take the themes and compare them with your own facilitation. What do you already do? Think about what that might be. Write an affirmative statement (a provocative proposition) that describes the idealized future as if it were already happening. For example:

    > To us excellent facilitation means …
    > We continually learn as we facilitate by …
    > We devote time to update our workshops by …
    > We ask our participants to tell us their needs by …
    > We stimulate all the learners' senses in the facilitation process by …

4. To write the proposition, apply 'what if' to all the common themes. Then write affirmative *present tense* statements incorporating the common themes.
5. Check that propositions are provocative and link to the best learning experiences described by participant facilitators.

The facilitator needs to help group members challenge their assumptions about themselves, their work, and their behaviour. (Assumptions are often implicit rules that explain what group members generally believe and why they behave in a certain way. Uneasiness may stem from the fear of doing something differently or making mistakes.)

4   Reviewing provocative propositions

Hammond (1996) suggests that you check your propositions against the following criteria:

- Is it provocative?
- Does it stretch, challenge or innovate?
- Is it what the facilitator participants want?
- Will facilitator participants become passionate about it or defend it?
- Is it stated in affirmative, bold terms and in the *present tense* as if it were already happening?

5   Innovation and action planning

Link statements to measurable results. Work out:

- Who will do what?
- When?
- Where?
- How?
- With what resources?
- How will you know if you are successful? Work out critical success factors and how you will evaluate them as you go along as well as at the end.

Outcomes

The outcomes are that members of a group of facilitators have directly tackled their own strategies for improvement based on their own positive experiences.

Advantages

When the facilitator asks appreciative questions, participants do not just give politically correct answers; they give heartfelt answers in response to 'searching questions'. Positive energies are generated as positive stories are told and heard. People feel good about themselves and their work. The process is based on adult learning theory: adults like to tell stories about their own experiences.

Disadvantages

The downside is that if a group is self-satisfied, the members may fail to see new ideas or processes that contradict their beliefs, and they may miss an opportunity to improve their effectiveness.

4

Strategies to enable multicultural teams to be more effective

Introduction

No culture can live, if it attempts to be exclusive.

Mohandas Karamchand Gandhi

The purpose of this chapter is to provide facilitators with a variety of processes to enable culturally diverse teams to be more effective in working together to achieve their goals. This may be effected by exploring and 'mapping' the cultural backgrounds of individuals, finding similarities and differences, and exploring how differences might be valued and bridged. In this way people can work together in a culturally mixed environment in creative ways, where the richness of differences is acknowledged and valued.

How can we alert ourselves to our own cultural biases and blindness? We know that culture is not a product that we can put under the microscope, but a living, changing entity. It is taken for granted much like the air we breathe, yet if someone violates our unwritten codes of behaviour we all react emotionally as well as intellectually.

In this chapter you will find discussion of:

- cultural socialization, cultural values (or drivers) and behaviours;
- characteristics of effective culturally diverse teams;
- intercultural leadership and sensitivity;
- the MBI model;
- different interpretations of the word 'culture', the petal model;
- purpose and rationale of the cultural values card pack;
- explanations of driver cards and card-sorting exercise;
- cultural bridge building and integrating bridges into systems;
- other participatory processes to map cultures;

- previously mapped cultures (commercial packages);
- simulation activities for cultural awareness;
- mapping cultures of stakeholders who work together;
- facilitative bridging strategies in culturally diverse groups.

Cultural socialization

Cultural socialization takes place through intensive interaction in the family, with peers, in school, in the local community and via the media. We learn 'social scripts' or 'codes of behaviour' which may vary from one generation to the next. Cultural values and behaviours, such as how to address our parents, elders, peers and children, will vary even within a single culture, according to context, time, space, between generations and locations (rural or urban). However, there are some generalizations that can be made by discussing the following terms.

'Cultural values' are widely held significant driving forces (sometimes called 'dimensions'). Some values are 'implicit', subconscious and unseen. Various discussions on these have been developed by Abdullah and Pedersen (2003), Abdullah and Shephard (2000), Hofstede (1980, 1991, 2001), Trompenaars and Hampden-Turner (1997), Hall and Hall (1990), Hogan (2002, 2003) and others (see Figure 4.1 and Appendix 1).

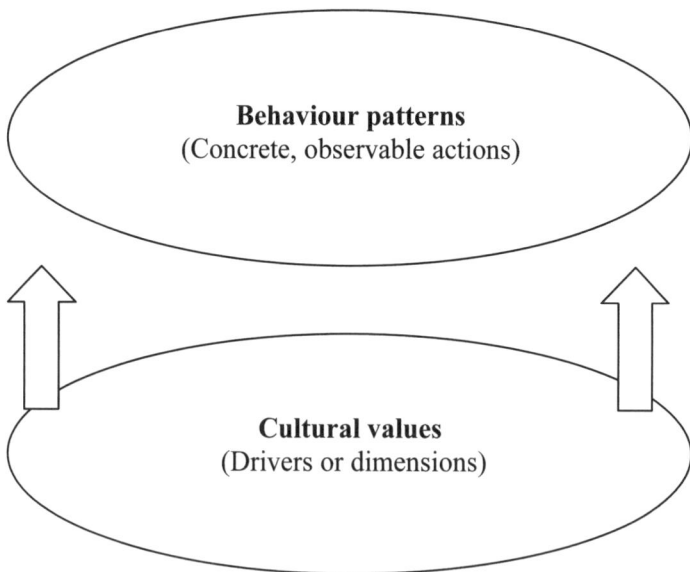

Figure 4.1 Cultural values and behaviour patterns

'Behaviour patterns' or' social scripts' result from the cultural values (drivers or dimensions of culture). See Appendix 2.

Cultural values are formed over time and are influenced by environmental factors, historical, social and economic factors, the media and contact with other cultural groups. Likewise behaviours or social scripts are formed by similar factors, but may be quicker to change. The values are like the hidden engine of a car (the parts that drive the motor), and the behaviours are like the parts of the car you can see, hear and touch.

Explanation of cultural values (drivers)

> A value system represents what is expected or hoped for, required or forbidden.
>
> Maybury-Lewis (1992: 7)

It is difficult to look at the ways of life of others without bias, since we all look through our own cultural spectacles and lenses at the world without even realizing it. It helps to invite everyone to stand back. In some workshops I use a poster of the 'world from outer space' (see www.postershop.com). I invite comments on how participants perceive the world from this angle: for example the variety of climates, no visible country boundaries, landscapes, oceans, and that people developed diverse lifestyles in order to cope with their dissimilar environments. No one response is better, they are just different. (See also John Lennon's song 'Imagine'.)

When explaining the meaning of terms used to describe values, it is useful to give examples from the cultures of the participants present in the room and from across the world. This enables participants to take a more detached, helicopter view, and illustrates that none of us live and work in isolation. I ask about the values of their grandparents. Are they the same as theirs? Discussion follows about cultures and change, with comments like 'Cultures and cultural values are not stagnant.'

Some participants may show resistance. The argument by some inward-looking fundamentalists from different creeds that 'Some things are part of our culture and therefore should not be open to discussion or criticism' is not valid, as values and views on values, human rights and responsibilities change over time. The power of the past is used in many cultures to maintain cultural identity. Things are done a certain way because that is the way it has always been done. One way of opening up this discussion is by inviting participants to read a quotation like the one made by anthropologist David Maybury-Lewis in the television series and book entitled *Millennium: Tribal wisdom and the modern world*:

> It's walking in their shoes to understand them better, to put your own prejudices on hold and give them a fair hearing. It may be that at the end of the day you'll find a lot of things that they do are quite unacceptable.

> That's all right. The most foolish sort of relativism is that which suggests
> that 'If they do it then it must be alright because it's part of their culture'. I
> think a serious relativism is one that doesn't take values for granted. Values
> are not something you pledge allegiance to in primary school. Values are
> something you are constantly worrying about. They're decisions that
> you're constantly making but you can't just make them and put them on
> hold. They should be reviewed in the light of new evidence.
>
> (Maybury-Lewis, 1992: 7)

During discussions, comments like 'values are not straightforward' and
'values are slippery' emerge. The whole philosophy of facilitation is for
people to be engaged in determining their future, the values they want
to keep and the ones they want to adapt or discard. There is a distinct
difference between 'cultural preservation' (which implies that culture is a
static object which can be locked in a tightly sealed exhibit in a museum)
and 'cultural survival', where people have a say in keeping traditions and
having control over the evolution of their culture and their own future,
and preventing 'cultural extinction'.

Scholars in the area of intercultural communication have advanced many
different classifications, 'dimensions' or 'values' in order to help us make
sense of our own and other cultures (Hofstede, 1980, 1991, 2001; Hall and
Hall, 1990; Trompenaars, 1993; Trompenaars and Hampden-Turner, 2000;
Abdullah, 2001). Table 4.1 outlines the many different descriptors used by
these authors to compare cultures. There is some overlap. However, the fact
that there are ongoing changes by authors and such variety illustrates the
difficulties involved in describing and comparing cultures. Note that the
cultural values are not all opposites, and they are not all on a continuum,
which is why I have used the term 'cultural values' or 'cultural drivers'
rather than dimensions in this book.

For further ideas on differences in cultural values see the World Values
Survey Website: www.worldvaluessurvey.org/library/ and Stringer and
Cassidy (2003).

Anthropologist John Wilson (1961) analysed cases of community conflict
in indigenous groups in the Pilbarra area of Western Australia. As a result
cultural descriptors emerged out of the case studies including:

- humour as amusement and humour as jokes;
- specific (segmented and private) and diffuse (little private space) areas
  of life;
- superiority and mutual respect for 'the other';
- trust and distrust for 'the other';
- people are basically good/good and evil/evil;
- space: shared and private;
- independence/do own thing versus dependence;
- capitalization/restraint versus consumption;
- central–peripheral;

- traditional/conservative/'old people' versus 'innovative people';
- multilingualism and monolingualism.

Facilitators on the whole, however, do not have the luxury of long-term immersion in other cultures, and we need quicker methods to help people describe their cultural values and behaviours.

Characteristics of effective culturally diverse teams

Research by Adler (1997) and DiStefano and Maznevski (2000) concluded that diverse teams tend to perform either better or worse than homogeneous teams, with more of them performing worse than better if attention is not given to the needs of individual members. DiStefano and Maznevski divided multicultural teams that they studied into three categories (destroyers, equalizers and creators) as described below.

Dysfunctional teams (destroyers)

I use the term 'dysfunctional' as the term 'destroyer' used by DiStefano and Maznevski sounds so military and antagonistic. These teams were dysfunctional because the formal leaders in complex situations made decisions without genuine discussion among members. As a result, they destroyed the potential value of these multicultural teams.

Equalizer teams

These team members smoothed, compromised and suppressed any differences in ideas and perspectives. DiStefano and Maznevski's research led them to believe that most culturally diverse teams that thought of themselves as doing well were really equalizers.

Creator teams

These teams did more than use platitudes like 'We value diversity.' They actively explored their differences and took advantage of their diversity like a jazz ensemble. Brenson-Lazán calls this the 'humungous paradox of synergy': the greater the diversity, the greater the potential for synergy and the greater the difficulty in achieving it. The less diversity there is, the lower is the potential for synergy and the greater the ease of achieving it.

From their observations of these teams, DiStefano and Maznevski concluded that the key to being successful is the quality of the interaction processes rather than the team membership.

Table 4.1 Cultural values (drivers/dimensions) described by various authors

Authors:	Abdullah and Pedersen (2003)	Adler (1997)	Brislin (2000)	Hall and Hall (1990)	Hofstede (1980, 1991)	Hofstede, Pedersen and Hofstede (2002)	Hogan (2002, 2003)	Hooker (2003)	Lane, DiStefano and Maznevski (1997)	O'Hara-Devereaux and Johansen (1994)	Trompenaars (1993)	Trompenaars and Hampden-Turner (1997)
Cultural descriptors												
Individualism and collectivism	X	X	X		X	X	X	X	X		X	X
Context: low (explicit) and high (implicit) context communication	X		X	X			X	X		X	X	
Time (monochronic and polychronic; past, present and future oriented; slow and fast)	X		X	X		X	X	X	X	X	X	
Feelings/emotions shown (effective/emotional) and not shown (neutral)									X	X	X	X

Apollonian: equanimity/well-ordered life and Dionysian intense experience			X		
Ascription and achievement oriented	X	X		X	X
Confucian dynamism (perseverance, status pecking order, thrift, shame/face)			X	X	X
Control: internal and external	X	X		X	X
Weak (particularism) and strong (universalism) uncertainty avoidance	X	X	X	X	
Universal (rules for citizens) and particular (allegiance to friends and important people)					

Table 4.1 *Continued*

Authors:	*Abdullah and Pedersen (2003)*	*Adler (1997)*	*Brislin (2000)*	*Hall and Hall (1990)*	*Hofstede (1980, 1991)*	*Hofstede, Pedersen and Hofstede (2002)*	*Hogan (2002, 2003)*	*Hooker (2003)*	*Lane, DiStefano and Maznevski (1997)*	*O'Hara-Devereaux and Johansen (1994)*	*Trompenaars (1993)*	*Trompenaars and Hampden-Turner (1997)*
Cultural descriptors												
Space (territoriality; personal space)				X								
Information flow (path and speed of communications)				X						X		
Power distance: small (equality) and large (hierarchical)	X	X	X		X	X		X		X		
Masculinity (aggressive, division of sex roles) and femininity (nurturing, unisex, cooperation)			X		X	X	X					

Harmony versus control over environment and events (harmony and dominance)	X	X				X	
Doing and being (career success versus quality of life)		X	X	X			
Relationships and tasks and/or rules	X	X		X	X		X
Shame (face) and guilt	X			X	X		X
Linear and circular thinking and speech				X			
Religious/ spiritual and secular nature of human beings	X			X		X	
Polite (feelings) and rude (justice over courtesy)					X		X
Humour as amusement and humour as jokes					X		X

Intercultural leadership

There is also the style of leadership to be considered. Dr Shobhana Chakrabarti used the ancient Sanskrit word *Sangam* as a metaphor for the style of 'inclusive leadership' she believes is required for leaders of culturally diverse teams:

> Sangam signifies the meeting point of different rivers coming from diverse sources ... whilst you can still see each river with its own separate identity, at the same time you experience the dramatic impact as the rivers flow together and see the strength that is generated in that confluence – that togetherness – as the rivers merge and join the ocean.
>
> (Chakrabarti, 2005: 5)

Shobhana describes the need for leadership of culturally diverse teams to radiate from the centre of the organization rather than top-down authoritarianism. After interviewing 12 women leaders of multicultural teams from around the world, she concluded that the ideal characteristics of intercultural leaders are:

- vision and dreams with a purpose;
- winning hearts through supportive, respectful relationships, solidarity;
- cultural sensitivity, promoting and celebrating differences, learning from each other and enriching life through intercultural contacts;
- leading and coaching for change and transitions;
- empowerment, taping into the power within people;
- being a role model and mentor.

Intercultural sensitivity

There are managers who minimize differences, so the model shown in Figure 4.2 can come in useful during workshops as a means of assessing the sensitivity of participants or confronting managers who deny the need to look at cultural differences.

The model of intercultural sensitivity developed by Bennett and Bennett (2004) is a six-stage model which helps facilitators to understand the worldview of participants and organizations. The model attempts to show the development of intercultural sensitivity as experience of difference increases.

The first three stages are ethnocentric, in that people are thinking from their own cultural perspective. In the 'denial' stage, people believe their own culture is the only one, and avoid contact with people from other cultures. Organizations in 'denial' have no systematic diversity recruitment systems or policies.

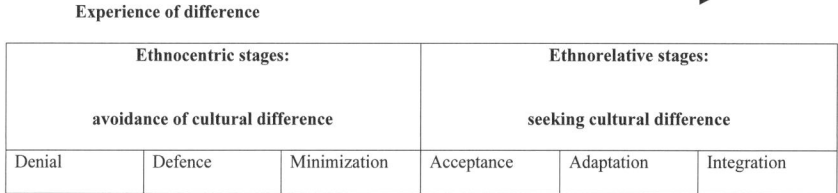

Figure 4.2   The developmental model of intercultural sensitivity

Source: Bennett and Bennett (2004: 153).

In the 'defence' stage, cultural difference is still downplayed and one's own culture (or an adopted culture) is experienced as the only good one. Organizations in the defence stage may be seen as over-confident or arrogant and insensitive to locals. They see cultural difference as a problem to be avoided.

In the 'minimization' stage, elements of one's own culture are seen as common to all, universal. There is an assumption, deep down, that people are all the same (and like the person making the assumption). Organizations in this stage claim to be tolerant but are seen as hypocritical. There is a strong pressure to conform to the organizational culture.

The second three stages are ethnorelative: people now see their own culture in the context of other cultures. In the 'acceptance' stage, other cultures are included as other possible realities. Organizations in this stage recognize the value of diversity. There is awareness and talk, but little training or action.

In the 'adaptation' stage, a person can swap perspectives. Organizations in this stage encourage training in intercultural skills. There is respect for diversity, and use is made of the diverse resources and perspectives of multicultural teams.

In the 'integration' stage, a person can shift in and out of different cultural worldviews and can also stand back and objectively take a 'helicopter view'. Organizations in this stage have integrated multicultural policies, procedures and rewards for using diversity creatively.

The model of course has its limitations. It assumes that intercultural sensitivity increases as experience of difference increases, and this unfortunately is not always the case.

Cultural mapping

Cultural mapping means different things to different people. (Anthropologists use the terms cultural or social anthropology, or social mapping.)

It involves researching and documenting information about a culture, like a jigsaw puzzle, to create a whole picture of both visible and invisible elements that intrinsically make up that culture.

Information may be collected by insiders through their own cultural lens, or by outsiders who need to consider the cultural lens through which they view another culture.

The process can begin with no information or guidelines, and allow insiders to name their cultural elements using their own terms. Or it can start with some trigger words, checklists of indicators or frameworks, choosing those descriptors that best fit a culture at a given moment in history. The elements may include visible elements like behaviours, language structures, sayings, ways of interacting, child rearing and educational practices, clothing, architecture, laws and policies towards insiders and outsiders, and invisible things like values, stories, spiritual beliefs and unwritten codes of behaviour.

While mapping, ideas may be illustrated by simple drawings, lists of words, sayings, photos, songs, and collections of art and/or craft. Or elements may be comprehensively collected in a database (such as a geographical information system – GIS) or a website with links to other websites with relevant portals, web pages, reference books and/or other information.

The process of cultural mapping enables individuals to appreciate their own and other people's perspectives, ways of being and motivation. The results may be used to design policy, living and community spaces, education programmes, work environments and ways for team members to interact.

See the Asia Europe Foundation (ASEF) 'Culture360' website:
www.culture360.org (website being updated at time of publication)
and the UNESCO 'Cultural lens' website:
www.unescobkk.org/fileadmin/user_upload/culture/Cultural_lens/
CDPL_Toolkit-August_Workshop.pdf

The MBI model

As a result of their research, DiStefano and Maznevski (2000) developed the mapping, bridging and integrating (MBI) model shown in Figure 4.3. In their research they observed that 'creator teams' actively:

● *mapped* and tried to understand their differences;
● *bridged* their communication and took differences into account;
● *integrated* team-level ideas by carefully monitoring participation patterns, solving disagreements and creating new perspectives.

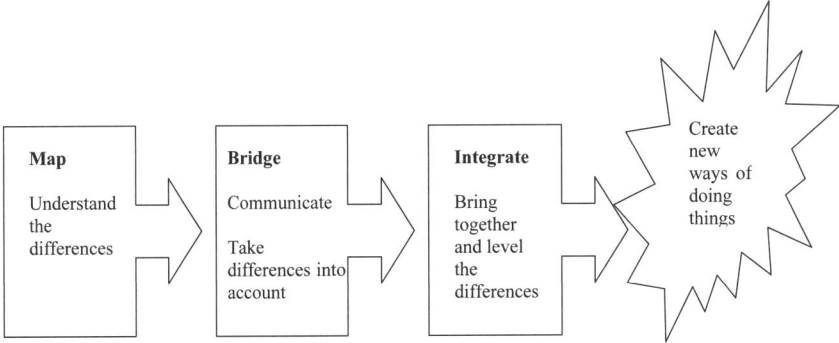

Figure 4.3   Mapping, bridging and integrating (MBI) model

Source: DiStefano and Maznevski (2000).

A facilitator may take a group through each stage of the MBI model in turn; if there is any confusion, it may be necessary to revert to a previous stage.

This section focuses on a three-stage MBI model and processes to enable multicultural groups to focus on diversity, and thereby to maximize the potential of the individual members of the group to achieve their common goals.

M: Mapping to understand the differences

Participants are invited to 'map' or plot their own cultures in some way. A useful preliminary exercise is to ask participants in small groups to discuss the question 'How many different ways could you use to describe your culture?'

The metaphor of 'mapping a culture' may need careful explanation first. Most multicultural teams do not take the time to map cultural differences openly; they just rely on broad generalizations (stereotypes) (Reese, 1997, 2001). The important aspect of mapping is identifying which differences will affect interactions and decision making: for example, cultural values, thinking styles and ways of achieving goals.

There are many different methods that can be used to map cultural differences. Among them are learning basic words or sayings in the languages of group members (Reese, 1997, 2001); discussing the cultural iceberg (after Brislin, 1981); developing cultural suitcases (source unknown); using cultural card sorts (Kohls and Knight, 1994; Abdullah and Shephard, 2000); videotaping meetings and analysing interactions (if culturally appropriate) using a mirroring process (Satir, 1983; Hogan, 2000, 2003).

B: Bridging

Bridging requires individuals to communicate, while appreciating difference. It is discussed in detail at the end of the mapping section.

I: Integrating

Integrating refers to bringing together new ways of being and behaving into the team norms.

Different interpretations of the word 'culture'

It is important to clarify which interpretation of the word 'culture' you are using. The word 'culture' has now been used very loosely in the English language. We may belong to many different groups with different 'cultural' norms. We have to learn what is acceptable and not acceptable in each, and be able to 'code switch' communication patterns, behaviours and even values at times. For example, children may have a very different family culture from their school and classroom culture. Teenagers may need to behave and dress differently when they get their first job. Students who study overseas have to learn to behave differently on return to their home culture. A football team and indeed football crowds have distinct modes of behaviour very different from a quilting group or a music group. This is illustrated in Figure 4.4. An individual, represented by a smiling face in the middle, may belong to or interact with many different types of cultural groups as shown in the petals. As the petal model illustrates, human identity is very complex. I am an Australian citizen, of English origin (and citizenship), with distant Irish ancestry, a liberal, a woman, a wife, a facilitator, a teacher, a learner, an author, a heterosexual, a believer in human rights and responsibilities, a musician and a community member. Each facet of my identity requires different codes of behaviour.

Which culture do you describe?

Before 'mapping' a culture, it is important that facilitators clarify which culture is being placed under the magnifying glass. In the context of this book I am focusing on the culture/s that has the most influence on the values and behaviours of the individuals in a team or workshop group, but these techniques are transferable to mapping other types of cultures.

In workshops I use coloured circular cards held together by a pin in the centre to explain the petal model. In this way I can separate the petals to indicate which 'culture' is being spoken about. It is a useful visual and movable model. Participants often like to identify the different groups they belong to. The groups are numbered to enable participants to move around the model and aid discussion.

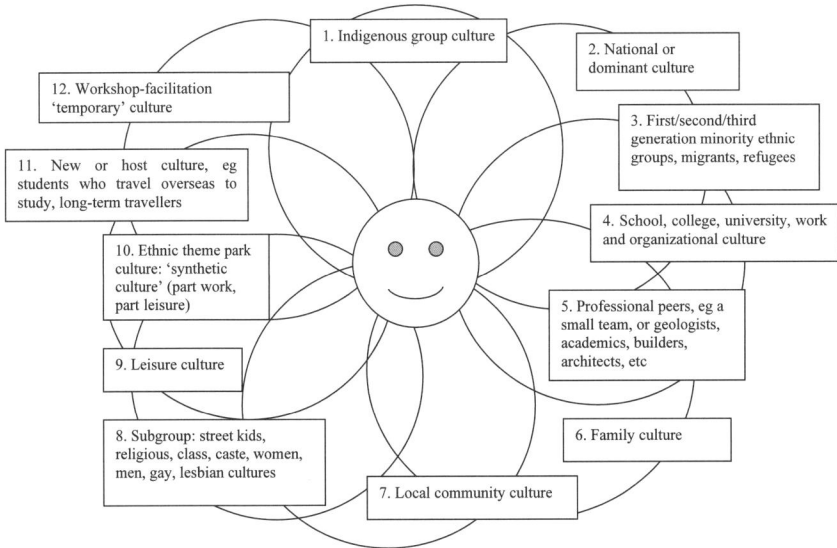

Figure 4.4   The petal model of different cultural groups

Workshop-facilitation culture

Facilitation is not value-neutral. Generally speaking workshop-facilitation culture includes:

- participation by everyone;
- participation seen as speaking;
- listening to everyone;
- the more ideas the better;
- ideas with equal worth (not in accordance to who said them).

Some participants may have to do a lot of code switching and feel very uncomfortable in a workshop as a result.

In some cultures the norms include control, obedience to authority figures and various degrees of paternalism. Silence is valued as a mark of respect, and does not mean that people do not have anything to say. As facilitators we encourage participants to speak loudly, yet in some cultures speaking softly is a cultural norm and sign of politeness. Often we design a process knowing it might not be completed, but that working on it will illustrate certain points. In many South-East Asian cultures there is a strong desire to complete exercises, and people focus on the content rather than the process itself.

The values espoused in many participatory workshops are in the list on the left of Table 4.2. The boundaries are not distinct. Compare these norms with societies where the participants regard themselves as a group (rather than individuals) and do not begin until the leader or power figure arrives. Then the leader states the goals of the session and assumes the right to dominate discussion.

The same type of table may be used to identify the values of a project in a developing country, to compare the values of the project with those of the local population/s, and to compare the 'espoused theory' and values of facilitation to the 'espoused theory' and values of participants (Schön, 1983). (See also Table 4.2.)

Ethnic (synthetic) theme park culture

Tamar Gordon produced a thought-provoking DVD highlighting the genre of cultural representation in cultural villages in China and Japan. She described 'contact zones' where performers from one culture meet tourists from other cultures in simulated orchestrated, controlled environments and 'imagined communities' (Gordon, 2005).

Facilitation dilemma

Should facilitators give cultural descriptor words for participants to choose from or just ask for ideas? If you are asking participants to describe their culture, you may experience a dilemma. Should you start with a totally unstructured approach with open-ended questions, for example 'Please tell me about your culture'? In response participants chose their own words and frameworks. Or should you give some prompts to trigger thought? For example, the questions 'Would you tell me what you think others should know about your culture?' or 'What should I pack in my

Table 4.2   Comparison between 'facilitation values' and possible 'cultural values'

Espoused theory: workshop-facilitation values	*Espoused theory: possible cultural values of one group of participants*
Equity: participation of all	Hierarchy: highest participation rates given automatically to power holders, males and elders
Direct: low-context communication. Differences of opinion encouraged.	Indirect: high-context communication. No open differences permitted. Harmony at all costs.
Value cultural diversity	Homogeneity. Do things our way (according to the culture of Head Office or donors).

cultural suitcase if I was going to visit your country?' will result in very different answers.

There may be a number of constraints. Respondents are likely to give the aspects they want outsiders to know about and/or the parts they think the others want to hear about: the 'good' side rather than the 'shadow side' which all cultures have. It is worth noting that participants who belong to the dominant culture often find it harder to describe their own culture than minority groups. This is perhaps because the dominant culture is so pervasive, while the members of minority groups have to 'code switch' regularly.

Purpose/rationale of the cultural values card pack

Card packs of key words have been used by many authors, including Hopson and Scally (1984), Kohls and Knight (1994), Abdullah and Shephard (2000) and Hogan (2000), to:

● stimulate thought and discussion;
● make abstract ideas more accessible and tangible;
● enable participants to cluster, rank, add or alter ideas;
● engender a sense of playfulness to lighten what could be quite difficult or contentious issues.

The 'cultural values card pack' is similar to the 'Power cards' I introduced in *Facilitating Empowerment* (Hogan, 2000) in that they have been produced in a format that is easy to photocopy. I want participants to be able to take a pack home to use alone and/or with family and friends. The card pack has been evolving over time and will continue to do so. The cards are also easily adaptable: I want facilitators to be able to adapt cards based on their own levels of confidence to 'handle' certain issues in a group, depending on the stage of development of that group. Some of the cards described below contain topics which it might be productive or prudent to omit, depending on the ability, at that time, of some groups to converse in a mutually respectful way about certain issues. It may not be culturally appropriate to discuss certain topics in mixed gender groups. In some cultures some topics are just not discussed openly. There are some topics where there may be no agreement and there is tacit agreement *not* to raise those topics openly within a group: for example, multiculturalism and monoculturalism.

The cards also rely on the written word, and words of course mean different things to different people, even among people who share the same mother tongue. Words are symbols of meaning designed to sensitize us to a concept. In themselves they cannot define a concept so that we all infer the same meaning (Festinger, 1957). Deriving a common meaning in groups has to be worked at, and at times it is a struggle.

If I add symbols and pictures in multicultural situations, these may cause misunderstandings. However, it could be useful for facilitators to ask participants to illustrate *their* understanding of these concepts through mime, story, metaphor, sayings, drawings, song and photos.

The pack is designed to map diversity rather than to increase stereotypes. The heading cards are designed to enable participants to be more aware of and sensitive to their culture, and to examine how it may be changing for the better and/or worse (in their eyes). As a result they can, if they wish, highlight changes they would like to embrace and those they would like to discourage.

There are no hard and fast rules on how to use this card pack. Some different ideas are explained below. However, what is important is that the facilitator encourages and ensures that everyone adheres to agreed ground rules to enhance cultural safety.

Cultural values cards

Scholars in the area of intercultural communication have advanced many different classification names, such as 'values', 'drivers' and 'dimensions', in order to help us make sense of other cultures and our own, as shown in Table 4.3.

It helps if we understand cultural values. We have to be careful about generalizing too much about our cultures. You will find some highly individualistic people in collective societies and some highly collective people in individualistic societies. I use the phrase 'cultural values' as some descriptors are dimensions on a continuum, whilst others are values and impossible to measure or quantify.

Some key points worth adding include:

- There are underlying patterns or values or dimensions in all our cultures.
- All cultural values have advantages and disadvantages.
- Cultures change over time.
- We must be careful not to make assumptions and stereotype others.
- There is a bell curve in each group. Some people on the left of the bell curve have a characteristic in a small way; others on the right of the bell curve may be extreme.
- The values are not necessarily on a continuum (of task and relationship), nor are they opposites.

Table 4.3 Cultural values in the card pack

NB: You may wish to edit the pack according to the workshop context.

A1 Individualism 'I' focus	A2 Collectivism 'we', 'group' or 'team' focus
B1 Respect rules of behaviour and protocol	B2 Casual politeness informality
C1 Hierarchy many levels in society, status, protocol	C2 Equality few levels, equal treatment and access
D1 Control over assertive, competitive	D2 Harmony with cooperative, avoid conflict
E1 Indirect communication Diplomatic, circular, metaphor, analogies	E2 Direct communication To the point, blunt
F1 Kinship systems not important	F2 Kinship systems important
G1 Task (doing) oriented efficiency, success, on the move	G2 Relationship (people) oriented friendly, hospitable
G3 Being oriented content to relax	G4 Having oriented materialistic, possessions oriented
H1 Time: flexible	H2 Time: tight punctuality/deadlines
I1 Time: past oriented history, stories, ancestors important	I2 Time: present oriented in the here and now, spontaneous
I3 Time: future oriented forward thinking, planning, imagining	I4 Time: cyclical seasons, events, rhythms of life and death
J1 Religious/spiritual religious practice permeates whole life	J2 Secular work separated from religion
K1 Shame Save or gain face: individual, family, culture	K2 Guilt individual responsibility for wrongs
L1 Karma	L2 Fate
M1 Universalism One way of doing things (our way) is transferable to all cultures	M2 Particularism There are many ways of doing things in different cultures
N1 Multiculturalism is valued	N2 Monoculturalism is valued
O1 Multilingualism is valued	O2 Monolingualism is valued
P1 Risk taking	P2 Risk avoiding
Blank: Please add your own	Blank: Please add your own

Table 4.1 (pages 112–15) details the many cultural descriptors used by authors over time. I have chosen the ones that I have found useful in a workshop context. In some ways it is better not to cover all areas, as participants like to be able to add or rename their specific cultural values to the pack.

Explanations of cultural values cards

There are many concepts here, some of which may be unfamiliar and may need explanation for participants. I write these concepts out on large coloured cards. I find it useful to go through each of the above groups of concepts with co-facilitators, acting out examples in quick role plays or using sayings or short stories to bring these concepts alive. Some are obvious. I have illustrated some of the more obscure concepts below.

Hierarchy and equality

Gerte Hofstede (1980) called these values 'high power distance' and 'low power distance'. Asma Abdullah used easier terms, 'hierarchy' and 'equality' (Abdullah and Pedersen, 2003). I usually draw two pyramids to help to explain these concepts (see Figure 4.5).

Respect and basic politeness

The ways in which people show respect vary from one culture to another. In some cultures, direct eye contact shows respect. In others, such as Australian Aboriginal society and many South-East Asian cultures, children and adults must show deference to people of higher age and status.

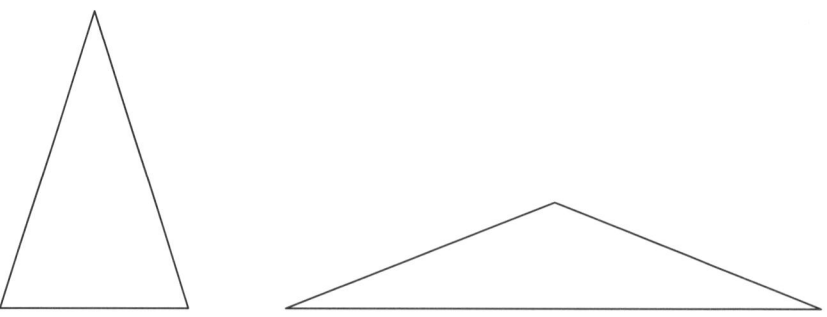

Figure 4.5   Hierarchy and equality

In Australia casual politeness may appear disrespectful to foreigners. However, some Japanese visitors commented that they liked it, as they thought Australian friendliness to strangers was more genuine than the elaborate Japanese protocols.

I spoke to an HRD manager at a hotel in Perth, Western Australia, which was part of an international chain. She commented, 'We had an edict from Head Office in the UK that all hotel staff should be trained in being less formal than in the past. As you can imagine there was an outcry from the hotel's branches in Japan, but also there is a need for staff to be trained in "situational politeness and respect". They might be far more formal with our Japanese customers than those from Australia. So our training materials need to be adapted.' This piece of advice is useful for facilitators and culturally diverse participants.

Task (doing) and being

Sayings may help to explain certain cultural values, for example 'Don't just sit there, do something' (task (doing) oriented) compared with 'Don't just do something, sit there' (*Thich Nhat Hanh*: being oriented).

> We are human beings, not human doings.
>
> Loretta Di Rozario

Participants may have their own culturally specific examples.

Shame and guilt

The strength of 'shame' is often not understood well by some Westerners. It is not only necessary to protect oneself from shame, as a Lao student who had just arrived in Australia told me.

> Lao student: 'I wandered around the campus lost for two hours when I first arrived in Australia, It was so hot, about 40 degrees, I was exhausted.'
>
> Chris: 'Why didn't you ask for help? Your English is so good!'
>
> Lao student: 'It took me some time to get used to the accents here. I was worried in case they would not understand my English, and if so I would bring shame not only on myself, but also my family and country.'

Harmony/cooperation and control/competition

In 2002, on the same day that Germany and Brazil played in the World Cup Final in Japan, the national teams of Bhutan and Montserrat met in an official Federation of International Football Association (FIFA) sanctioned friendly match in Thimphu, the Bhutanese capital. Ranked at the very bottom of international soccer, 202nd and 203rd respectively, they showed terrific sportsmanship. The prime minister of Bhutan was asked beforehand, 'Who do you think will win?' He answered, 'I don't know but I know it will be a great match.' At the end, the two captains held up the cup between them and it magically split literally down the middle, indicating the way sport can unite peoples of different cultures and the sporting attitude of both sides. Yet the match was rejected by all commercial sponsors. (See the video entitled *The Other Final*: Kramer, 2002.)

Religion/spiritual values and secular values

It was Asma Abdullah in Malaysia (1996) who first wrote about the importance of recognizing the influence of religious and secular values in multicultural business settings. Consideration of these issues is so important, especially given world events and sensitivities. As facilitators we need to take religious as well as secular needs into consideration in planning workshops, and be prepared to contract for cultural safety and address issues of prejudice if they arise. See Chapter 7 on 'Facilitating difference'.

Karma and fate

Karma relates to cause and effect, how past deeds impact on one's current life. The concept is central to belief systems like Hinduism and Buddhism that incorporate the concept of incarnation or cycles of rebirth. Fate or destiny refers to the inevitable course of events that we are powerless to influence, no matter what we do.

Time cards and an ethical dilemma

There are many cards representing time. I heard somewhere that some indigenous Native American groups, when making decisions, try to imagine the impact on the next seven generations.

In one workshop, I was put on the spot as a facilitator when participants were discussing the 'future orientation' card. A representative from one minority group said, 'I'm so worried, our group does not have a future and our language is dying.' At the time I was not sure what to do, given the political context of the workshop. I acknowledged his concern, but did not write up his point on the flipchart. As it was time for morning tea I called for a break. Later I went to speak with him privately and voiced my concern for his well-being. I asked how he would like to proceed after the break. He acknowledged that he was pleased that given the people present, I had not delved further.

Indirect and direct communication

Indirect communication has also been described as 'high context' and direct communication as 'low context' by Hall and Hall (1990). I renamed them as these terms were difficult for some participants to differentiate. Indirect communication can relate to feedback, and it is one of the hardest cultural values for Westerners to learn. Wajuppa Tossa, a wonderful Thai storyteller, illustrated indirect communication with a story.

THAI MYTH: INDIRECT COMMUNICATION

A young boy was courting a young woman. She invited him to her house, saying she would cook food for him. He was ravenously hungry and quickly ate his meal. He was hoping there would be some more rice, so he picked up his empty plate and said, 'What beautiful china this is, what exquisite design and colours.' The girl stood up, gracefully walked into the kitchen and returned with the empty cooking pot, saying, 'See this beautiful pot! It has been in our family for centuries.' He immediately understood that the family had produced as much food as they were able, and he did not ask for more.

To outsiders this may appear to be 'beating around the bush'. Indeed many outsiders would not even pick up the clues about the family's lack of food given by the girl. Direct communication may seem very rude to some, but it is a cultural norm in some societies, as shown by sayings such as 'Say it as it is', 'Call a spade a spade' and 'Don't circle the hot porridge' (a Dutch proverb meaning be direct and to the point).

Indirectness may also relate to signage and instructions which are either not written up or not very noticeable. In Thimphu in Bhutan I was stopped by the police for driving up a one-way street the wrong way. When I apologized and explained that there were no signs, the police officer patiently told me that they did not need a sign as everybody knew it was a one-way street.

People in high context societies take in information from the whole environment. This has been born out by research by Richard Nisbett, whereby Chinese and Americans of European descent were asked to look at photos. Each image had a striking central figure set against scenery. The American students spent much longer looking at the central object, while the Chinese participants' eyes tended to dart around, taking in the background (Merali, 2005).

Comments from facilitators who have used the cards

Careful briefing

The explanation of the cards and examples by the facilitator may impact on people's understandings of the cards. Kevin Kettle commented to me:

> At a workshop in Manila for museum staff from nine nationalities the Vietnamese group added 'communal spirit' and at first I did think this could come under the individual/collectivist category, but they explained that it was a bit different and described it more as an inherent feeling of communal spirit that went beyond family to include neighbors in the street and thus thought processes always being community-driven. I suppose that the way in which the cultural values are explained prior to doing the activity and what examples are given determines the outcome here. I think I had explained individualism and collectivism in more of a work context and this could explain the Vietnamese group offering of 'communal spirit' in a day-to-day context as opposed to a work context.

It is important that participants can add and rename cards (Alia, 2006).

Large cards

I use large coloured cards (A4 size in landscape format with letters 10 centimetres high) to aid the verbal explanation of the cultural values. I am careful not to put the cards which could be construed as typically 'Western' under one another. I jumble them up.

Mixed groups

Often if there are only one or two participants representing one culture they decide to link up with others. In a culturally diverse workshop in Myanmar there were a number of Westerners, one each from Canada, Denmark, the United Kingdom and Australia. They decided to join up, and spent most of the time arguing noisily. It was a very useful example of how collective nouns like 'Western', 'African', 'Asian' can be too general.

Useful additions

An Indonesian group added 'local leadership' and 'local laws'. They pointed out that this was not applicable to larger cities, but that in rural communities local leadership and customary or traditional justice systems surpassed any national directives.

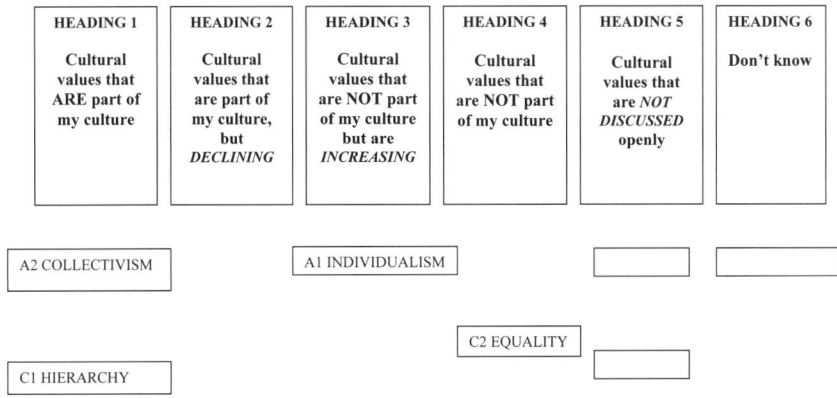

Figure 4.6 Layout of heading cards

Sorting the cultural card pack

In the cultural card pack there are four different kinds of cards. It makes identification of them easier for you and participants if they are photo-copied in different colours:

- 'Heading cards' (green). Spread these out from left to right as in Figure 4.6.
- 'Cultural values' cards in capital letters, such as 'HIERARCHY' (yellow) (see Appendix 1).
- 'Behaviour cards' or social scripts in upper and lower case, such as 'Written contracts are valued' (white) (see Appendix 2).
- Blank cards for everyone to rename and/or add cards. (See Appendices 1 and 2.)

Note that the cards are numbered in pairs and groups, such as A1, B1, or A2, B2, C2, D2. This numbering system indicates cards may be linked in some way, for example 'A1 INDIVIDUALISM' and 'A2 COLLECTIVISM'.

Card pack preparation

1. Cut up the cards to form a deck of cards. Make sure they are in sequence: A1, B1, A2, B2, and so on. You will need a pack of cards for each cultural group.
2. Prepare 'Cultural comparison charts' for each heading (see Figure 4.7). I type the words on the computer with 40 font size minimum and bold type as it easier to read, or use a data projector to display the information on a screen.

Heading 1 Cultural values that ARE part of my culture					
Cultural values ⇩	**Cultures** ⇒				
	a	**b**	**c**	**d**	**e**
A1 INDIVIDUALISM 'I'	x			x	
A2 COLLECTIVISM 'WE'		x	x		x
B1 RESPECT	x		x	x	x
B2 CASUAL POLITENESS		x			
C1 HIERARCHY	x		x	x	x
C2 EQUALITY		x			

Figure 4.7   Cultural comparison chart

Variations in setting up the card sort exercise

● In some groups you may wish to give out blank cards for participants to write their key cultural values or key values on before you give them the card pack.
● It is best to distribute the 'values' cards first. After these have been discussed you can choose which groups of behaviour cards to distribute next. Some participants get overwhelmed if there are too many cards.
● You do not have to use the heading cards. These were added to embed in the process the fact that cultures (like languages) change over time. You may prefer participants to just turn over cards from a shuffled pack and discuss each in turn.

Emphasize that groups within a culture vary. There are many shades of grey, but you are asking the participants to give the dominant trend in their group.

Equipment needed

Flipchart paper, Blu-Tack, one card pack per cultural group. (If there are more than six representatives of one group you may wish to provide additional packs.) Plenty of tables are required to lay out cards.

M: Mapping cultures with the card pack

Ask participants to state their 'culture of origin' or the culture in which they have most long-term connection and experience (or empathize with or feel part of).

Stages

Instructions to participants

1. It is useful to sort the cards on top of a sheet of flipchart paper on a large table or on the floor (if that is culturally acceptable). Once they are sorted they can then be attached with Blu-Tac and displayed or stored for later use.
2. Ask participants to turn the flipchart into portrait format and write the name of their cultural group at the top of the first sheet of paper.
3. Lay out the 'heading cards' from left to right. See Figure 4.6.
4. Discuss each card (or groups of cards) in turn and decide where to put them.
5. When everyone has agreed where to place them, attach with Blu-Tac so they can be displayed on the wall.
6. Ask a group representative to write down the letter names of the 'values cards' under Heading 1 and to fill in the 'Cultural comparison chart' (see Figure 4.7) so everyone can compare the results from different groups in the workshop.

Collating and comparing the data collected

When facilitating a multicultural team it is useful to collate the data to obtain a holistic view of the different cultural dimensions and values held by the group members. These may be collated on a flipchart or displayed electronically using a data projector.

Collect data on another chart for 'cultural values that are part of the culture but are decreasing' and on a third for 'cultural values that are increasing'.

Discussion

Facilitator questions might be:

- Can you identify any similarities?
- Are there any surprises?
- Are there any differences?
- Which differences might be useful to explore and build bridges?
- How could these bridges be integrated into your workplace and maintained?

Behaviour cards

The possible number of behaviour cards is enormous (see Appendix 2). In some ways it is best for facilitators and participants to generate their own packs based on the context and focus of the workshop. I have clustered them under the following headings:

- verbal communication;
- listening and silence;
- writing;
- reading;
- body language/feelings;
- time;
- performance/getting things done;
- food/drinking/dress and etiquette;
- family/gender/child-rearing practices;
- community.

These may then be dealt with in turn in different workshops. For example, comparisons of cultural aspects of family, gender and child-rearing practices may be the focus of induction programmes for migrants and could be summarized.

Debrief

Before going into the bridge-building stage, it is important to allow participants from each group to describe their perceptions. (Comments aired may include 'Oh, that's why we find that group rude: they are just more direct than us.') Also discuss what is added to the blank cards (these can yield some exciting discussions).

In Myanmar, the card sort triggered discussion among a group about 'Shame and guilt'. They related this to the Thai concept '*A nar tae*' (embarrassment, guilt, shame or uneasiness), with different examples such as arriving late for meetings, and feeling guilty when foreigners ask them to do things at weekends and they have to host or attend family functions.

We all belong to many different kinds and sizes of groups, each with their own cultures. When participants are faced with the negative or shadow side of their own culture we may feel 'cognitive dissonance' because as human beings we like consistency. If there are clashes between words, deeds or values we *may* react negatively (Heaney, 2001). For example, in one multicultural group in Perth, a man from Mumbai (India) admitted that to get things done in India you had to use bribes: 'You've got no choice.' But he added, most emphatically, 'Bribery is definitely *not* part of my culture.' He was experiencing 'cognitive dissonance', or discomfort at the gap between his personal values and the behaviours and values he observed. Some dissonance is inevitable. This may be especially obvious during times of conflict, such as between different generations in families of migrants and/or refugees. The card pack may be used for identifying each of these and for finding out areas of dissonance, so that groups can work on ways to resolve these disagreements.

Variations on uses of the card pack

At another time you may wish participants to use the card pack in different contexts to describe the dominant norms or codes of behaviour in other 'cultural groups', such as their family culture or work culture. See the petal model of cultures on page 121.

You could also give a pack to colleagues and friends from other cultures, and invite them to select cards that best describe your culture. Compare the different perceptions.

Observations regarding identity

I have noted that in mapping culture, individuals who are from blended cultures, or who are international people with semi-nomadic experiences, sometimes start to question who they are. For example, participants whose families originated in China, but who were born overseas, do not feel totally at home in China. Participants with dual or triple nationalities likewise sometimes during this exercise start to question where they belong. On a visit to Perth, John Heron, a facilitator, showed us an affirming 'holistic ritual'. Holistic exercises are those where there is an attempt to involve the whole person: the head or thinking side, the heart or emotional side, the body, and the 'self' or spiritual side.

'This is me': a holistic exercise

Stage 1   One whole

Participants form a circle. With arms down and palms facing out into the group, they say, 'I am.'

Stage 2   Collective

Joining hands and making a 'whoosh' sound, the group walk into the middle of the circle, raise arms and say, 'We are.'

Stage 3   Individual affirmation

The participants walk back and cross their arms across their chests. Each one says, 'This is me.'
  Repeat right through three times.

For children identity can be very confusing. A beautifully illustrated story book, *Tell Me Why* (Templeton and Jackson, 2004), tells Sarah Jackson's story. At seven years of age she started asking her mother (the artist of the book) questions like 'I know I am Aboriginal, but why am I white with freckles?' Mother and daughter wrote and illustrated the book.

B: Bridge-building processes and strategies

The metaphor of a bridge is an important one. We are often unaware of small ideas or twists of thinking that can help us learn new things. Facilitators have to act as bridges and help others to send information and understanding from one side of a bridge to the other.

Building bridges and integrating processes and strategies may be used by groups to discuss ways of overcoming differences and maximizing the inputs of everyone in a group. For some of the cultural values I have illustrated divergent participant perspectives followed by some bridge-building and integrating ideas for facilitators on pages 151–57. It is useful to invite participants to develop their own bridging and integrating strategies. The ideas for this section have been developed and adapted from the works of Beasley and Hogan (2003), Chang (2002) and Verghese (2003).

Bridging to communicate across differences

It doesn't work to leap a 20 ft chasm in two 10 ft jumps.

Proverb

Bridging requires trust building, development of ground rules, and motivation and confidence to discuss differences openly. Team members need to learn 'decentring', a skill similar to empathy and role reversal, which requires individuals to suspend judgement and value differences, using the information from the mapping stage and accepting that 'Difference just is. It is a fact of life.' It is similar to taking a 'helicopter view' or being a dispassionate observer from outer space in a flying saucer.

Bridge building may occur on different scales, eg, between countries, ethnic groups, offices and departments in different cultures, and between two or more team members. Bridge building is an important way to develop and/or restore understanding and harmony in groups and teams.

It may not be possible for all bridge building to occur between participants in a workshop forum. Some issues may be too difficult to discuss openly. The difficulty with bridging is that open discussion often favours the person with the most power: typically the manager, the donor agency representative or the person who speaks fluently the dominant language used by the group.

There appear to be at least three major standpoints on a bridge (and a thousand other places to stand):

- You come to my side.
- I'll come to your side
- Let us meet in the middle as a compromise.
- Let us generate totally new ways of doing things or norms for our group: transformative, creative ideas.

Discussion

Ask participants 'Is there a myth or traditional story from your culture or elsewhere to illustrate these positions?' and 'What other standpoints can you think of?' Authentic bridge building requires the facilitator to use processes to help participants reach the second standpoint wherever possible. Otherwise it may mean that those with less power continually have to move over to the side of those with power.

I: Integrating bridges into the existing system

Participants need to recentre back in the 'here and now', and build new ground rules and processes based on what they have learnt during the mapping and bridging stages in order to manage participation, resolve disagreements and build on ideas. People with different cultural backgrounds often have very different norms to manage participating, not participating and turn-taking. DiStefano and Maznevski (2000) provide some suggestions:

- Rotate a process leader or observer, provided this is not a threat and is culturally appropriate. In very hierarchical societies, it may be almost impossible for a participant of low rank to take the role of process leader.
- Vary modes of meeting and sharing information. For example, solicit ideas by e-mail before a meeting, talk to staff informally to gather ideas, have paired-group discussions during meetings, and have frequent breaks in meetings.
- Map ideas on flipcharts, mind maps or drawings.

You will have many ideas and suggestions of your own. One workshop participant suggested during the integration stage:

> We have to reflect on the various hierarchies both official and unofficial. If necessary we have to develop new structures with their own hierarchies. For example, in a community project to help women from slum areas, we

noticed that these women were locked out of community decision making. So we helped them to form a new group comprising all the women from the slum areas. They then decided on a leader who represented them at local government boards and meetings.

If difficulties occur, go back to basics to understand more fully what cultural perceptions and values are underpinning problems. For further exercises on cross-cultural conflict resolution, see Blainey, Davis and Goodwill (1995), and Brenson-Lazán (2003).

Bridge maintenance

Bridges need to be maintained and achievements acknowledged and rewarded. It may be necessary to ask and confirm the support of seniors to support and mentor others. Bridges require hard work and maintenance, and firm foundations: they need to be revisited and revised over time. Achievements in intercultural bridge building need to be acknowledged and rewarded.

The MBI model described above is a set of principles for helping team members to develop their own best ways to working together. It may be applied to debriefing a meeting or for analysing a videotape of a team meeting.

Comparing cultural ideals and cultural realities

We often see politicians and participants comparing the ideals of their own culture with the actual behaviours (including the shadow or negative side) of people from other cultures. This leads to high-minded, condescending thought patterns of 'we' are better than 'you'. Often we do not 'walk our talk'; there may be a huge gap that is not acknowledged. Chris Argyris and Donald Schön (1994) focus on the gaps between what people think they believe in – their 'espoused theory' – and their behaviour – their 'theory in use'. There is a perceptual gap here which often occurs when we compare our cultures (see Figure 4.8).

It is useful for facilitators to look out for participants who speak politically correct jargon while behaving very differently in real life. I have found this model very useful in workshops, and showing it to participants gives an opportunity for clear but strong indirect feedback. Naïve-sounding suggestions like 'Take a moment to reflect about your own life in relation to this diagram' can be very effective.

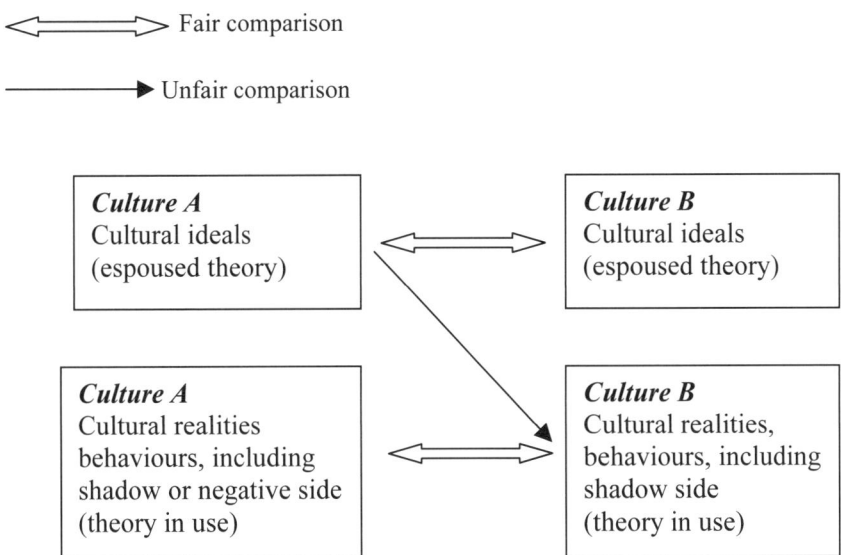

Figure 4.8 Comparing cultural ideals and cultural realities

Other processes and strategies to map cultures

This section describes a variety of processes that facilitators may use to enable participants to map or describe their own culture and values. In my book *Practical Facilitation* (Hogan, 2003: 171) I discussed an exercise which uses the metaphor of the cultural iceberg. It is useful as it raises awareness of both the seen and the less obvious aspects of a culture.

Develop cultural suitcases

Another exercise is to ask participants to join groups of similar cultural background and discuss what participants from other countries should pack in their 'cultural suitcases' in order to enable them to live and work in their respective cultures. The suitcase can be packed with basic 'dos' and 'don'ts' as well as songs, sayings and proverbs. Issues and contradictions that arise may then be used as starting points for developing bridges and integrating the views of participants from different cultures who are present.

Key words and sayings to describe core values

One interesting exercise in a multicultural group is to ask 'What key words or sayings describe your core cultural values?' For example, in Australia the word 'mateship' means more than just male friends, it means equal partners who share work or project journeys and watch out for one another. A 'fair go' means equitable opportunity, and signifies that everyone should have an equal and reasonable chance to prove themselves.

I noted that a gender group in Myanmar listed Myanmar sayings about sex roles and gender. They reported that the sayings were so one-sided that they felt depressed at first. For example, 'The sun does not rise until the cock crows': that is, the hen has no influence. Then they sat down to write humorous rebuttals or more egalitarian sayings, such as, 'Even if the cock doesn't crow the sun still rises.'

Cross-cultural exchange process

Author/background

The following exercise has been modified from the work of McKeen, Salas and Tillmann (1998). This process works best with groups comprising people from many different cultures. I added the use of participants' drawings which gave a colourful and dramatic stimulus to the 'inside teller' and the 'outside listeners'.

Purpose/rationale

The process may be used to enable groups to:

- identify different components of a culture;
- encourage cross-cultural exchange of ideas and values;
- feel pride in their own cultures.

Materials

Cards, felt pens, flipchart paper.

Stages

1. The facilitator of this activity should draw his/her culture first. It is not fair to ask your participants to take a risk that you are not willing to take. When I used this process with 40 newly arrived international mature postgraduate students (from 20 different countries) at Curtin University, I added in the dimension of using pictures. I demonstrated by showing them my view of England. Flipchart paper with the names of each county was displayed around the walls, and participants

were left to draw their own perceptions over a couple of days. Group pressure worked, and as students observed the pictures growing on the walls, they went and added to their sheets at breaks. Then each group was asked to present a summary of its culture. You can also send yourself up with the drawing, and show that you do not require participants to show artistic skills, but merely to convey simple ideas. (There is a photo of this on my website, www.hogans.id.au)

2. Ask participants to form groups with others from the same national culture or ethnic group.

3. The scenario is 'You have been invited to attend a meeting on the moon where you will meet people from different planets. You have been invited as a delegation to present key ideas about your culture at this very special meeting. The goal is to portray the colourful diversity of cultures on earth.

   A spaceship will arrive soon. Think about what is most important to people from your culture or ethnic group. Please collect ideas and items from your group which describe what you value most, as accurately as possible. They could include some of the following:
   - your favourite food and/or drink;
   - items of food and/or drink that are *not* acceptable in your culture;
   - symbols of religious or spiritual beliefs;
   - your beliefs about nature;
   - important historical events;
   - names of great artists, authors, leaders, singers, dancers and athletes;
   - a saying, story or myth which is passed from generation to generation;
   - famous cities, landmarks or buildings;
   - famous books and films;
   - anything else you think should be included.

4. Discuss in your group how you will present a 10 minute overview to the rest of the group. Please illustrate your ideas on flipchart paper with pictures and/or key words. Choose six things to represent your culture.'

5. Invite participants from the same culture to bring out their flipcharts in groups and to present together to the rest of the participants. I take care to place cultures in alphabetical order so as not to give precedence to any one group.

Debriefing questions

- What would it be like to describe your culture to people from another galaxy?
- What did you learn about yourself and your culture during this exercise?
- What did you learn about others during this exercise?

Advantages

This process enables participants themselves to choose from a variety of ideas to represent their cultures. It was noticeable how proudly they started to talk about their homelands, and how their enthusiasm was contagious. Comments included:

- 'I want to go to Mongolia and Samoa!'
- 'We can promote our own culture and learn about other cultures.'
- 'I like the cultural drawings, I appreciated more the things I saw every day at home.'
- 'You took us out of our cocoon and reserved state and made us feel great and important.'

This process is a starting point. The descriptions are the top of the iceberg of culture. However, it enables starting points for discussion and comparison and some safe ground for dialogue. For example, for the Philippines the discussion might range across the influence of Catholicism, the Spanish, dress, food, rice growing and the 'green revolution' of rice research innovations. Often students do not speak to each other much because they are afraid of showing their ignorance of 'the other'. They literally don't know where to start and therefore stay quiet in case they offend. After this exercise they had some safe starting points. At a later date discussion of deeper cultural 'dos and don'ts' may be added.

Cultural probes

Cultural probes are an experimental creative research method developed by designers at the Royal College of Art in London to encourage 'design inspiration'. The use of cultural probes requires facilitators to work in autonomous mode and to trust participants to go out and map their 'community' and 'culture' (see Chapter 3). A cultural probe is an information-gathering package containing flipchart paper, postcards, a camera, questionnaires, a tape recorder, a media diary, a photo album and so on. The packages are handed out to the target cultural group. It is an open way to involve the user group and their ideas and thereby to get to know them better (instead of using surveys or interviews).

In one example, summarized below, the European Union funded a project to increase the presence of elders in their local communities in Norway, Italy and the Netherlands. It was used by designers to provoke inspirational responses from elders from three diverse communities about their worlds and their needs, in order to make effective plans for future communities (Gaver, Dunne and Pacenti, 1999: 26). The designers wanted to challenge the elderly groups through both the probes and the resulting designs (without being condescending), and to ensure that functional areas were also aesthetically pleasing to the users rather than merely a luxury. They sent out stimulus postcards, disposable cameras and local maps (for participants to plot favourite meeting places and dangerous areas) and diaries to record activities, visitors, favourite television programmes and phone calls in and out.

The results provided the facilitators and the communities with inspirational, rich and varied ideas which stimulated the designers and enabled them to develop useful structures of relevance in local cultures. The elders captured particular facets of their lives in each culture. They learnt about their aesthetic preferences, beliefs, desires, fears, dangers and cultural concerns. The elders also learnt about their own and one another's lives, roles and pleasures, and to seek out new roles and behaviours. There were enhanced effective conversations between designers and user groups which continued through the project. Three very different urban designs emerged as a result.

Previously mapped cultures

There are also commercial packages available where 'cultural mapping' has been completed for you. This has some advantages and disadvantages. It is quicker, but may lead to stereotyping. Some questions to consider are:

- Who chooses what cultural values and behaviours are used to describe whole nations?
- Are these stereotypes, given that so many countries are now multicultural?
- Are these attributes of how some cultures would like to be seen by others?

Culture Active

Culture Active (available for a fee via the internet) is a comprehensive database on 'National Cultural Profiles' including detailed outlines of geography, history, politics, the economy, culture, languages, values and core beliefs, cultural black holes (disadvantages), concepts of time and space, communication patterns, language usage and listening habits. It also has useful tips regarding the expectations of audiences at presentations, concepts of status, gender, management language, manners and taboos.

For further information go to https://secure.cultureactive.com/info

Cultural Detective

The *Cultural Detective* series on each culture (available for a fee via the internet) includes a 'values wheel' including five to seven core values and a list of negatives as perhaps observed by outsiders. (See examples in Table 4.4.) The package on each culture contains the following:

- the 'detective' role taken on by participants who wish to solve sample case studies involving cross-cultural incidents;
- the idea of using a 'magnifying glass' to focus on cultures more closely;
- 'clues' or values which explain behaviours;
- key proverbs and sayings that illustrate the core values of a culture.

Each country module was developed by teams of writers including an 'insider' and 'outsider' for each culture (one of whom is a cultural expert). The problem here is that the key phrases given may appear as definitive descriptors. All three countries included in Table 4.4 are described as 'multicultural', yet the descriptors may lead to stereotyping of individuals from those countries. (Note that the diagram is meant to be read from top to bottom, not across.)

For more information see www.culturaldetective.com. To subscribe to a bimonthly newsletter entitled *Clues to Intercultural Effectiveness* go to www.culturaldetective.com/archive.html

Country-by-country background information

For country-by-country background information please see the Country by Country Information Resource List on the website.

Values, exercises and resources

For more resources and exercises on cultural values see Stringer and Cassidy (2003) and Inglehart, Basanez and Moreno (1998).

Review of intercultural training

For an in-depth study on approaches to training workshops on cultural issues see *Handbook of Intercultural Training* (Landis, Bennett and Bennett, 2004).

Behaviour cards

Examples of behaviour cards and the headings used to group them are listed in Appendix 2. Space does not allow them to be presented graphically

Table 4.4 Sample of country beliefs and values cited in *Cultural Detective*

Malaysia	Australia	United States
Religion and spirituality *Ugama* (Negative: conservatism)	Informality, laid back (Negative: insulting)	Speed (Negative: mechanistic)
Paternalism *Budi bahasa* (Negative: passive)	Forthrightness (Negative: rude, insolent)	Speaking up (Negative: competitive)
Consensus seeking *Mesyuwarah* (Negative: lack of initiative)	Independence, live and let live (Negative: disrespectful)	Law and order (Negative: rigid)
Face saving *Jaga air muka* (Negative: dishonest)	Give it a go, practicality (Negative: self -serving)	Capitalism (Negative: materialistic)
Group affiliation *Kawan* (Negative: cronyism)	Egalitarianism A fair go for all (Negative: adversarial)	Equality (Negative: disrespectful)
		Control (Negative: impatient)
		Self-reliance (Negative: self-centred)

as cards. These may be linked to the specific purpose of a workshop, or participants may wish to make up their own 'work behaviour pack'. The process of creating the pack in itself leads to a great deal of discussion and learning.

Cultural awareness in simulation activities

There are a number of cultural awareness simulation activities available commercially. My personal preference is to work in 'here and now' with a group and the diversity within it. However there are times when a more indirect approach via simulations is worthwhile, especially if the group is culturally homogeneous.

BaFá BaFá

In BaFá BaFá participants come to understand the powerful effects that culture plays in every person's life. It may be used to help participants prepare for living and working in another culture, or to learn how to work with people from other departments, disciplines, genders, races and ages. It is now available in English, Spanish and Portuguese (Shirts, 1975): see www.stsintl.com/business/bafa.html

Ecotonos: a multicultural problem-solving simulation

Ecotonos was designed as a tool for engaging in problem solving and decision making in diverse groups. Methods and processes of decision making are examined in four contexts: monocultural groups, multicultural groups, groups where one culture is in the majority, and groups evenly balanced in cultural representation (Nipporica Associates and Saphiere, 1997).

Randõmia balloon factory

In this simulation, a group of trainers representing a toy and game company from Richland (a wealthy and powerful Western country) travel to Randõmia, a traditional non-Western country, to train the Randõmians in techniques for improving product quality and productivity. The trainers have successfully conducted this training innumerable times in Richland. Because their company is just beginning to globalize, they assume that their standard training format will work equally well in Randõmia, the site of several of the company's new balloon factories. Wrong! The training is a failure (Grove and Hallowell, 2002). See www.interculturalpress.com

Barnga

Barnga is the classic simulation game on cultural clashes. Participants experience the shock of realizing that despite their good intentions and the many similarities amongst themselves, people interpret things differently from one another in profound ways, especially people from differing cultures. Players learn that they must understand and reconcile these differences if they want to function effectively in a cross-cultural group (Thiagarajan and Thiagarajan, 1990).

More information can be found on the website of Simulation Resources for Global Educators at www.augsburg.edu/global.Simulation%20Resources.%207-1-031.doc

Mapping the cultures of stakeholders

We all make generalizations about different groups. The 'them' and 'us' syndrome can lead to lack of coordination and teamwork across departments and organizations.

Stakeholder analysis

> A stakeholder analysis enables participants to share their work experi-
> ences, exposes the kinds of issues inherent in any development pro-
> gramme or project, and asks participants to consider how these issues
> arise between groups of stakeholders as they engage with each other.
>
> (Blackman, 2003: 20–26)

In any project a team does not work in isolation. So it is useful to analyse
the stakeholders in different ways: for example, who they are, their role/s,
their power or lack thereof, and their importance. The following exercise
is adapted from Blackman (Blackman, 2003: 20–26 and Kettle and Saul,
2004: 54–56).

The word 'stakeholder' rather depersonalizes the people who share an
interest in a project, such as the local community, local leaders, government
departments, donors, partners, consultants, INGOs, NGOs and private
companies. Each of the groups mentioned contains many subgroups identified by status, ethnicity, wealth and influence. Stakeholders include:

- user groups: people who use the resources or services in an area;
- interest groups: people who have an interest in, an opinion about, or
  who can affect the use of, a resource or service;
- beneficiaries of the project;
- power holders (formal and informal);
- decision makers (formal and informal);
- those often excluded from the decision-making process, such as the
  very poor, women and children.

Primary stakeholders are those who benefit from or may be adversely
affected by an activity. Secondary stakeholders are those people and
institutions with an interest in the resources or area being considered
(Bohm, Factor and Garrett, 1995). Project implementers have to be skilled
cultural translators and skilled code switchers as well as being able to help
to mediate or balance power differentials.

In Figure 4.9 I have placed the primary stakeholders at the top of the
pyramid, indicating that they are the most important.

Stages in stakeholder analysis

1. Invite participants to analyse the stakeholders in their project in small
   groups.
2. List the stakeholders in the Stakeholder analysis chart (Figure 4.10)
   down the left-hand column and repeat in the same sequence the horizontal headings (see examples in italics in Figure 4.10). Note that there
   is a diagonal of shaded squares where Culture A meets Culture A, and
   so on.

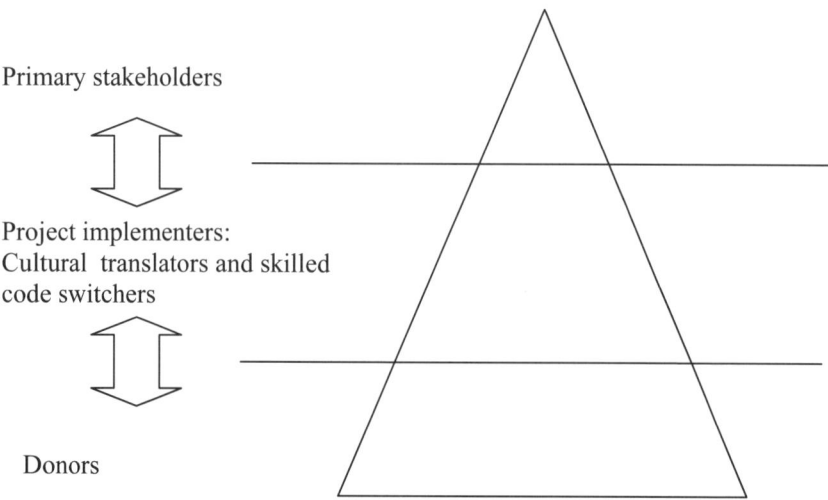

Primary stakeholders

Project implementers:
Cultural translators and skilled
code switchers

Donos

Figure 4.9   Groups of stakeholders

Stakeholders	Name A *Local community (culture/s)*	Name B *Government officials (culture/s)*	Name C *Local development workers (culture/s)*	Name D *Development workers from overseas (culture/s)*
Name A *Local community (culture/s)*				
Name B *Government officials (culture/s)*				
Name C *Local development workers (culture/s)*				
Name D *Development workers from overseas (culture/s)*				

Figure 4.10   Stakeholder analysis chart

3.   Invite participants to consider the issues that may arise between groups of stakeholders as they engage with one another, such as culture, power, relationships and language. For example, in Box 1 what issues may occur when members of the local community meet government officials? Fill these in on the chart.

Influence (power) and importance

Some stakeholders will have more influence on the project than others. While some are in a position to influence the project so that it is successful, there might be others who feel threatened by it or wish to sabotage it for some reason. A facilitator may wish to ask participants to consider how to approach those whose interests will be negatively affected, in order to avoid conflict and possible failure of the project. While the primary stakeholders usually have the highest priority, the table will help identify which stakeholders require time and energy: for example, either those who are allies of the project, or those who might cause problems for the project. It is important not to neglect the primary stakeholders.

Exercise to compare importance with the power and influence of stakeholders

Figure 4.11 combines the influence and importance of stakeholders so that participants can analyse their positions in relation to each other.

Influence is the power that stakeholders have over the project.
Importance is the priority given by the project to satisfying the needs and interests of each stakeholder.

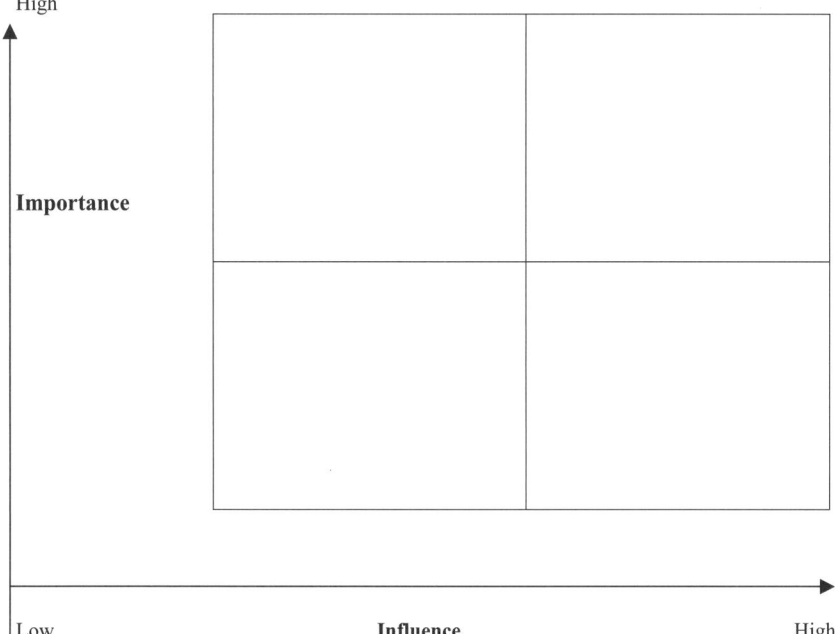

Figure 4.11   Power: influence and importance of stakeholders

Stages

1. Copy Figure 4.11 onto a large sheet of flipchart paper.
2. Go through the list of stakeholders on the stakeholder analysis chart (Figure 4.10). Think about the amount of influence they have and the extent to which they are important to the project.
3. Write the names of the stakeholders in the appropriate spaces in Figure 4.11. If they have high influence, place them towards the right of the figure. If they are of high importance to the project, place them towards the top of the figure.

Debrief

1. Ask for observations. Who are the key stakeholders of the project?
2. Boxes A, B and C are the key stakeholders of the project. They can significantly influence the project or are most important if project objectives are to be met.
3. Box A are stakeholders of high importance to the project, but with low influence (such as villagers). They need special initiatives to ensure their interests are protected.
4. Box B are stakeholders of high importance to the project, who can also influence its success. It is important to develop good working relationships with these stakeholders to ensure adequate support for the project.
5. Box C are stakeholders with high influence who can affect the project impact, but whose interests are not the target of the project. These stakeholders may be a source of risk. Relationships with these stakeholders are important and will need careful monitoring. These stakeholders may be able to cause problems for the project, and without their support it may be too risky to go ahead with the project at all.
6. Box D stakeholders are of low priority, but may need limited monitoring and evaluation to check that they have not become high priority, for example after a natural disaster.
7. Identify appropriate stakeholder participation methods. Participation is essential in development work, but in practice it is a concept that has been misused. Participation means different things to different people in different situations. In its widest sense, participation is the involvement of people in development projects. For example, people can be said to participate by attending a meeting, even though they do not say anything, or taking part in the decision-making process.

For more activities for exploring differences in values, see Stringer and Cassidy (2003).

Facilitative bridging strategies

If as facilitators we are asking multicultural teams to build bridges, then as facilitators we need to be able to build bridges to accommodate the different cultural values and behaviours of our participants. This section is devoted to illustrating some possible bridging strategies developed for facilitators. Please add your own. (Adapted from Chang, 2002; Beasley and Hogan, 2003; Verghese, 2003.)

Individualism and collectivism

Participant perspectives

A1 Individualism	A2 Collectivism
• Group activities are a nuisance because there are bound to be people who will not put in their fair share of the work. • It should be up to me whether I want to contribute in the workshop. It's my problem and I should be able to do what I am comfortable with.	• Group discussions are a chance to work together and draw on others' expertise and viewpoints. However, it will be annoying if people do not contribute, as the whole team will suffer. • Should I contribute? Only if I am adding value and have something worthwhile to say. Otherwise, I might waste everyone's time. • I like doing group work, it feels safer somehow.

Some bridge-building ideas

- Invite participants to contract for desirable group norms by asking questions like 'How can we all get the most out of our time together?' Ensure these ideas are written up and clearly visible in case you wish to refer to them later. I usually add 'the right to say "no" and participate by observing'. People can participate in groups in so many different ways: by listening, thinking, and supporting non-verbally as well as by talking. This ground rule is very freeing for participants who feel shy.
- Explain or invite participants to discuss the advantages and disadvantages of individual versus group activities and competitive and cooperative behaviour. Ask participants to raise their concerns at the beginning, and invite them to develop ways of dealing with 'social loafers', language constraints, poor timekeepers, dominating and/or dysfunctional behaviours and so on. Show evidence of the potential productivity of diverse teams (Adler, 1997).
- Invite members of small discussion groups to come out to present their ideas together, with everyone saying something.

- At other times, ask for a representative to report back to the whole group; at the end, ask if any other group members want to add anything.
- Ensure there are face-saving mechanisms in place for mediation if a group is dysfunctional. Some highly individualistic people find it very hard to work productively in a group environment.

Harmony and control

Participant perspectives

D1 Control over	D2 Harmony with
• I like to have an argument in a workshop and then carry on our debate over lunch or even later over a few drinks.	• I don't like to disagree too much in a workshop or seem to be in conflict with other participants. I'll just go with the flow.
• I like to volunteer in workshops or to lead discussions because that's how I learn.	• It's hard to be friends with participants in the workshop who think so differently to me.
• I like to challenge ideas in a workshop just to see what happens.	• I won't speak out as it's better if I let others have the opportunity to 'gain face'.

Some bridge-building ideas

- Explain to participants at the beginning of your workshop how to 'dialogue' rather than 'debate' about ideas: see Chapter 7.
- Show participants how to look at all sides of an issue to gain the whole picture, using, for example, 'pluses, minuses and interesting points' (PMI), or 'six thinking hats' (de Bono, 1985).
- Encourage reticent participants to express their ideas and responses, and make sure that each participant is given the opportunity to contribute something to the discussion. A round robin process takes away the need for participants to think about interrupting, as 'turn taking' is highly structured.
- Build in written processes to assist quieter participants and those participants with English as their second or third language. Writing gives everyone time to think and reflect. This equalizes participation and generates many ideas quickly. For example, this can be done with card sorts (Geschka, Schaude and Schlicksupp, 1973; Hogan, 2003) and brain writing (Hogan, 2003). For brain writing, participants write one idea per card; the facilitator collects them and redistributes them anonymously so that individuals can add positive ideas. Eventually, all cards are displayed, clustered and discussed. This is an equalizing

process, as everyone is participating at the same time, there is no turn taking and people whose first language is other than the one used in the workshop have a chance to think and write (it is far less stressful for them than having to think and speak on their feet). In contrast, brainstorming is a totally verbal process, slows down idea generation as only one person can speak at a time, and favours the participants with good verbal skills who can think on their feet and who are not afraid to verbalize what may at first be considered as crazy ideas.

● Working in pairs maximizes participation and builds confidence. Pairing the power holders and more dominant participants ensures that quieter participants are more evenly matched and have an opportunity to voice their ideas and opinions.

Hierarchy and equality

Participant perspectives

C1 Hierarchy	C2 Equality
(high power distance)	(low power distance)
● Mmm … OK. You are the facilitator, but what are your qualifications and areas of expertise?	● The facilitator can't expect respect just by being a facilitator. Hope she knows what she's doing!
● The facilitator has been employed by the company and deserves some respect. How should I address you: Mr Steve or Ms Chris or Ms Hogan or Dr Hogan?	● Well, what do you mean, and why do you want us to use this process? ● The facilitator is here as a guide and should provide a service to me and the group.
● The facilitator is the expert and should provide the answers or tell us what to do.	● Everyone should offer his/her ideas and exchange information.

Some bridge-building ideas

● Make your own roles as a facilitator clear (for example, that as facilitator, you are not going to enter into content; or when you are going to go into content, explain that you are putting on your 'trainer' hat).

● Ensure that the participants are clear about their roles before the workshop.

● In some hierarchical cultures it may be useful to ask a senior executive to introduce you and indicate your qualifications and experience (especially if you are an outsider or a female facilitator in a male-dominated culture and/or workshop).

● Write about your experience, qualifications, family and interests in the workshop handout. This saves you from having to give a long introduction about yourself.

- Take an interest in the participants, and show that you are flexible. Recognize the participants as individuals who may have very different backgrounds.
- Be patient with participants from societies that are different from your own, and remember that it may take them more time to feel at ease if you are from a culture different from theirs.
- Participants from low power distance societies may feel quite happy to speak out, so build in equalizing processes such as round robins to give structured opportunities, especially in hierarchical societies, for everyone to speak out.
- With participants who show low power distance behaviours and are too familiar, or show lack of respect, you may need to draw the line in a friendly but firm manner. (This comment may be more applicable to female facilitators.)
- Do not take personal questions as an affront. It is often good to tell participants a little about your family background as they then see you as a person as well as a facilitator. Also encourage participants to ask questions related to the workshop.
- Some people from strongly hierarchical societies may not value participation and facilitation. Sometimes workshops are not suitable and a form of 'shuttle diplomacy' and discussions with small groups including people of similar rank may be more appropriate.

Task (doing) and relationship (people) oriented

Participant perspectives

G1 Task (doing) oriented	G2 Relationship (people) oriented
<ul><li>Ice breakers are a waste of time.</li><li>I'm really busy, so I just want to get the work done in the minimum amount of time and with the least amount of fuss.</li><li>I like to know exactly what to do and complete it in time.</li><li>I like to have specific ground rules about what we have to do in workshops.</li></ul>	<ul><li>I need to get to know my fellow group members before we get down to work.</li><li>I work best with people I trust and feel comfortable with.</li><li>It's more important to be able to work well with my colleagues than to show how clever I am.</li><li>I like to have specific ground rules about how we should relate to one another in workshops.</li></ul>

Some bridge-building ideas

- Design 'warm-up' activities that are related to the goals of the workshop so that participants can get to know one another, but do not feel they are doing activities without a purpose. Do not use the term 'ice breaker'.

- Ensure that pre-workshop refreshments, lunch and breaks are provided adjacent to the workshop room so that participants mingle and chat and do not return to their offices.
- Arrange tasks and group activities so that participants from diverse backgrounds work together and have to discuss and share different perspectives and experiences.
- Change the composition of groups regularly for different tasks.

Time-flexible (polychronic) and time-tight (monochronic)

Participant perspectives

H1 Time-flexible (polychronic)	H2 Time-tight (monochronic)
<ul><li>We start when we are all ready.</li><li>I like it when a workshop develops and we can explore different ideas on a topic as they arise.</li><li>I like to have the time to be able to explain the context of an example.</li><li>I think that facilitators should be more flexible over deadlines and schedules.</li><li>We all like to talk at once, so what?</li></ul>	<ul><li>I expect to start and finish on time.</li><li>I like a detailed workshop agenda.</li><li>The facilitator should keep to the scheduled break times and course schedule.</li><li>I dislike it when some participants jump in and do not wait their turn.</li><li>We should elect a time-keeper to keep everyone on schedule.</li></ul>

Some bridge-building ideas

- When you generate ground rules in the first workshop, discuss with participants the cultural issues surrounding time-keeping and punctuality, especially when time is short.
- Acknowledge different cultural perspectives of time and punctuality, but give your expectations and reasons clearly for your workshops.
- Praise or reward the participants who come back on time.
- Go with the flow: in some cultures, at times things just won't start on time and there is nothing you can do about it.
- At the end of a break, play a piece of music that is a signal to everyone that you will restart in five minutes. This enables participants who have been chatting to make a quick toilet stop or whatever.
- Explain the rationale behind turn taking and one person speaking at a time.

Indirect communication and direct communication

Participant perspectives

E1 Indirect communication (high context)	E2 Direct communication (low context)
<ul><li>I find it hard to express how I really feel in a workshop. Anyway, surely the facilitator can see how I feel from my body language?</li><li>The facilitator will know I disagree because I will remain silent.</li><li>It's my job to build my case by giving all the background circumstances, but not to tell someone else what to think.</li></ul>	<ul><li>I just like to say it as it is.</li><li>It's important to stick to the point and not beat around the bush.</li><li>It's my job to make my case clearly and directly and to back it up with facts and sound arguments.</li></ul>

Some bridge-building ideas

- Present good models of report structure and oral presentations to illustrate the framework required for expressing opinions and arguments in the context in which you are working.
- Acknowledge that different cultures and languages have different ways of agreeing, disagreeing and expressing opinions.

Religious/spiritual and secular

Participant perspectives

J1 Religious/spiritual	J2 Secular
<ul><li>I feel embarrassed when people swear, especially if they use the name of God.</li><li>I feel that my spiritual beliefs should be treated seriously.</li><li>I feel awkward on a Friday when I want to pray and we only have a short lunch break.</li><li>I wish they had gone to the trouble of finding out my dietary needs; there is nothing here I can eat.</li></ul>	<ul><li>I think religious ideas and beliefs are a private matter and should play no part in workshops.</li><li>I don't see why we should have to finish a workshop early so a small number of participants can go to prayers.</li></ul>

Some bridge-building ideas

- Ensure that the workshop venue can cater for different religious and other dietary needs of participants. (It may need to provide kosher, halal and vegetarian meals, as well as low-salt, vegan, low-carbohydrate and gluten-free alternatives. Provide fruit for morning tea, as people with diabetes cannot eat biscuits. Nuts are also a major danger for people with allergies.)
- Check that there is a private room for prayer. Build in a long lunch break or discussion activities for secular participants when others are at prayers. Check to see that those who are at prayer do not feel left out.

Shame and guilt

Participant perspectives

K1 Shame	K2 Guilt
• My family members will all feel so shamed if I make a mistake or if I fail. I will also let down my town and my country.	• If I speak out and upset someone in the workshop, I will feel guilty.
• I feel nervous about speaking out in a workshop in case I get it wrong and lose face.	• As long as my conscience is clear, I will do whatever it takes to succeed, even if it means using the ideas of others and claiming them as my own.
• I am concerned with what others (especially the boss) may say about me if I say something stupid.	
• As the boss, I will lose face if I do not say something (even if I have nothing to say).	

Some bridge-building ideas

- Explain to participants that with many processes designed to generate creative ideas – for example, brainstorming and brain writing – there is no such thing as a right or wrong idea. Brain writing is anonymous and reflective and less likely to cause 'loss of face' than brainstorming.
- If participants are required to write something, explain clearly and show examples. Try to help them 'get it right' first time.
- Allow participants in training sessions to have extra reading time, and provide opportunities to resit tests and resubmit reports to avoid stress and fears of failure, which may inhibit their thinking processes.
- Use brain writing so participants can write ideas anonymously.
- Build an atmosphere of trust.

5

Metaphors, stories, music and dance

Introduction

This chapter describes ways in which facilitators can utilize metaphors, stories, case studies and case stories, music and dance with culturally diverse groups. It is an extension of a chapter entitled 'Processes to involve all the senses' in *Practical Facilitation* (Hogan, 2003).

Metaphors

> If a picture is worth a thousand words, a metaphor is worth a thousand pictures.
>
> Gary Brewster

A metaphor is a figure of speech in which a word or phrase is applied to an object or action to clarify understanding. The abstract concept of 'culture' is difficult for some people to understand at first, and as a result a number of metaphors have been used to describe it. For example, culture is like:

- The air we breathe: it's automatic and we don't notice it.
- An iceberg: we only see 'surface' behaviours, what is obvious, a tiny proportion above sea level. Beneath the waves are the not so obvious deeply held truths upon which behaviours are modelled: values, wisdom.
- An onion: we at first see outer layers and as we learn more we peel back layer after layer (Hofstede, 1991).

Metaphors do not always translate easily

> Metaphors are considered by some to be an interdisciplinary Rosetta Stone.
>
> Source unknown

But metaphors are only useful across cultures if they can be understood cross-culturally. Even the quote above is culturally based, since in some cultures the Rosetta Stone (a metaphor in itself) is not known about. (It was found in Egypt in 1799 and contains the same information in three different scripts, which provided the key to unlocking the meaning of Egyptian hieroglyphics).

Metaphors that are useful across cultures

The weather is a very useful metaphor for introductions. 'Tell us how you feel today by telling us today's weather and the forecast for the next 24 hours.' Sport also provides us with useful metaphors and discussion topics across cultures. Check gender issues, as male sports *may* not appeal to some women and vice versa.

See also the metaphor drawing ideas in Chapters 6 and 7, and the 'Sangam' river metaphor in Chapter 4 (page 116).

Culturally inappropriate metaphors

> No single metaphor will appeal to everyone. If the tool or metaphor isn't helpful, move on.
>
> Deal and Masman (2003: 16)

Metaphors that are successful in a workshop in one culture may not always be useful in other cultures. I observed a Western facilitator at a facilitators' conference in Kuala Lumpur. As a discussion starter he asked us to divide up into groups in different corners of the room, depending on which of a choice of animals we identified most with: a horse, an elephant or a St Bernard dog, and then discuss why we had made the choice. Everyone looked puzzled. Someone asked him to repeat the instructions and there was again stunned silence. I asked him to explain what a St Bernard dog is (these huge dogs were once used as rescue sniffer dogs by monks on a pass across the Alps now called the St Bernard Pass). Needless to say, not many people from Malaysia and Singapore had even heard of these Swiss dogs. But there is another twist: dogs in Malaysia are considered dirty, and in the past some carried rabies, so people are taught not to touch them. Nobody in the workshop would have chosen to identify with the dog. Facilitators need to be careful to check out metaphors beforehand with cultural informants.

Stories

> Everyone is a storyteller. We are our stories.
>
> Marie Finlay, storyteller, Perth, Western Australia

Different cultural perceptions of story

The important thing about storytelling is 'story listening'. In listening we show respect to the teller. The use of story is an accepted part of a facilitator's toolkit: either telling anecdotes, stories and myths, or generating stories and myths from the participants. Our role is to facilitate listening. But our cultural perceptions of 'story' and 'storytelling' may not be the same, as the following story illustrates.

Story: What is a story?

I was trying to 'understand' the lives of the rural women I was working with in the Sudan. I asked them to tell me the stories of their lives. They looked at me with great puzzlement. 'What stories do you mean?' For an hour we tried to establish mutual understanding about what we meant by stories. Eventually I told them the story of the Loch Ness monster in a lake in Scotland, and how the story was that it was a prehistoric animal left over from thousands of years ago, and occasionally people still see it. Suddenly they seemed to understand, and shyly and tentatively a woman began a story about their tribe . . . .

Sandra Bernhardt, English facilitator in Sudan

The process of storytelling varies from culture to culture. In some countries, the location is important, and storytelling means sitting under the stars. One story may take many hours or even all night. Perhaps also there are some stories that cannot be told to 'outsiders' and others that require a different time and space.

Stories to illustrate concepts: impermanence

One of the very powerful teachings of the Buddha is that of constant change: impermanence, and as a result the uncertainty of life. This teaching is illustrated beautifully in the traditional stories, 'The pious son-in-law'(MacDonald and Tossa, 2004) and 'The old man and the horse' (Hogan, 2000).

Inviting participants to tell their stories

A facilitator may discover that a person has a personal story relating to the workshop context. These stories can become major teaching points and a focus for discussion or role plays.

Emergent stories

In a 'Managing cultural transitions' workshop for postgraduate students, one participant confided in me that one young Muslim female student had a story about the first night she arrived in Australia (a few days previously). I asked her privately at the break if she would be prepared to tell her story to the whole group so we could discuss it. She agreed.

She was being put up in a hotel, and the first evening went into the bar to get some water and to sit with the other students. At the bar a man saw her veil and immediately confronted here about the Schapelle Corby case. (A young Australian woman had just been sentenced to a substantial jail term in Bali for drug smuggling, and it had resulted in a media circus in Australia at the time (April–July 2005).) As a result of her telling her story, a culturally mixed group of newly arrived postgraduate students had a very productive discussion, and took part in a variety of role plays on the different ways to handle strangers.

Respecting the right to refuse to tell a story

Facilitators have to handle people's right to divulge their stories with care, as illustrated in the following incident.

STORY: TELL US YOUR STORY

In an Asian country, a visiting facilitator was conducting a gender workshop. She heard that a man had a story about his wife who had not had any post-secondary educational opportunities. In front of the whole group she invited him to tell the story without checking first. The man hesitated (he was a member of a minority group and his story was extremely sensitive). He resisted and looked down.

The facilitator misread his body language and assumed he was shy. She pushed and encouraged and waited for the story to begin. Eventually with some embarrassment he told his wife's story. For him it was a culturally sensitive story to tell openly in that context in front of his work colleagues, who were from the dominant culture.

Chris Hogan, 2003

In this instance the facilitator was insensitive. We must be careful either to check privately at a break whether a person is willing to tell his/her story, or to invite him/her in a way that gives 'choice' and the right to say 'No' without feeling embarrassed. There is a fine dividing line between encouragement and coercion.

Personal story process

The following process is a team-building exercise to help team members learn more about one another, to develop deeper understanding and mutual trust.

Author/background

The strength of storytelling is 'story listening', especially when a personal story is being listened to in respectful silence by colleagues. The personal story process is a storytelling process developed by Bob Dick and Tim Dalmau in Queensland (1994). It is a way of honouring a person, his/her past and stories.

Purpose/rationale

Through self-disclosure people grow closer and come to appreciate each other more as people rather than the mask of their job roles and titles. It is important that all participants stay in the group until the end of the process, and that no latecomers interrupt the flow of the process. The group decides at the beginning whether stories are to be kept confidential to the group.

Size of group

Small groups of three or four people maximum. In cultures that are very hierarchical, participants may feel more at ease to be with people at a similar level.

Venue layout

Participants form small groups and sit in a circle or around a table.

Time

Two hours minimum. Each story takes three or four minutes per person. You may need to allocate at least 10 minutes per person in groups where people know each other well, as 'deeper' stories involving higher levels of intimacy often take longer. Also in certain cultures the circuitous method of discourse will make storytelling a much longer process.

Stages

The introduction to the workshop is important. If participants are new to one another, during a warm-up it is useful if they tell their name and the story of how that name was chosen. This sets the tone for a little disclosure and storytelling.

Give a brief explanation about the process and ask whether they are willing to attempt it. If the answer is 'yes', complete your explanation of what is required.

1. Take some moments to look back and choose six turning points in your life.
2. Choose three stories you feel willing to tell the group in the workshop space.
3. There is no time limit.
4. Other participants actively listen and attend as fully as possible to the teller; they do not ask questions or interrupt in any way.
5. Go around the circle again so that each person tells his/her second story; then again for the third story.
6. At the end of the story it is useful for each person to say:
   - why it was a turning point;
   - why it made a difference;
   - what it says about him/her now.

There is often a respectful silence between each story. During the second and third rounds a shift occurs, as people take a little more risk, based on what has been divulged in the first round.

Debrief

Some groups will finish ahead of the others, so it is useful if you brief everyone beforehand. For example, 'If you finish early, please start your debriefing discussion. Reflect on what happened for you in each round of the stories. Did the telling change in each round? Did your choice of stories change, and if yes, why? Has this process changed the way in which you viewed people before and after?'

Outcomes

The outcomes are that members of each small group develop increased intimacy. All stories have metaphorical hooks which the listeners tune into in different ways and on different levels. Even if individuals become tearful, afterwards there are deeper levels of empathy as they tap into aspects of common experiences.

Advantages

> A good story is a bridge between our particular lives and the universal, it connects our individual life to the patterns and wonders of the whole.

Marie Finlay

The personal story process takes participants to a deeper psychological level, and therefore the transition between this and the next stage of a workshop needs to be carefully facilitated. It is necessary to bring people from the past to the present, and to identify what and how they can bring what they have learnt into the next stages of the workshop.

In a hospital which was being privatized, I was facilitating a 'Managing change and transitions' workshop. I asked team members to tell of major transitions in their lives. One woman told of the hardships she had to overcome to leave her war-torn homeland, and the additional work she had to do as a refugee on arrival in Australia to get her family established. Her colleagues were in awe as they had never heard (or asked for) her story before. As the facilitator I could see their increased admiration of her courage and tenacity. The next stage was to discuss the skills and attitudes they had learnt during those transitions. I watched in admiration as the previously quiet migrant woman taught the other participants many skills based on her own life experiences.

Disadvantages

The personal story process is time-consuming. Some groups finish earlier than others. It undermines the process to cut some groups before they have finished, so it is important to explain how groups can start their own debriefing discussion while others finish.

Case studies created by outsiders

The problem with canned or old case studies is they may be:

- 'dead' or perhaps dated, and participants may feel detached or even that they are irrelevant to their world (Mumford, 1999);
- culture-specific, as many case studies are developed in the West and may not be relevant to the local cultural situation and work culture;
- divorced from reality, and therefore learning transfer is more difficult or may not even occur.

Learning is contextual, and as facilitators we need to chose and/or adapt case stories appropriately.

Case stories created by participants

Background

I developed this exercise as a result of requests to create relevant case studies in different countries and cultural contexts. Table 5.1 illustrates the pluses, minuses and interesting points (PMI) evaluation process (de Bono, 1987).

Purpose

The purpose of engaging participants in developing personal case stories is to engage them in:

- storytelling which is in tune with adult learning theory (Knowles, 1984);
- story writing, which encourages participants to think and reflect more deeply about an issue (Honey and Mumford, 1992);
- joint problem solving;
- developing 'live' studies which are relevant to their local work and national culture/s.

Case stories may be used to:

- highlight cross-cultural issues in demonstrating best practice in management or examples of poor practice;
- illustrate the need for change to meet new issues or demands;
- introduce a new technique or approach to management or teaching and the potential issues in different cultural settings;
- show the rise of e-business and online education.

This exercise can be conducted with any size of group.

Stages

1   Explain or ask participants to describe what is meant by a 'case story'

One definition adapted from the work of Alan Mumford (1999) is:

> A description (in words or video) of a situation, specifically written for learning and analysis, which exists, existed or might exist within a school, organization and/or community.

Participatory video case development has been used very successfully to enable participants to film, edit and present their 'case' to authority figures

Table 5.1　Comparison of participants' case stories and prepared case studies

Type	Pluses	Minuses	Interesting points
Participants' case stories	Personal. Very popular with participants. 'We are our stories.'	It may be harder for the storyteller to analyse the story in an objective way. Participants may already have filtered their own stories through their own values filter, so it is already judgemental: there is 'lateral inference' based on their assumptions.	The writing and telling process sometimes leads to serendipitous learning
	When given a choice participants tend to want to tell and listen to their own stories	May not meet the teaching need exactly	
Prepared case studies	Participants all approach the same story at the same time	May not be so applicable for participants	
	There are fewer assumptions and interpretations made	May make transference more difficult	
	Can be designed to develop certain learning points	May feel 'dead' or 'outdated' or irrelevant to participants	
	Can be tailored to the group members' context/s and culture/s		
	Can be long and detailed, eg for in-depth analysis at university level, or short to stimulate discussion		

(Braden and Huong, 1998). This process has been used in Africa, Vietnam and the United Kingdom (Chase *et al*, 1999).

2   State the ground rules

When developing a case study it is important that participants:

- focus on relevant issues;
- change personal and place names to preserve confidentiality where necessary;
- seek advice from the facilitator if there is a chance that a story may create difficulties for others who are not present.

3   Explain the components of a case story

The facilitator describes what is needed. 'Please choose a story from your experience or that of your colleagues, which has happened and puzzled you. Or make up an incident regarding something you hope does not happen, but where you would like help in order to manage the situation effectively.' Ask participants to consider the following:

- A title. This should not give the story away by stating the perceived main issue, so, for example, 'Growing tensions at the office' is preferable to 'Miscommunication problems at work'.
- The cultural context: the location, community and cultural mix: city, village, rural or remote.
- The organizational cultural context: government, private, NGO and so on.
- Characters: the key players with pseudonyms, roles, gender.
- Story: sequence of events. Explain the lead-up to the incident/s and the current situation.
- Size: maximum length two pages.
- The beginning, middle and end.

4   Participants form pairs

It is useful if the facilitator directs the formation of groups, and pairs up participants of equal rank, similar interests and experience. Each pair must decide on a story, preferably from their own experiences, and write it up together. Some may prefer to write alone.

5   Participants show their cases to the facilitator

It is important that the facilitator checks the case stories as they are developing, and is available to check with participants regarding potential issues and anonymity.

6   Facilitator distributes cases to participants

It may be necessary to cull some of the cases handed in by participants as some may be more relevant to the focus of the workshop than others.

Ask participants to generate the stages they think they should go through when analysing a case study. Or if the participants are not used to generating their own problem-solving stages, give them a list of stages to follow, for example:

- Read through once.
- Read again and highlight key words/issues.
- Ask yourself what are the presenting problems. In other words, what is known?
- Ask what are the underlying problems. In other words, what is not known, but may contribute to the problem? Asking 'what is missing?' is an important skill in many situations. Point out that we often jump to the wrong conclusions in real life, so we must be careful when analysing case studies to separate what is known and not known, and to identify what extra information would be needed in real life.
- Point out that there is often no 'one right answer' in real life. Many issues are just so complex.

7   The debriefing process

Allow plenty of time for the debriefing session. Useful questions at each stage of the story are:

> What would you do and why?
> What are the potential ramifications, advantages and disadvantages of action 'x' versus action 'y'?

There are two levels of debriefing. The first level is the facilitation of the cases themselves. Note how the discussion often jumps quickly into solution giving rather than first analysing the cause/s.

Facilitators should restrict participants to discussing observable actions (and non-actions) described in the case story itself. It is best to confront them early if participants try to interpret and guess the causes and/or results of behaviours, as this is what happens in real life, and we often jump to the wrong conclusions when we make assumptions and generalizations. Indeed one of the main learning points to come from case studies and case stories is how much our brains like to complete unfinished stories.

The second or higher level is to engage the participants in listing the stages and/or questions to ask when trying to solve a problem case:

- What are causes of the problems?
- What information don't you know that you ought to find out? (Even in real life there are some aspects of a situation that you do not know.)
- What are the effects of the problem/s?
- What are the cultural issues behind the problem/s?
- What are the cures for the current situation in the short term that are culturally acceptable and non-acceptable?
- What could prevent this situation from being repeated in the future?
- Does this link to any theories or models you have learnt so far? Are these theories or models relevant in your culture?
- Are there any key insights that are relevant to your job and/or organization?

Advantages

This process is based on adult learning principles (Knowles, 1984) and action learning (Revans, 1982). As it contains real potentially 'live' stories it is more likely to engage the feelings of learners, as do real-life experiences (Kolb, 1984).

The language of the locally produced case stories is more likely to be understood by, and appeal to, the participants. Case studies drawn from another country or culture may be rejected by participants: 'Oh, that would never happen here' (Mumford, 1999).

This process develops reflection as well as analytical skills, and enables participants to share their knowledge and experiences.

Disadvantages

Some participants in some cultures may feel that it is the facilitator's responsibility to provide content and the case stories. Therefore this process needs to be used with careful explanation and after some presentation of content by the facilitator. Mumford (1999) suggests that the facilitator should think carefully about the position of case studies in a workshop. One option is for the facilitator to make a short presentation first, including some models and questions, followed by a case story (similar to the transitional learning model: James, 2000). In other words, in cultures where participants are used to receiving some input first, it is best to ease everyone into participatory learning step by step. The other approach is to invite participants to analyse the case story first, then give a presentation followed by a re-analysis of the case applying the theory that has been learnt. See Figure 5.1.

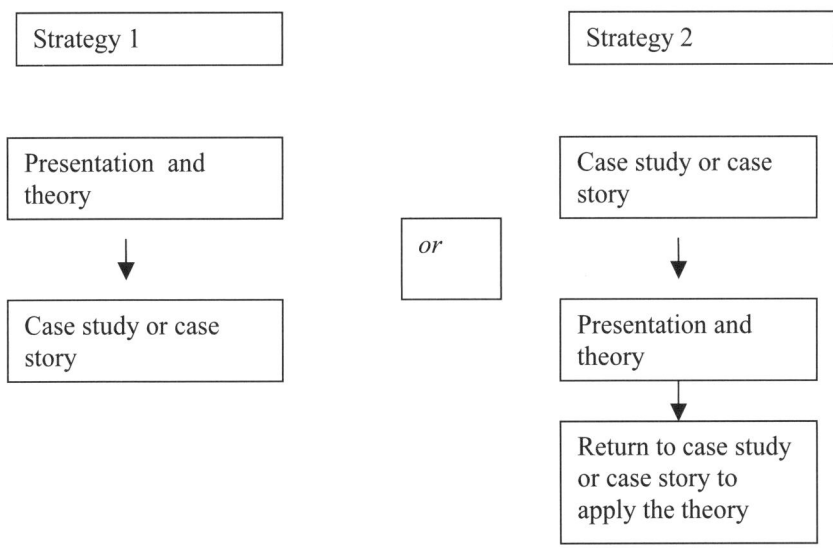

Figure 5.1   Alternative ways of locating case stories in a workshop

Role-reversal stories through the eyes of 'the other'

Use of role reversal is a powerful way to jolt participants out of their ethnocentric thinking patterns. It can lead to awareness raising about values and behaviours which individuals take as normal for them and often perceive as normal for everyone else.

STORY: THE ZORTOCIANS HAVE LANDED

'The Zortocians have landed' is a role reversal story used by Tim Muirhead to enable participants to 'de-centre' and divert their thinking from their current lives, and imagine what it would be like to be invaded and colonized by the inhabitants of the planet Zortoc. It helps if there are two facilitators to follow up with a role play. If there is only one facilitator he/she can always brief a participant beforehand.

Imagine you suddenly meet strange-looking people from the planet Zortoc. They have arrived on Earth saying 'Our planet Zortoc is overcrowded; we need the Earth, space, resources and water for our people. Do not resist, let us show you our weapons. We are going to move the people of xxx [the capital city] to xxx [a country town or village]. Don't worry, we will give you allocations of Zortocian biscuits to sustain you while you get established. You will not be able to return to the capital city without a permit, and if you are seen on the streets of the city at night you will be arrested . . .'

Many of these experiences evoke feelings that may have been felt by Aboriginal people living in Australia when the 1905 Act was enforced. (The Act established the Chief Protector as legal guardian of all Aboriginal children under the age of 16. It resulted in many children – now called the 'Stolen Generation' – being removed from their families. This story will have resonance for indigenous peoples and minority groups in the United States, Canada, South Africa and New Zealand. It may be adapted to countries that have been colonized or administered by ethnic groups from outside.

Debrief

After telling the story, the debriefing discussion could focus on the following:

- In 60 seconds with a partner, discuss how you felt when you heard the story. List on flipchart paper the words that come out , such as 'angry', 'lost', 'resistant', 'depressed', 'sick', 'I'd like to kill the bastards', 'resentful'.
- The two facilitators can role play. For example, 'I'm the Zortocian Expert in Earthling Affairs and my colleague here is an Earthling to whom we have given the role of Earth Manager of Agriculture (under our supervision, of course). We would like you to tell us how to create a 'culturally safe environment' for us to communicate and work together.'

Participants can then discuss the kinds of behaviours that lead to building of trust, mutual respect and open communication, and some of the many issues involved.

Role-reversal video: *Babakiueria*

This is discussed in Chapter 8.

The hand pump story

'The hand pump' is a story written by Geoff Griffith, an English development worker, during a contract in Cambodia. Because it is written through the eyes of a Cambodian poor farmer, it makes a very useful case study for analysis by facilitators to examine their behaviours and practice. Unfortunately it is too long to include here, but it can be found on my website, www.hogans.id.au

Role-reversal stories to help participants to decentre

STORY: BODY RITUAL AMONG THE NACIREMA

This story by Horace Miner (1956) is a classic among anthropologists, demonstrating how one society's customs can appear entirely incomprehensible to another. Even for non-anthropologists, it is a fascinating and amusing study in cultural differences. It was published in 1956 by the *American Anthropologist*. Miner describes Nacirema attitudes to their bodies. (The word 'Nacirema' is 'American' spelt backwards.) It is a great story for examining how our culture has an effect on us in ways we may not be aware of. See the extract. The whole story is retrievable from: www.msu.edu/~jdowell/miner.html

> Nacirema culture is characterized by a highly developed market economy which has evolved in a rich natural habitat. While much of the people's time is devoted to economic pursuits, a large part of the fruits of these labors and a considerable portion of the day are spent in ritual activity. The focus of this activity is the human body, the appearance and health of which loom as a dominant concern in the ethos of the people. While such a concern is certainly not unusual, its ceremonial aspects and associated philosophy are unique.
>
> The fundamental belief underlying the whole system appears to be that the human body is ugly and that its natural tendency is to debility and disease. Incarcerated in such a body, man's only hope is to avert these characteristics through the use of ritual and ceremony. Every household has one or more shrines devoted to this purpose. The more powerful individuals in the society have several shrines in their houses and, in fact, the opulence of a house is often referred to in terms of the number of such ritual centers it possesses.
>
> (Miner, 1956: 503)

Music

Music, singing and dancing unite human beings, enabling us to express feelings and meaning, and celebrate life. Music impacts on our brain waves, heartbeats, feelings and states of mind. There is a vast amount of research now available describing the different ways in which people perceive and process new information, learn and behave. We need to cater for these differences by stimulating all the senses during workshops.

> Music is embedded in all cultures and its reputation as a universal language is well deserved.
>
> Eric Jensen, 2000

I gained my love of music from my father, who had an amazing appreciation for and collection of music of all types from across the world, even though he was not a musician. He always played various types of music in his school in inner London as children were gathering for assembly. He maintained that if one child took an interest later in life in music it was worthwhile. I use music in workshops because I believe it helps both the participants and me. It is an integral part of my life.

Facilitators can use music for 'emotional switching' in groups: that is, raising or lowering energies, changing feelings, thoughts and behaviours and so on. Some tunes are found all over the world, including 'Happy Birthday', 'Auld Lang Syne' and 'Frère Jacques'. 'Lao Pengyou' (Old friend) is a popular song to the tune of 'Auld Lang Syne' in China. In northern Thailand, many villagers know the tune of 'Frère Jacques'.

It can be said that music:

- is an integral part of all cultures;
- improves the quality of life;
- can improve harmony and social bonding between people playing or listening to it;
- can move us: it can change our mood: can cheer us up or depress us, can temporarily transport us to another world and time;
- helps us to identify our feelings;
- can help to decrease stress by slowing heartbeat, reducing blood flow and stimulating stress-reducing hormones;
- brings people together more than language can ever do.

Music and brain waves

We all know that music has the capacity to transport us temporarily into other worlds, spaces and time dimensions (Jensen, 2000). It helps if facilitators know about the link between brainwaves and a person's activities, and the way in which we can use music to change brainwaves. Brain waves affect how well we can perform different tasks. One way we can change our brain waves is by using music and sounds. There are four types of brain waves: alpha, beta, theta and delta. These altered states can be measured in cycles per second (cps) of brain-wave activity, as shown in Table 5.2.

Brain waves are not the same as musical beats per minute (bpm). However, the greater the number of beats per minute, the greater the arousal and energy generated.

Cross-cultural considerations in choosing music

When participants listen to 'exotic' music, which is from a tradition outside their own cultural background, their interpretation may be very different

Table 5.2   Types of brain waves

Brain wave	Our experience	Cycles per second (cps)
Delta	Deep sleep state; deep breathing; unconscious; cannot hear consciously.	1–4
Theta	Twilight zone; half awake and half asleep; we are creative and imaginative; can see things from different angles; may feel stress; can be stimulated by very slow music, for example, ethereal harp or flute music.	4–7
Alpha	Relaxed, but alert, reflective; clear, calm thought processes; focused concentration; brain open and prepared to take in new information; also called 'super consciousness'; the dreaming state rapid eye movement (REM); can be stimulated by music with a slower beat, for example Baroque music, *Kitaro* (Japanese group), singing bowls. Or other techniques like meditation, staring at a relaxing computer screen saver picture.	8–12
Beta	The most common state during consciousness; alert; able to critique information; make decisions; solve problems; busy classroom activities; discussion; can handle many thoughts at once; can be stimulated by upbeat music: pop, bouncy instrumentals, some dance and jazz music.	12–25
Super beta	Intensity; high drama; exercise.	25+

Source: adapted from Brant and Harvey (2001) and Jensen (2000).

from what you, the facilitator, intended. We all have a learnt cultural template for music as well as many other aspects of our lives. Javanese pentatonic scales and gamelan music may sound very strange to some Western ears, and European music may sound equally strange to some Africans and Indonesians.

According to Davies (1991), there are some culture-free aspects of music based on the physics of the music, for example:

● loud sounds represent higher energy or a more aroused state of mind;
● high frequency tones represent higher energy than lower tones;
● faster music represents a faster rate of information flow than slower music;
● there are no known groups or societies anywhere in the world that are without music of some kind.

Music fulfils different needs in different locations around the world, and we are all prisoners of our cultural assumptions and expectations

(Millbower, 2000). There are 'cultural and psychological templates' which we learn from birth. Imagine how you would respond to a Western major scale in contrast to the Javanese pentatonic scales used in gamelan. On the other hand, the increasing popularity of so-called 'world music' has meant that many people have diversified their tastes in music in recent years. The term was coined by marketing companies in the 1980s to bring music from Asia, Africa, Eastern Europe, South and Central America, and the Caribbean closer to the mainstream of Western popular music.

Singing songs

In the West, television has eroded the pastime of communal singing in the home to a large extent, and music is seen to be performed by 'others', professionals. In many Asian and African countries, however, singing a local song is an easy and pleasant way to start a workshop, as singing is still so much part of these cultures. The rise of karaoke in South-East Asia, for example, has increased the popularity of singing in public.

At the beginning of my first workshop in Kuala Lumpur over 10 years ago, I was quite nervous. The rows of heavy wooden desks were immovable in the training room. I faced a large group of Muslim women in traditional dress sitting in straight rows. The introduction I was given was very formal and respectful. As a warm-up exercise I asked if they would be kind enough to sing me a traditional Malaysian song, and was quickly amazed at their smiling faces and lack of inhibition. Their singing helped to put both them and me at ease with one another.

Choosing music to energize

Music that energizes us usually has many of the following characteristics:

- It is written in a fast tempo, 75 or more bpm, so each beat is shorter than one second.
- It is written in a major key. (Note that minor keys in Western music sound sad, for example they are used in Beethoven's Fifth Symphony and *Moonlight Sonata*.)
- It contains strong, heavy, deep, drumming and rhythms which stimulate and temporarily increase muscle energy. It is used by aerobics students, swimmers and runners. (Heavy metal and some quiet New Age music reduces muscle energy.)
- It contains violins or flutes for inspiration.
- It has strong associations (for example, a movie theme like *Born Free*, Handel's 'Hallelujah chorus', 'Land of Hope and Glory' and 'Waltzing Matilda'). It is useful if facilitators try to find local cultural examples).

Music as background during group work

Instrumental music is best as a background to group work as lyrics can be distracting. When using music as a background during small group discussions it is best to use a straw vote (a non-binding show of hands) to check whether all participants are happy with and not distracted by music. Some people may feel distracted by music and may choose to sit at a distance from the source of the music. If there are major objections, then do not proceed. If there is acceptance, check with groups near the source of the music regarding their comfort with the volume of the music, and show them how to adjust it if needed.

It is useful to choose music that does not have a wide range of volume changes, as otherwise you will have to keep adjusting the controls. Some Baroque, New Age music, flute, harp and pan-pipe music is useful. I find flute music is performed all over the world as flutes can be made from so many different materials such as bamboo, wood, metal tubing and clay. Cheerful or soothing flute music is usually well received.

Advantages of lyrics

Songs may be used to link to the workshop topic. There are albums of work and life songs which may be used as discussion starters. There are many Beatles songs that are known world-wide, including 'Power to the people' and 'We can work it out'. Additionally songs by international artists like Miriam Makeba from South Africa are recognized by different age groups from many cultures.

When I am overseas I ask local cultural advisers for ideas. 'Mama Temba's wedding song' (from the musical *The Warrior*) is a rousing song which South African colleagues have suggested. We used it at an International Association of Facilitators (IAF) conference, and the locals led the song (plus drumming accompaniment) at the beginning of the workshop. Similarly 'Rasa Saya Heh!' (a song know to Malaysians) was well received at the beginning of an IAF conference workshop in Kuala Lumpur, with 60 participants from all over the world. In South America *Gracias a la vida* ('Thanks for life') by Chilean diva Violeta Parra evokes strong passions. These songs are simple and visitors soon pick them up if the words are clearly displayed.

Disadvantages of lyrics

Facilitators need to take care when choosing songs. Millbower (2000) describes several difficulties with the use of songs:

- Lyrics may trigger personal memories (both good and bad).
- Some lyrics have a hidden meaning which may not be appropriate to the situation or culture.

- Lyrics can make concentration difficult, so they are best used as the focus for discussion, not background music
- Language barriers and some metaphors may be difficult for some participants.

Songs about work and social issues

Songs have been written in all cultures both by people working on physical and often tiring and repetitive tasks, and by those who wish to send a message to make us think about social issues. Work songs were created to:

- reduce feelings of boredom;
- help people synchronize with the rhythms;
- reduce the fatigue of physical labour;
- energize physical movement;
- enhance a feeling of camaraderie amongst workers;
- tell stories of achievements and abuse: improvised verses sung by slaves had verses about escaping, while improvised verses sung by sailors had verses complaining about the captain and the work conditions.

Social issue songs have been written to:

- provoke thinking about current and past societal issues from different angles;
- promote empathy with others;
- stimulate action to improve situations.

Hints for facilitators

Preparation

- Try out music on yourself beforehand, and note your own physical and emotional reactions.
- Select your music based on the goals you wish to achieve, your own favourites and those of the participants.
- An understanding of the history of musical periods helps in the selection of music for different purposes (see further information on my website, www.hogans.id.au).
- When choosing music to accompany reading from a text, select items that match the emotional intensity and pace of the text (see further information on the website).
- For background music, select items that have a balanced and predictable beat, rhythm and volume. Remember lyrics are distracting.

- To enhance creativity, select music that is more expressive and stimulating.
- When choosing songs, make sure the lyrics are clear. If you are using the song as a stimulus for discussion, print the words on an overhead projector transparency (OHPT) or reproduce the words on handouts.
- If you want participants to join in with songs, make sure you choose songs that are 'catchy' and easy to sing or hum.
- When choosing songs, ensure the lyrics are culturally and politically suitable. For example, many Western songs reflect the values of 'individualistic' societies and may not be suitable in more 'collective' cultures.
- Try not to be dogmatic and exclusive about the music you choose. There is no 'right' music for a particular topic or group. It is 'right' if it creates the impact you are aiming for: it helps relaxation, increases alertness, or whatever is needed (Meier, 2000).
- Use an audio/cassette player; some canned or piped muzak can feel very shallow.
- Compile a table of your favourite tunes.

Use of language

- Choose techniques with which you feel comfortable. There are, however, always going to be times when you try something new and stretch your own comfort zones. After all we ask participants to do this, don't we?
- It may be useful to use centring and breathing techniques (Heron, 1999; Hogan, 2002).
- The way a facilitator chooses words to introduce an exercise is important. For example, 'I feel a bit worried about whether this will work' is less convincing than 'I wonder whether you would perhaps mind trying this out?' (Heron, 1999: 239).

Explore the web

- If you are looking for the words of a song, try typing the title into an 'exact words' search with the Google search engine. The words of very simple songs can be found at www.djmorton.demon.co.uk/scouting/campfire.htm
- Visit the Musicmaker site at www.musicmaker.com. Musicmaker.com is a provider of customized music CD compilations on the internet. The company's website allows you to order custom-compiled music CDs. You can digitally download songs from the company's online library directly to your computer.

Ground rules and group dynamics

- Generate music ground rules; for example, invite participants to give you feedback regarding use of music. Some people find background music distracting, and others such as individuals with hearing aids may be disadvantaged, as hearing devices pick up and amplify background noise.
- Invite participants to bring in their favourite music, but explain what kinds of music are suitable: that is, have music ground rules. Check and approve choices; otherwise music that is sexist or racist may offend or defeat your purpose.
- Offer a variety of music.
- Ensure that during some activities music is not used in order to cater for people who prefer to work in silence.
- Observe the group and if something isn't working, ask why and discuss what to do next and/or try something else.
- Explain to participants why you are using music. If you are enthusiastic about music, often they will be too.

Monitor and research

- Conduct some action research yourself and with participants and other facilitators.

Check purpose and context

Evidence of the power of song is in the stories of those who have been persecuted, imprisoned or expelled from their countries for their songs. So facilitators need to choose lyrics with care according to the goals of the workshop and the cultural and political context. John Lennon's 'Power to the people' might be a very useful discussion starter for a workshop on 'Empowerment' in some cultures, but be totally inappropriate in others.

Useful websites

The CD album *Work Songs* (Drog, Ontario) can be found on www.drog.com/albums/work.htm

Look for the works of Ewan McColl, Peggy Seeger, Mercedes Sosa, Miriam Makeba, Violeta Parra, Roy Bailey, The Beatles, John Lennon, Woody Guthrie, Pete Seeger and Bob Dylan, to name but a few. (See BBC Radio Ballads Series of Programmes at www.bbc.co.uk/radio2/radioballads) They include songs about work, jobs that have disappeared, HIV/AIDS, and other social issues.

Music to find jobs by: see www.planningcommunications.com/jf/work_songs.htm. This website includes a list of songs that may be used as discussion starters, for example, '9 to 5' by Dolly Parton.

Over extended workshops, it is interesting to be able to play music from different traditions. For example see the CDs:

- *Routes: Africa, Asia and the World;*
- *Routes: Britain, Ireland and North America* (Nascente label), a set of four CDs which give a comprehensive coverage of world folk music;
- *Music for the New World* (a mix of music from Africa, Bangladesh, and Sufi, Tuvan and Gaelic traditions).

Processes involving music and sound

Before designing an exercise it is important that facilitators ask themselves, 'What is the purpose of the group exercise?' and then consider the music/ sound process to achieve this purpose. Below is a list of choices I give participants for various team-building workshops.

Write the words to a song with your group

Use a tune that many people are familiar with, for example 'Happy birthday', 'Frère Jacques' or 'Auld Lang Syne', compose the words of a song on a topic of your choosing, preferably to do with people and facilitation, the workplace, team work, or the conference themes. Work out how you can demonstrate your song to the other participants and involve them if you (and they) wish.

Design sounds for a creative visualization/ guided imagery exercise

Use music or sounds to accompany a progressive relaxation exercise. Take participants to a serene and peaceful setting of their choice. Use a singing bowl, simple drum beats or tingshaws to evoke thought. A singing bowl is a metal bowl comprising many metals which is struck with a wooden beater. Then the edge is stirred and a haunting sound emerges. Singing bowls and tingshaws were transported across the caravan routes of Asia and traded in ancient times. They are now traded in markets all over the world.

Create a team percussion using sounds created by you and the props you can find

Look around you at the different things and materials that can be used to create sounds (such as parts of your body, hands beating on table, clicking glasses and hands on different clothing textures). Create a soundscape together to represent a work theme of your choice.

Create a team percussion using the small instruments available

Build a theme or story through percussion sounds using the small instruments available. Create a soundscape together to represent a work theme of your choice. One group facilitated a soundscape with all participants in a circle. They invited everyone to make sounds to illustrate a summary of feelings during the workshop whilst they gave a verbal overview of each process (see Table 5.3).

Table 5.3   Examples of percussion instruments

cymbals	rattles in the shape of fruit	djembe drums
small drums	wooden water buffalo bells	bells
tambourines	drum sticks	conductor's baton
tins with beans	zills (belly dancing cymbals)	tingshaws (cymbals)

Wherever I travel I buy small instruments from different cultures. A primary school in Johannesburg generously lent me boxes of percussion instruments for a conference. It is easy for participants to make their own too out of tins, plastic containers and beans.

Please note that it is not advisable to distribute wind instruments like kazoos, pan pipes, whistles and ocarinas because of the potential risk of spreading disease. If you buy plastic kazoos, it is a good idea to obtain one per participant and invite users to write their name on them with a permanent maker pen.

Add sounds to accompany a story

Choose a teaching story or myth from your culture. I usually provide some examples to prompt memories. Work out the sounds and noises you can interweave with your story. See examples of myths in this book, or see Finlay and Hogan (1995) and Hogan (2000) for ideas.

Create a rap or chant

Create a rhythmic rap or chant to represent a work theme or message of your choice. It might have a question and answer format or a repeated message every few lines. You could accompany it with clapping or stamping or whatever you choose.

Observing reactions and sensations

Prepare a variety of sounds, for example using tingshaws and a singing bowl (singing bowls induce alpha brain waves and a sense of relaxation) and music from your collection of workshop CDs (I take a collection of about 30 CDs). Play short sequences of each and invite participants to report their responses and how they might use, adapt or reject these pieces of music in their work.

Bring in your favourite piece of music

A colleague, Gill Baxter, invited a class of postgraduate psychology students to bring to class a piece of their favourite or most important music or a song of their choice in order to explore the potential use of music for individuals and groups.

> We were looking at how music changed mood, brought back memories, set a scene and communicated at a different level. I asked the class to think about a meaningful piece of music and to bring an example in. Some brought their own music, some brought CDs that inspired them, relaxed them or stimulated them. One lady brought the copy of her song that she sang for her brother's funeral. That had us all in tears. Another brought in a song his wife had written and sang to him at their wedding. He described how nervous he had been and then how captivated he was by his wife singing about her love in front of everyone and how her song drove away his fears. Music is a strong therapy tool and can be used consciously or unconsciously. We discussed how people play music to get rid of strong emotions, eg anger and sadness as well as connecting with others. I think a book could be written on just this topic.
>
> Gill Baxter, psychologist and facilitator, Perth, Australia

This type of exercise may be quite emotional. The facilitator needs to have skills to manage this. It requires uninterrupted time and a commitment by the group to honour and listen to both the music and each individual's story behind the music. This exercise is a very useful tool for team building.

Develop a song or music to represent your organization

Facilitators can provide simple props and simple percussion instruments. Invite participants to join small groups and produce a song about their organization in the style of their local culture/s, rock and roll, country and western, blues, folk or rap. This activity is useful as an end-of-year activity with school teachers or at the completion of a phase of a project. It is a great way for people to let off steam.

Song words which parody current work practices

The Shiny Bum Singers (so called as they have shiny bottoms, because they are government workers who sit on office chairs for many hours a day) have published four booklets of words which parody current work practices in Australia (Shiny Bum Singers, 1999, 2000, 2001, 2002). They also have a CD, *An Audience with the Shiny Bum Singers*. See website www. fasfind.com/p/borisbooks

Licensing information

If facilitators are using music or songs to enhance the environment of their workshops or business, many Western countries require the purchase of a licence. This is to ensure that musicians and composers receive proceeds for the use of their intellectual property. Some large organizations buy an annual licence to cover all use of music in the workplace. Regulations vary from country to country. A most useful website containing addresses of copyright offices in countries across the world is at www.csmpro.ch/ Promotion/copyright.htm

Dance

In countries where I know that social and traditional dancing is popular, I invite participants to show us all a dance. Sometimes it is useful to have a dance to break the ice. Others might volunteer to teach a dance once they see that people join in.

I have used a very simple circle dance entitled 'Nigun Atik' (also known as 'Zemer Atik') with multicultural groups in Malaysia, Myanmar, South Africa and Australia as an opening or closing ritual with up to 300 people. The title means 'ancient melody' and it is a traditional Middle Eastern wedding dance (where the couple stand in the middle of the circle). The music and the dance are simple and seem to resonate with many different kinds of people. A circle in many cultures symbolizes unity, strength and equality. Many different artists have recorded the music; CDs can be bought via the web. See instructions for Nigun Atik on www.hogans.id.au

If I am in a country where some women might feel awkward at holding hands with strange men, I either invite women to dance together on one side of the circle (asking female acquaintances to be at the front and back of the women's line next to the men) or have women in a circle in the middle. If there are some who prefer not to dance or who are not able to dance, I invite them to drum on a table or use drums and percussion instruments if I have them with me. I always give choices.

6

Visual techniques

Introduction

A visual aid does not need to be a piece of art – it just has to pass on a message.

Petra Röhr-Rouendaal (2006)

In culturally and linguistically diverse groups the use of visual techniques is even more important to enliven communication, interaction and understanding. You cannot rely on oral communication alone. This chapter contains discussion of:

- a comparison between group (community-based) media and mass media;
- pictures and cartoons as discussion starters;
- useful visual literacy research for facilitators;
- questioning processes for facilitators to use with participants;
- graphic facilitation;
- participants' mindscapes and concept drawing;
- empowering use of participants' participatory videos;
- idea generation in three dimensions;
- resources to help participants see things from different angles;
- how to avoid death by PowerPoint;
- learning how to draw.

Group media (community-based media)

Silvio Waisbord (2001) suggested that the term 'group media' is based on Freire's work, whereby small groups can use community-based forms of communication such as songs, theatre, radio, video and locally developed media to develop a critical attitude towards the reality of self, the group, community and society through participation in group interaction. They are used to:

- disseminate information;
- identify common problems and solutions;
- reflect upon community issues;
- mobilize resources to change the status quo.

As with any tool, group media are dependent on how they are used, the skills and sensitivity of the facilitator, the appropriateness for the participants and the context.

See the Center for Media Literacy website, www.medialit.com, for more information on group media.

Increasing uses of visuals

Robert Horn (1999) claims that visual language is already a global language and that it will rapidly become an international auxiliary language (IAL) in the 21st century. (An IAL is a language that is used in addition to our native languages.) Visual language is certainly already aiding communication across cultures. Visuals help us process the escalating masses of information that emerge daily in our lives.

Social marketing

Media are used to inform and change behaviours. 'Culturally adapted social marketing and research' is the adoption and more importantly adaptation of successful marketing strategies (mass and group media) into non-marketing contexts to inform and change behaviours to achieve socially desirable objectives. Unfortunately, in the past mass marketing has usually been imposed in a top-down approach. The resulting media may have little impact unless they are designed after careful research at micro-cultural levels. In the field of health education, for example on HIV/AIDS, researcher/facilitators are involved in researching traditional beliefs and cultural norms, and the previous impact (and reasons for lack of impact) of visual media intended to instruct people about HIV/AIDS and to change behaviours. See the excellent manual written by Scarlett Epstein (1999) and the work of Kotler, Roberto and Lee (2002).

Flows of communication with pictures

There are many ways to interact with pictures.

One-way communication

Visuals that 'stand alone', forms of one-way communication such as posters and pamphlets, always need to be pre-tested. Why? Because you cannot assume that your message is understood unless you get feedback. However, you can send messages indirectly by leaving posters on display on the walls at workshops.

Two-way communication

Visuals may be used in a participatory way with questions and answers between the facilitator and participants (see 'Facilitated discussion framework' on page 192). For example, a series of pictures that tell a story may be held up as a stimulus for either facilitator-driven questions or participant-driven questions.

Multi-way communication

Multi-way communication means that the facilitator takes a more minor role and by staying silent enables the participants to discuss a visual. Multi-way communication is enhanced if everyone, including the facilitator, is sitting in a circle. The facilitator only intervenes to guide discussion when needed.

Alternatively, the participants may be divided up into small groups and left to discuss a picture on their own first. This is particularly useful if some participants are less fluent in the dominant language of the workshop.

> Pictures can help people to read the world. Suitably designed visual aids can initiate the process by which oppressed people develop a critical awareness of their own reality. Reading the world is the first step towards taking action to change reality. Paulo Freire wrote that 'people must learn to read their own reality and write their own history'. Pictures can help both these processes.
>
> (Linney, 1995: 2–3)

Useful visual literacy research findings for facilitators

As facilitators we need to be aware of the research into visual literacy, as it will make an impact on how we develop, use, choose and analyse pictures with groups. One of the most comprehensive pieces of visual literacy research was conducted in Nepal by UNICEF in 1976, where six visual styles were tested (photos, photos with background blocked out, stylized drawing, line drawings with shading, line drawings without shading, and silhouettes). Simple line drawings plus shading to show three dimensions with little or no background were found to be most effective. See pictures on www.hogans.id.au

In some villages, pictures are only seen to illustrate politicians, local gods and advertising. (In Islamic cultures pictures of the Prophet Mohammed are not allowed. In Quaker groups, symbols are not allowed.) Studies conducted in many different cultures (Holmes, 1963; Fussell and Haaland, 1976; Dudley and Haaland, 1993; Bradley, 1994; Linney, 1995) have yielded similar results with villagers who are illiterate and/or who have little exposure to pictures being used for educational purposes. These results and suggestions are summarized and expanded upon below.

Setting up a discussion

The tone and body language of the facilitator is so important. Patronizing or condescending attitudes can easily be sensed by participants, who all have very good 'phoney detectors' working.

Visual literacy

Reading and understanding pictures and symbols is not automatic. Reading pictures is easier than reading words, but some people do not automatically know how to do it and may need to be taught. Messages in pictures are not always obvious. One-way communication is least effective. There is a need for two-way communication of pictures in brochures and posters.

Picture style

- Villagers tend to 'read' pictures very literally, so draw literally. They might recognize objects and people, but not attempt to link them or read a message in the message.
- Avoid abstract ideas. Try to move from concrete examples to abstract ideas rather than vice versa. Abstract ideas in pictures can cause confusion.
- Perspective and depth are sometimes not easily understood, so for example an adult in the background may be perceived as a child.
- Use three-dimensional techniques enhanced with shading and/or cross-hatching.
- Avoid unnecessary detail. Unnecessary background detail can be distracting and cause confusion.
- Scale may confuse. In one anecdote, a development worker produced an enlarged picture of a fly and described how it carried disease. A villager said, 'That won't be a problem for us as we don't have flies that big.' In fact the villager was the local comic; he was fully aware of the scale issue, and was making fun of the development worker, who perhaps was being a little patronizing.

Symbols and conventions

● Do not assume that people will automatically understand symbols. Help people to develop visual literacy by explaining pictorial conventions like crosses, ticks, arrows, speed lines, ♀,♂,!,?.
● Avoid unfamiliar conventions. If people are unfamiliar with a convention, they will try to read the picture literally: for example an arrow may be perceived as an arrow rather than a symbol indicating direction.
● Explain symbols. This helps people to develop visual literacy skills in interpreting graphic conventions.

Sequences and connections

● People do not necessarily identify a sequence of pictures on one sheet of paper as was intended by the artist (say, left to right or in a circle/cycle). Where possible, avoid them. Images are generally read individually.
● When explaining the cause and effect of problems, it may be necessary to use a storyboard or sequence of pictures. The idea of linked pictures and ideas needs to be explained.

Cultural associations

● Identify important needs in the community by asking what is important as a starting point.
● Identify local icons/items/people/heroes and heroines of cultural importance that people like to see in pictures.
● Avoid things from outside the known environment. (Some clip art is very confusing in some contexts.)

Gender

● Pictures need to be gender-sensitive. For instance, if you are trying to communicate the importance of women's land rights and names on land titles, then illustrations need to show pictures of women, not husband and wives jointly holding a land title.
● If the message is aimed at women, the facilitators should, if possible, be women and vice versa.
● Be aware that youths and men may laugh at women who give 'wrong answers'. This can be very upsetting for women who have summoned up the courage to speak, so be careful to set up some 'ways of listening' to one another before you start.

Use of text and language

- Give names to ideas. To adopt a new idea we need to be able to put a name to it. The evolution of a visual vocabulary must develop hand in hand with an understanding of the local verbal vocabulary (Dudley and Haaland, 1993). For instance, ask people to give an appropriate local name for behaviours that would equate to 'domestic violence'.
- Use text which makes sense. As far as possible, the text should make sense when reading aloud.
- Print desired text and/or questions on the back of pictures as prompts for the facilitators and to ensure similar stages of desired interactions.

Local differences

Ensure that familiar objects are used. If necessary, visuals may need to be redrawn for use with participants from the city, from rural areas and from different ethnic groups (adapting clothing, house styles and so on). Ensure the message is the same. If one image is meant to serve for the whole country, it will usually involve making so many compromises that it could be close to useless (Dudley and Haaland, 1993).

Colour

Uses and interpretations of different colours have different meanings. For example, silhouettes of people may be perceived as ghosts, devils or representing evil. In Nepal, orange and yellow were well liked and people thought of them as colours of gods.

Size

Pictures produced should be A3 size minimum (that is, twice the size of A4) so that they can be seen from a distance).

Training

Training is required in the use of pictures, storytelling and the use of question-and-answer techniques. Facilitators need to be aware of the need to explain and summarize key messages, symbols and so on. See 'Facilitated discussion framework' on page 192.

Pictures and cartoons as discussion starters

Cartoons are ambiguous. They are meant to be.

Michael Leunig, Australian cartoonist

There are many ways to gain attention and stimulate a discussion: a carefully worded provocative question, pictures, stories, role play and puppet stories. Pictures and cartoons are also useful, especially if they are drawn to focus on local issues. They do not show causes or solutions: these are left open for the participants to discuss and with the prompting of the facilitator to dig deeper. Discussion starters can be very effective in teaching participants how to develop logical, analytical thinking and problem-solving processes.

Comparing cartoons from various different cultures, Havet (1987) suggests that humour and the lack of words allow cartoons to present the unacceptable face of reality to people within the same culture in an acceptable manner. They are in some ways similar to the court jester of earlier eras.

Do not assume that people understand the indirect messages and intended humour behind cartoons. Also conventions like speech and thought bubbles may need to be taught in a non-patronizing way. People may feel resentful if presented serious information in a cartoon strip or if they feel they are being drawn in a 'funny way'. Cartoons may not be good way of conveying educational messages (Dudley and Haaland, 1993).

The Hungry Man and There You Go

Oren Ginzburg is a committed aid worker, and author and illustrator of two delightful, punchy cartoon books entitled *The Hungry Man* (2004) and *There You Go* (2005). See pictures on www.hogans.id.au. In *The Hungry Man*, a villager who is portrayed as not hungry at the start of a development project becomes hungrier as well-meaning development workers focus on their tried and tested 'process' – needs analysis, report writing, organizing workshops and so on – while forgetting about people's everyday need for food. It makes fun of the saying 'If you give a man a fish, you feed him for a day; if you teach a man to fish, you feed him for a lifetime' (Lesley, 2005).

The series of cartoons would form the basis of a useful discussion for development groups. I usually ask everyone to point into the air with their forefingers (remember pointing at others is very rude in some cultures). Automatically three fingers point back at themselves! It's a useful way of stopping blaming and getting everyone to review his/her own practice.

In *There You Go*, Ginzburg challenges the arrogant assumption that Westerners can teach 'sustainable development' to tribal peoples by introducing (imposing) impractical and short-sighted 'income-generating' projects which ultimately lead to economic collapse of the environment or bare-faced theft of mineral, timber and other resources by companies from outside. In the *Cambodia Daily*, Ginzburg commented, 'There is a huge distance between what we do and what we say we do, between how we experience our actions and how the people we are targeting experience them' (Melamed, 2005). These booklets may be ordered from: www. HungryManBooks.com or e-mail: contact@hungrymanbooks.com

How to make grassroots comics

World Comics-Finland has a very useful website: www.worldcomics.fi/howto_grassroot.shtml

Facilitated discussion framework for picture analysis

We have to be careful that participants understand the message that we are giving. If the cartoon is using ironic humour and is 'tongue in cheek', do the participants realize this? How can we tell? Questions should be open-ended, so they result in a variety of different answers. Closed questions (those that get 'yes' or 'no' answers) are not so useful (see Table 6.1).

Once you have all the answers to your questions, it is good to repeat them all to the participants once more, to confirm who is who and who is doing what.

Table 6.2 provides a suggested framework of questions as a rough guide. It is only a guide. Not all the stages may be needed, depending on your purpose. Some ambiguity in the picture is useful, and may lead to unexpected but useful discussions.

Table 6.1   Good and bad facilitation questions

Good questions (open)	Bad questions (closed and either/or)
What do you see here in this picture?	Do you understand this picture?
What is happening in this picture?	Is this a xxx or a xx?
Who is the person in the front who is speaking?	
Who are the people sitting down?	
What are these people doing?	

Table 6.2 Facilitated discussion framework

Stages	Description	Possible questions
1. Describe	Encourage participants to describe what they see in the picture	'What is happening in this picture?' or 'Can anyone tell me what this is?'
2. Explain	Symbols or artistic devices	'These people are in the distance. That is why they are so small.'
3. Summarize	Key elements in the picture	'The key things in this picture are …'
4. Relate to own lives	Invite participants to relate what is shown in the picture to their own real-life situation.	'Does this happen in your area/village?' 'Has anyone seen this happen?'
5. Identify the problems	Ensure that everyone is clear about the main problems illustrated in or suggested by the picture. Allow 'think time'. Ensure that people dig deep to the root causes. This relates to Paulo Freire's concept of conscientization. Ensure a variety of 'sectors' are discussed, eg not just health.	'So the main problems here are …, related to health, communication systems, transport …'
6. Identify the consequences of these problems	Try to help participants relate the problems to their own experiences	'What effect could this have in your community?'
7. Look for causes	Invite participants to look for causes of the problems. This is a very important stage in the development of critical awareness	'What makes this happen?' 'But why?' 'But why?'(see below in next section)
8. Look for solutions	Encourage participants to suggest solutions that correspond to the causes they have found.	'Are there things that need to be done immediately?' 'Are there any things that can be done over many years?' 'Do you need to talk to others in the community?' 'Are there any solutions where you might need outside help/training?'
9. Plan action	Participants draw up an action plan to put solutions into practice.	'Who is going to do what, by when and with what resources?' 'Do picture posters need to be made?'

Source: adapted from Linney (1995: 93).

Photo analysis

Another technique to develop empathy involves questions like:

- Can you tell me what is going on here?
- Can you imagine what it would be like to be the people shown in the photo?
- Imagine you are this person in the photo. Using the first person – 'I' – can you say what he/she might be thinking or going to say to the people around?
- If you talked to these people what do you think they would tell you?

Photolanguage

The Photolanguage concept was originally devised by Pierre Babin and his colleagues in France in 1968. *Photolanguage Australia*, 130 black-and-white pictures on values by Cooney and Burtin (1986: available from Innovative Resources, www.innovativeresources.org), has many uses. The pictures were taken in Australia, though most are not culture-specific. These photo sets can be used for values clarification, spiritual development, moral leadership courses for the armed services, youth programmes, social awareness groups, migrant and student induction programmes and cross-cultural awareness courses.

It is noticeable that having a picture to talk to enables individuals to speak more freely. The other participants look at the photo, so an individual speaking feels less inhibited.

Alternatively, make your own culture-specific picture packs using digital photos and evocative pictures from calendars and postcards that depict human values, feelings and issues. Digital cameras enable you to take and print your own pictures. You may need to test and filter pictures based on how they are chosen (or not chosen) and interpreted by participants.

Graphic facilitation

Graphic recording and facilitating combines pictures, symbols and words to represent the ideas participants generate in workshops. A graphic facilitator is a person who may work in conjunction with a facilitator to record the ideas of participants in the form of symbols, simple drawings and key words in bright colours on flipchart paper. The images are created in real time, and as participants converse in this way they can check if ideas have been expressed correctly. (Alternatively the facilitator can take this role and employ these techniques.) There are four stages (Agerbeck, 2004):

1. *Listening*. Listening to the group as an outsider, gathering points and details at a meta level, above the politics of the group.
2. *Thinking*. Thinking about what information and what level of detail is most salient to facilitate the group, and deciding what is put on the map (and what to leave out).
3. *Organizing*. Organizing the conversation, giving it structure, using critical thinking and spatial skills to create a whole, integrated image.
4. *Drawing*. Drawing images and symbols to create narrative and appeal to the visual and emotional parts of our brains, while adding supporting structure through colour, arrows and groupings.

See examples in Schuman (2005).

Symbolary

A symbolary is a collection of symbols and word meanings, similar to a dictionary. In order to build up your repertoire of symbols it is useful to keep an address book and keep adding key words/concepts and simple drawings to illustrate them in alphabetical order. To get started see the symbolary in *Visual Thinking* by Margulies and Valenza (2005).

Mindscapes and concept drawing

Author/background

One way to help participants learn about concepts is to ask them to draw what they already know about a concept: in other words, to apply adult learning theory (Knowles, 1984). Asking participants to draw concepts brings them (the concept and the participants) to life. This process may be used to map changes in understanding and perceptions by asking them to redraw later: that is, before and after a workshop session. The following draws on the work of GATT-Fly (1983) and Kettle and Saul (2006). Margulies and Valenza call these pictures 'mindscapes': visual representations of ideas using pictures and words:

> Making ideas visible, using both words and images, means that we are making our very process of thinking visible. Often we go about thinking and attempting to solve problems without a conscious awareness of our own process.
>
> (Margulies and Valenza, 2005: 8)

Sylvia Downs, who works with the long-term unemployed in the United Kingdom, developed a very simple mnemonic to describe how we learn: MUD. We learn by Memorizing, Understanding and Doing (Downs, 1981). There are many documented techniques to help people to develop 'memorizing', 'understanding' and 'doing' (skills-based learning) techniques (Downs and Perry, 1984; Downs, 1995). Developing understanding of concepts is a higher level of learning and is the most difficult.

Purpose/rationale

The process may be used to enable groups to:

- identify different components of a concept, such as 'culture', 'development', 'participation', 'power and 'empowerment', 'co-facilitation', 'journey' and 'plan';
- realize the many different meanings others have of concepts which they think everyone understands in the same way;
- learn from one another;
- give facilitators insight into the levels of understanding of participants.

Materials

Crayons, felt pens, flipchart paper.

Stages

1. Brief the group and bolster confidence along the lines of 'No previous experience is necessary, just make some marks. We are not looking for Leonardo da Vincis here.'
2. Ask groups to draw their understanding of the concept under discussion at the workshop.
3. Start anywhere with a visual symbol of key word to represent the topic (or start with a mindscape template, see below).
4. Invite individuals to walk around if they wish to view the work of others and/or join other groups if they wish.
5. Facilitators should stand back and allow participants to get on with the exercise, observing but not directing.
6. Remind everyone that you are not looking for works of art, but ideas. It is useful to display some of your own efforts to create some laughter.
7. Invite groups to display their sheets in a 'gallery'.

Debrief

1. Ask the 'artists' to remain quiet while the participants focus on their particular picture and give their interpretation of its meaning.
2. Invite the 'artists' to describe their intended message/s and meaning.

3. Optional: after all the pictures have been discussed, invite participants to vote on which they think is the 'best' or 'most thought-provoking' portrayal of the concept by putting a dot on the bottom of their preferred choice.
4. Remind participants that they cannot vote for their own picture. (In some cultures, such as in Myanmar, it is perfectly acceptable in workshops to vote for yourself.)
5. Ask participants to explain why they voted for a particular picture.

    The last two stages are not mandatory, but mean that participants look at pictures and listen to explanations more intently.

At the end of the workshop you may wish to return to this exercise and ask participants to add new concepts/ideas learnt in the workshop as a way of seeing whether their concepts have enlarged.

Pluses

Visual methods have many advantages as they:

- enable everyone to take part by watching, talking, drawing and/or adding to or adapting visuals (Linney, 1995);
- are fun;
- are relatively stress-free, enjoyable and playful if completed in a group;
- enable both people who are literate and those who are non-literate to participate (Heslop, 2002);
- allow people to represent complex things simply;
- allow participants to use their own artistic styles, traditions and folk-lore symbols to represent their ideas (such as a woman who used the picture of Ganesh, the Hindu elephant god, as a symbol for attributes of a facilitator: see www.hogans.id.au);
- provide a clear focus for debate and discussion;
- help people analyse information carefully, and compare their views with others;
- are flexible: new information and perspectives can be added;
- are open-ended since visual ambiguities attract attention and stimulate discussion (Heslop, 2002);
- are colourful and energizing;
- may be used by facilitators, or with groups and individuals.

In groups, visuals often lead to lively debate, and help highlight clearly the differences and similarities between the views of different people. For example, the same issue can be discussed separately with women and men, or older and younger people.

Minuses

The drawings illustrate the levels of current understanding of participants. Facilitators may need to draw out further explanation and discussion of the concept and/or add further reading and other information later in the workshop.

Interesting points

- Visual exercises can also be rerun during monitoring and evaluation, to see what changes have occurred since the first visual record was made.
- Remember the most important outcome is not the picture, map or diagram being created, but the discussion that takes place in creating it. Pictures tell us things about the people who construct them.

Mindscape templates

Another approach is to start with a mindscape template which often relates to commonly known metaphors.

Drawing mindscapes: 'rivers of life'

There is a commonly used activity called a 'life line' where participants draw a graph with years on the horizontal axis and highs and lows on the vertical axis. Alternatively this may be drawn as a mindscape or landscape picture. Participants draw their lives thus far as a river from its source (birth) to the sea, with all its twists turns, rapids and waterfalls, sluggish points and obstacles. It is a process that can be used to highlight decision points, and show how people overcome problems (rocks).

Drawing mindscapes: 'journeys to achieve goals'

The metaphor of the journey is common to all cultures, and the metaphor of climbing a mountain may be used for goal setting and action planning. Large picture templates on flipcharts of a simple landscape or 'mountain trek' (Margulies and Velanza, 2005) can be drawn and filled in (see Figures 7.1 and 7.2, pages 215 and 216).

Stages

1. Draw a simple landscape with a mountain in the distance.
2. Add a cloud sitting near the mountain top. This can include the goal/s as words or symbols.

3. Draw footprints at the bottom of the picture to represent first steps.
4. Next add big boulders and fill in names of possible obstacles.
5. Add signposts and write in milestones to be celebrated.
6. Add possible side paths going off the main track which represent 'doing nothing' and 'becoming disheartened'.

A mindscape does not have to be a scene, it can include a mix of metaphors and shapes. Other useful metaphors that may be built into mindscapes follow.

Rainbows

Rain colours, clouds, raindrops refracting light, sun, pot of gold, future goal, paths, floods, calm and peace after the flood or storm, local legends. 'Rainbow Nation' is a term coined by Archbishop Desmond Tutu to describe post-1994 South Africa, after apartheid rule had officially ended. The term was intended to encapsulate the unity of multiculturalism and the coming together of people of many different races, in a country once identified with the strict division of white and black.

Ladders

Steps, stages, hierarchy, degrees of difficulty, power, participation, empowerment. (See Arnstein's ladder (page 84), the empowerment ladder (page 87) and the ladder of assumptions or inference, page 226.)

Landscapes

Journeys, goals, travel up paths to the mountain or down a river towards the sea.

Trees

Roots, solid, branches, leaves, growth, stability. Roots may represent cultural roots; branches and leaves, growth and individuality.

Bridges

Linking, conflict resolution, cultural bridges, ideas, process, temporary, permanent (see Chapter 4).

Onions

Layers within layers, research. See also Russian *Matryoshka* dolls (page 209).

Participants design pictures

In Chapter 4, I described how the cross-cultural exchange process can be adapted to incorporate participants' drawings of their own cultures. Additionally the drawing process enables participants to express some things they might not say directly to a group.

Bob Linney acknowledges the shortage of good suitable pictures in the development field, and criticizes the design of visuals by outsiders in a top-down approach. Involving local people in the process of designing visuals is a major way of educating people about your message while developing a people-centred approach to visual aids production. See Linney (1995) for an excellent description of how to do this.

While I was working in Lao PDR, I invited government workers to design their own pictures to educate villagers about their project. In Lao Loun culture (that of the dominant group in Lao PDR), traditionally the youngest daughter inherits from her parents as she is the one who frequently stays home to look after them in their old age. It follows therefore that visuals should reflect this and prominently show pictures of women holding their land titles. Other visuals are required to illustrate couples and/or single males who have bought land holding their land titles. Without any training, the workshop participants designed very useful pictures: see www.hogans.id.au

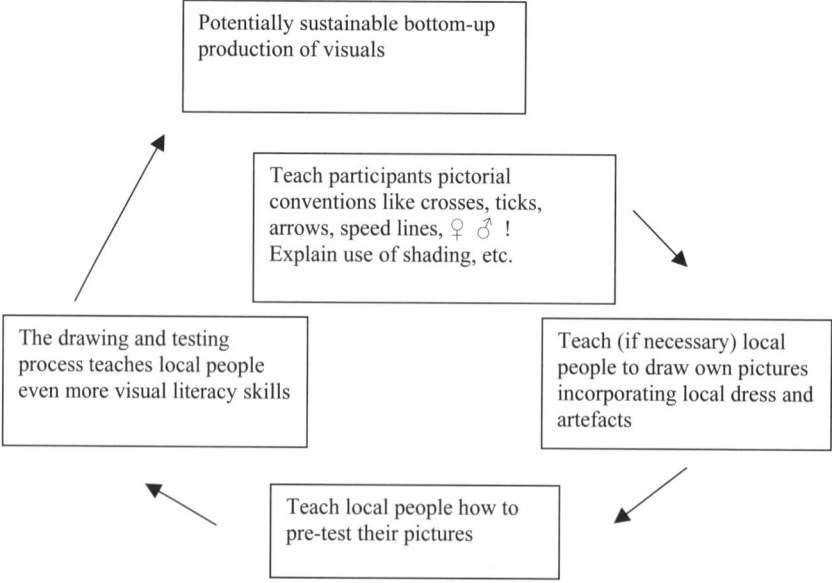

Figure 6.1 People-centred production of visuals

Multi-purpose visuals

Calendars as storyboards

Some organizations produce an annual calendar to promote their work with visitors and officials. These can be multi-purpose, in that the large pictures may be used as storyboards about the project. See www.hogans.id.au

Pre-testing visual aids

Pre-testing means finding out how well the visual aid is understood by asking questions about it. You need to pre-test before the visual aid is finalized.

- Test drawings and words separately (the drawings first on their own and then with the text).
- Ensure that the text relates to the drawing being shown.
- Always test, as many visuals fail. New materials should be tested repeatedly with representative samples of the target audience.

Conducting pre-testing

Pre-test in pairs: one person asks questions and the other notes answers. If the message is aimed at women, the interviewers should if possible be women. Choose a suitable time and place. Explain to village leaders that villagers may feel intimidated by their presence.

Who should do pre-testing?

Involve district teams and community members in the research process as local people will be less threatening to villagers. Researchers should:

- ask a village leader or elder to do the introductions (and then preferably be left to it);
- be courteous and show respect to the villagers, who may feel very nervous as they may feel their village is being judged;
- introduce themselves and ask the names of villagers (if this is normal cultural practice);
- engage the villagers in talking about their village to gain their confidence;
- go slowly;
- since people often think it is they who are being tested, explain they are testing visual and/or audio aids for their project;

- explain that the villagers are the experts and only they know whether the message will be understood in their community.

Remember: people often feel embarrassed to say what they really think. Be sensitive and tactful. Some people do not like to criticize a picture designed by strangers, as they do not want to offend.

Pictures

The questions will vary according to the type of material being tested. Try to keep to a few simple questions. Decide on your questions beforehand so that all researchers use the same questions and the same words. Examples of questions include:

- What do you see here?
- What message is the illustration trying to give?
- What do you think about the message?
- Can you do what this message asks you to do (yes/no)? If not, why not?
- Is there anything you like about the message?
- Is there anything you dislike about the message?
- What do you think about the illustrations?
- The illustration is trying to ... [tell the villager the intended message]. What improvement can be made to make the illustration communicate the message better?

Written materials

Ask participants to read the words aloud, and note any words they find difficult to read. Questions will vary according to the type of materials you are testing. Examples of questions include:

- Can you state in your own words what you have just read?
- What is the text telling you?
- Is there any word you do not understand?
- If yes, please explain. What other word/s do you suggest are easier to understand?

After you have tested your materials, they can be mass-produced.

Different ethnic groups

When you are planning and designing your visual aids, think about how they may be translated into different languages. For example, with a brochure keep words to the minimum in a space away from a picture so that translations can be inserted easily.

Distribution and follow-up

- How will the materials be distributed to outlying groups?
- How will you know whether they are being used?
- How will you know whether they are being used properly?
- How will you know when they need to be reprinted?

Picture card packs

Even simple pictures work as visual metaphors by adding meaning and power to words. They act as visual 'conversational prompts'.

> Many people can identify life-changing experiences that have been ignited by art, symbols, music, poetry and even silence.

> Russell Deal, Innovative Resources

Innovative Resources card packs

Innovative Resources is a creative publisher in Bendigo, Australia, which produces a wide range of delightful card packs, each with a facilitator's guide. It has an electronic newsletter and a fantastic website: www. innovativeresources.org

Feelings cards

Feelings cards are extremely useful for exploring what individual partici-pants are feeling at the beginning and end of workshops, and during them. They may be used for developing emotional literacy, vocabulary and storytelling. *The Bears* (Deal and Veeken, 1997) was developed initially for use in family therapy, and contains adult and child bears with different expressions, but no words. Likewise the delightful *Koala Company* (Deal and Jones, 2005) contains pictures only. *Stones Have Feelings Too* (Deal and Masman, 2003) is a card pack where each card has three words which give possible interpretations of the feeling of the stone character on the other side, such as 'smug, satisfied, pleased ... or?' The stones are particularly useful with adolescent males.

> Use carefully and respectfully, the cards may generate lots of questions and emotions. As a powerful conversational prompt, they can assist conversations to evolve in different, even unexpected ways.

> (Deal and Masman, 2003: 19)

Strengths cards

It is better to focus on positives – to build strengths – rather than focus on weaknesses (see literature on appreciative inquiry, such as Hammond, 1996). Card packs from Innovative Resources – for example *Strengths in Teams, Strength Cards, Strength Cards for Kids, I Can Monsters* (for kids), *Mates Traits* and *Our Scrapbook of Strengths* (for family and group work) – are very useful. Some packs may need careful editing as some concepts may not be culturally transferable or translatable. Some useful questions to ask yourself before using cards (Deal and Masman, 2003) are:

- What is the purpose for introducing the cards?
- How do you think they might help?
- Are the cards culturally relevant to the participants? If not, do some need to be removed, added or a new pack developed?
- Is it the right time to introduce the cards?
- Will the cards get in the way of communication that is already occurring?
- Is there a trusting, respectful relationship between those who will use the cards?
- Has the issue of confidentiality been discussed and a policy agreed?
- What is the energy level?
- Is there sufficient time to work through the insights, issues and vulnerabilities that might be raised?

Graphic tools

For free articles on graphic tools see www.newhorizons.org/strategies/graphic_tools/front_graphictools.htm

Three-dimensional idea generation and development of prototypes

Author/background

Idea generation in three dimensions was developed by Azim Pawanchik in Kuala Lumpur, Malaysia.

Purpose/rationale

The purpose of three-dimensional modelling is to enable individuals and groups to explore ideas in a playful and creative way. It favours learners with a preference for kinaesthetic (touch) learning, who often get left out in workshop process design. Most adults do not have time to put cares aside and enter into play mode, yet we know that creativity and a relaxed mind are stimulated by play.

Size of group

This activity can be used in large groups divided into smaller groups of up to six participants.

Materials

Plasticine (two or three colours only to keep things simple) or playdough, flipchart paper, felt pens. Some small sample Plasticine models to show scale.

Venue layout

Participants sit in groups around tables and may move around as they like to gain ideas from each other.

Time

90 minutes.

Stages

1 Setting the scene: mind movie

The scene setting might include 'Imagine waking up long before sunrise and then walking for more than two hours to the nearest river or borehole carrying a two-litre bucket full of water on your head all the way home.

'Now imagine you are a woman or a young child and it is your responsibility to carry this heavy bucket of water every day of your life.'

2 Instructions

'Develop a medium-term solution for transporting water say over the next one to three years. There are two constraints. First, the villagers cannot relocate and the solution must be simple and cost-effective. Second, the villagers are extremely poor and cannot afford to invest in draught animals.'

3 Conception: the rationale, need and urgency for change

Try to imagine yourself in the villagers' shoes. Ask yourself:

- How do these people feel?
- What are their constraints?
- What do they want or value?

Make a model of their current situation.

4 Creation: exploring the possibilities

Each person needs come up with two ideas. Try to think creatively: that is, use out-of-the-box thinking. Use the Plasticine to make at least five promising prototypes.

5 Conversation: select and make the idea happen

Out of the five different ideas, select the best or make a combination to produce the most promising prototype.

Advantages

Working in three dimensions is unusual for many people. As participants work the plasticine, they chat and joke. Plasticine is a very calming and relaxing medium for many. This is particularly useful in cultures which favour indirect communication: for instance, Azim Pawanchik comments, 'Malaysians tend to be less direct; we do not tend to speak out on things. I tested this on over 200 people over five different sessions and I found the process to be highly engaging and memorable for the participants.'

Plasticine is cheap and can be recycled.

See also the work by Sue Baldwin (2002, 2005).

Empowering uses of participatory video

Who represents who? What medium is best?

Participatory video can be used with the poor and/or people who feel powerless to enable them to represent themselves and communicate directly with the powers that control the world beyond their community. Video is the only medium which records both images and sound. With carefully trained facilitators, it can be an empowering process whereby people and especially women gain an opportunity to represent themselves to others, the health of themselves and their families, their workloads, access to markets and the education of their children.

In an experiment in Vietnam in 1995, a team of NGO facilitators (from Vietnam, Canada and the United Kingdom) were trained in the use of video for participatory community development. The team then collaborated with local people to make three programmes about issues which the villagers identified themselves (Braden and Huong, 1998). To make the video required close daily contact between the facilitators and the people, something that does not always occur in participatory rural appraisal (PRA) workshops. The facilitators first used participant observation while joining in everyday chores like getting water. This gave ample opportunity for the villagers to be the teachers and also for them to ask questions of the NGO workers.

Issues

There were of course a number of issues to be managed or overcome:

- No one could participate without ruling party approval. Therefore the team did not always reach the poorest villagers.
- The process took time. The team facilitated evening 'cinema sessions', and further discussion at night with villagers as they reviewed the day's filming led to further and deeper information emerging. Songs and poems were added.
- There was a need for a strategy for conflict resolution, as some disagreed with comments made on film.
- Editing in camera led to confusing footage.
- There was an issue of outsider versus insider knowledge.
- Leading questions were asked by the facilitators.
- When women saw themselves in close up they felt the camera was burning their faces, so some footage had to be reshot.
- There was a need for transparency to find out the meaning of what is being said, as well as the identity and motives of the speakers.
- The Vietnamese NGO facilitators were all outsiders, as they were educated city dwellers, and it took time to gain trust.

Outcomes

> There is no point in practising conscientisation [*awareness raising about power*] and participation for their own sakes: they must have outcomes.
>
> (Chase *et al*, 1999)

The process of developing programmes, from research to filming and editing, encouraged the villagers to take a critical approach to their problems. The finished videos were shown to the local authorities, and as a result new funds were allocated to improve conditions and resolve some of the issues. Community-made video can be used locally for the purposes of conflict resolution and advocacy, and internationally for fund-raising and staff training.

Outcomes of participatory video might include:

- exchange of views between the local community and the world beyond;
- some progress towards claiming rights of representation (see Rocha's empowerment model in Chapter 3);
- stored information, a recording of what had been said that the group can retrieve and discuss at a later date (if they have access to the appropriate equipment, of course);
- enhanced awareness of issues of equity of representation;
- enhanced self-confidence.

Serendipitous outcomes

Villagers saw their own environment differently on television, saying, 'We live in a beautiful place. We did not realize before as we have been so busy with the daily grind of living and working.' A change in appreciation of the surrounding environment may lead to the valuing of local scenery, rivers, wildlife and so on.

Participatory video is also used to encourage insiders to film their own culture.

For more information see Ashmore (2000) and Kaiser and Wood (2001).

Resources for seeing things from different angles

Mandalas

Mandalas can be used in many different ways. They may be produced before a workshop and used to focus the minds of participants, or a facilitator can use a meditation to focus the minds of the participants on a particular topic. At the end participants start to draw using circles and spirals to represent the thoughts generated during the meditation.

The Convention on the Rights of the Child as a mandala

UNICEF Bhutan has translated the guiding principles of the Convention on the Rights of the Child (CRC) into a mandala blending the Buddhist approach to life with the basic framework of the CRC. In Sanskrit, 'mandala' means circle or centre. It is traditionally a vehicle used for concentrating the mind so that it can pass beyond superficial thoughts and focus more precisely on valued concepts, progressing towards enlightening the mind. See www.hogans.id.au

Russian dolls

Wooden painted *Matryoshka* nesting dolls were first made in the late 19th century in Russia. They may be used to illustrate the layers within layers of understanding of a concept. The tactile process of undoing the dolls can provoke thinking about complex problems.

Talking sticks

The following description is from Carol Locust:

> The traditional talking stick has been used for centuries by many American Indian tribes as a means of just and impartial hearing. The talking stick was commonly used in council circles to designate who had the right to speak. When matters of great concern came before the council, the leading elder would hold the talking stick and begin the discussion. When he finished what he had to say he would hold out the talking stick, and whoever wished to speak after him would take it. In this manner the stick was passed from one individual to another until all who wished to speak had done so. The stick was then passed back to the leading elder for safe keeping.
>
> Some tribes used a talking feather instead of a talking stick. Other tribes might have a peace pipe, a wampum belt, a sacred shell, or some other object by which they designate the right to speak. Whatever the object, it carries respect for free speech and assures the speaker he has the freedom and power to say what is in his/her heart without fear of reprisal or humiliation.

> (Locust, 2006)

Talking sticks may be created by groups, whereby individuals place on the stick something of themselves that is culturally or otherwise significant. The stick then has the power of the group and may be used to enable individuals to speak from the heart.

Japanese *Daruma* dolls

Daruma or 'make a wish' dolls from Japan date back to the 18th century. Sometimes they are used when making New Year wishes. They are made of papier maché and are constructed without eyes. When a goal is set, one pupil is painted and the doll placed in a significant spot to remind the person of the goal. (Traditionally it was put in a Buddhist or Shinto altar in the home or workplace.) When the goal is achieved the other pupil is painted, and in a small ceremony thanks are given for the achievement. The doll is kept as a reminder of goals achieved. See www.onmarkproductions.com/html/daruma.shtml

The earth from outer space

The NASA photo entitled 'The earth from outer space' made a major impact as it clearly showed that we are all linked and that climate change and pollution know no boundaries. It can be found on the website www.postershop.com (search for 'earth from outer space').

The earth from above

Yann Arthus-Bertrand has produced superb air photography in *Earth from Above* (www.yannarthusbertrand.com). The pictures really do help us to stand back and take a helicopter view.

World maps and different projections

Map projections are really points of view or ways of seeing the earth. These images shape our world view. Because the earth is round it is impossible to show it on a flat surface without distorting shapes, areas and direction.

Peters Equal Area Projection

This projection was drawn by Dr Arno Peters, a German historian, in the late 1970s. It was designed to correct some of the distortions of commonly used maps such as the Mercator projection. The Peters Equal Area Projection is an area-accurate map that is fairer to countries in the south (for instance, in Africa), many of which are portrayed as smaller than their actual size by other projections. See www.petersmap.com/index.html

Dissected pictures

Ursus Wehrli has playfully deconstructed the art works of famous artists and reconstructed them to fit his own whimsical view of the world (Wehrli, 2003). These pictures can be powerful metaphors to help participants take apart frozen constructs, systems and so on.

Posters

Posters around the walls can be used to challenge people's views and perspectives. Posters of doors are useful as a stimulus for discussion: for example, for future planning, and asking which door they would choose and what is behind it. A large picture of a tree and extensive root systems might be used with roots symbolizing culture, the trunk growth, and the branches individual development. See the website www.art.com

Suppliers

Pinpoint Facilitation, website: www.pinpoint-facilitation.com
Vista visuals, website: www.vistavisuals.com.au

How to avoid death by PowerPoint

As a facilitator I do not use PowerPoint. Facilitation requires gathering information from the participants rather than presenting to them. Facilitation requires multi-way communication, whereas a presentation is predominantly one-way. However, there may be parts of a workshop where a facilitator and/or participants change hats (roles) to that of presenters in order to provoke deeper dialogue about their own situations. Photos of the participants' work and its context can enable them to present their problems to other participants to gain from group wisdom. However, it is how PowerPoint is used (and abused) that is the issue. See 'How to avoid death by PowerPoint' at www.hogans.id.au

Learning how to draw

It is cheaper and often more exciting for you to produce your own visuals rather than purchase ready-made ones. It also helps participants to have a go too. If you want to improve your own skills then I recommend as resources Linney (1995), Linney and Wilson (1988), Röhr-Rouendaal (2006), Sonneman (1997) and Westcott and Landau (1997).

Website

Visualpractitioner is a website for people who use visual methods to assist learning and communication between groups and individuals: www.visualpractitioner.org

7

Facilitating difference

Conflict is a sign something has to change.

Source unknown

Introduction

In this chapter I have included a wide variety of stories and issues from around the world regarding difference and dialogue. The following chapter focuses on reconciliation. To me they are all interrelated.

Differences exist everywhere, and are necessary and valuable resources for the sustainability and evolution of all systems. There are degrees of difference in all groups regarding opinions, values, physical and mental capabilities, feelings and gender. Culture is but one area of difference. There are degrees of cultural difference in all groups. This is normal and in most cases useful. Some degrees of prejudice and stereotyping (either positive or negative) are normal. We all have to be on our guard on these issues. Some stereotypes may have some basis in reality. But when they lead to discrimination and racism either in school, work or community contexts, this form of bullying is not permissible.

Facilitation cannot solve the world's problems regarding conflict and cultural difference, but it may offer some strategies to enhance dialogue and reconciliation (if people are willing and able to talk and to listen to one another). Even then we know that people's memories and hurt are often carried through generations. What we do know is that violence is not the way to end conflict. Talking and listening may be hard, but for human beings they are the only rational alternative. There are different levels of talking and listening that we can harness.

There are no such things as quick and easy ways out of conflict situations. It takes hard work and determination on all sides. There is no simple recipe book or process for facilitators to follow. Facilitating differences so that participants (and facilitator) remain open to ideas and listening for possibilities requires time, supportive, safe environments and space. Discussing cultural unmentionables may be uncomfortable.

This chapter includes discussion of:

- constructive and destructive paths and choices (mindscapes);
- ways of talking and listening;
- facilitating dialogue in culturally diverse groups;
- warm-up activity to alert participants to sources of conflict;
- raising awareness of assumptions and stereotypes;
- perception and misunderstandings;
- when dialogue stops and learning stops;
- use of superordinate goals to unite disparate groups;
- facilitating cultural inclusivity;
- holding up a mirror to 'others.'

Constructive and destructive paths and choices

Life and indeed every day presents us with innumerable choices, some conscious, some not. If we consider these as journeys and pathways we can see how certain paths may lead us on a constructive road and others on a road that could be destructive.

The mindscapes illustrated in Figures 7.1 and 7.2 are central to this chapter. They illustrate different paths and choices marked by milestones, which warrant pause and reflection of both where we are coming from and where we are going to.

Facilitators may use these pictures in a number of different ways. Examples include distributing a template for discussion, then asking participants to draw the scene again and fill in milestones based on their experiences of how to break the destructive path. These can then be compared, ideas clustered, and if required the new figure added to the collective wisdom of the group. The exercises which follow elaborate on aspects of the milestones shown in these mindscapes.

Generally, in the course of a long workshop, the relationship between facilitator and participants gets stronger, and in a way more intimate. As trust builds, more and more difficult issues can be explored. However, there is a constant tension between freedom of speech and cultural sensitivity. Hence the discussion earlier about setting norms for 'cultural safety' whereby conflicting issues may be discussed while still valuing and respecting the person/s with other viewpoints.

A workshop which deals with conflict and discrimination involves participants in taking a journey. It is a long journey which cannot be rushed; it requires adequate time, processes, skills and resources to make the trip.

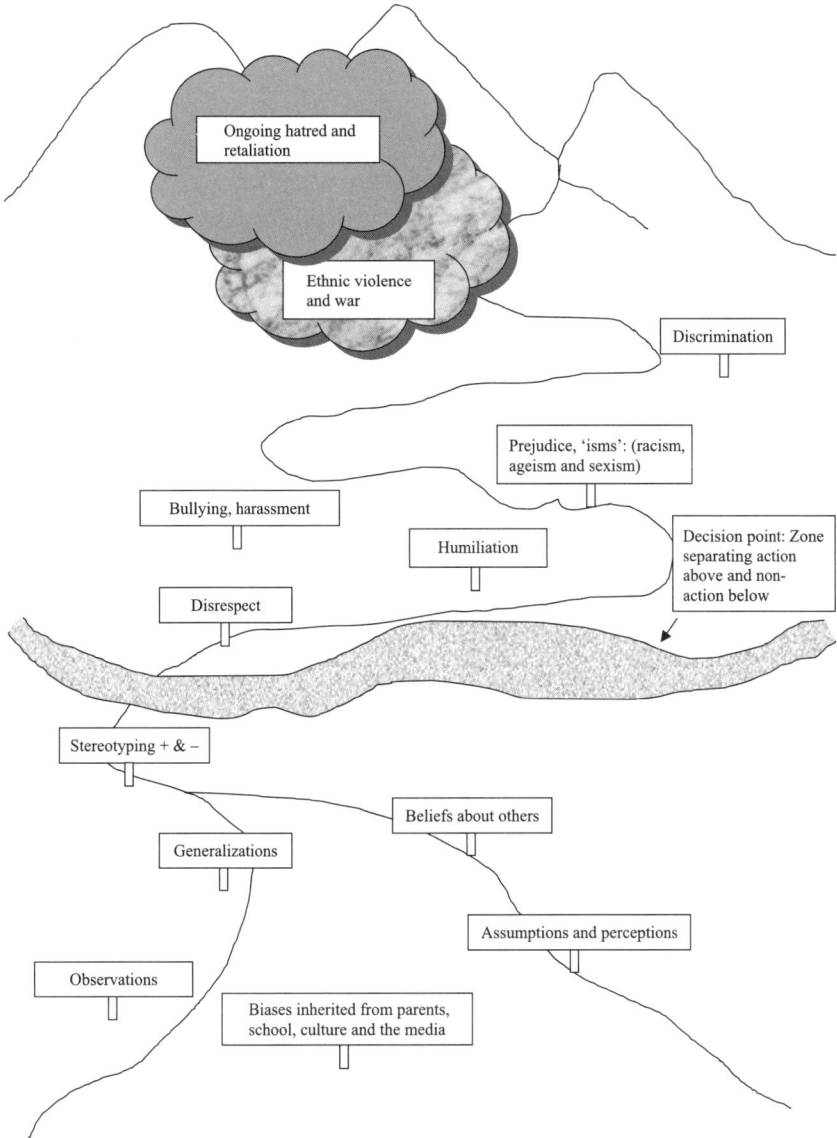

Figure 7.1 Potentially destructive paths and choices – we could stop at any time, why don't we?

Regarding the potentially destructive paths and choices, we could stop at any time, so why don't we? Or perhaps we should ask what role/s facilitators can play in enabling individuals and groups to stop, take stock and develop more constructive ways of dealing with conflict. Conflict just is; it's the way we manage it that is the issue.

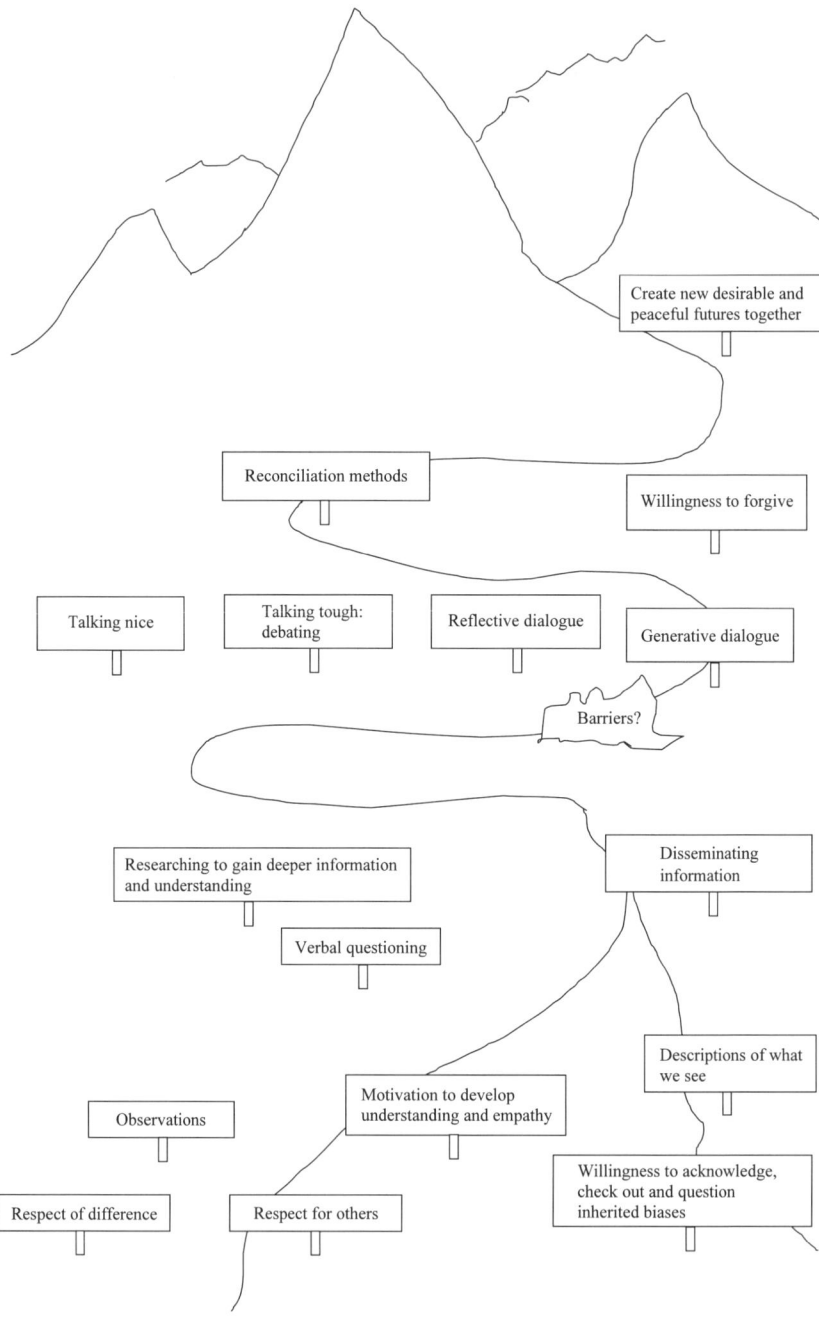

Figure 7.2 Constructive paths and choices

Ways of talking and listening

> The significant problems we face cannot be solved at the same level of thinking we were at when we created them.
>
> Albert Einstein

Four fields of conversing

One of the most necessary things for facilitators is to persuade participants that there are different ways of talking and listening, and to open them up to try these different modes. I find it useful to show them and invite them to discuss Figure 7.3.

Otto Scharmer (2001) and Adam Kahane (2002, 2004) first described four ways of conversing with others, which I have synthesized with some additional ideas in Figure 7.3. However, it is not as simple as it looks. Even 'talking nice' is different in different cultures. Some are far more open and forthright even to strangers. Like any taxonomy, the stages are not linear or sequential.

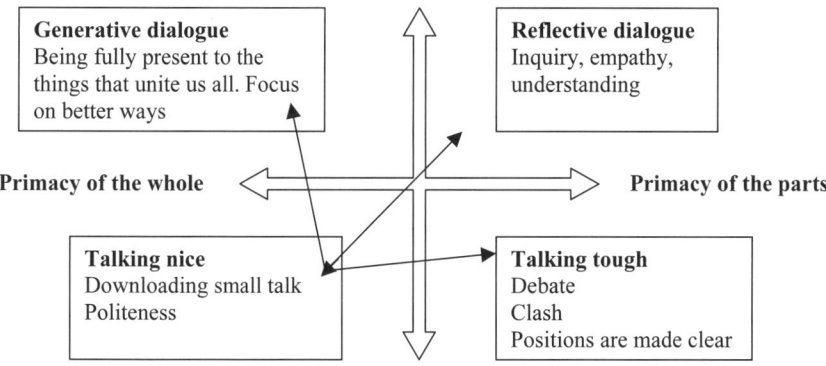

Figure 7.3 Four fields of conversation

Source: adapted from Scharmer (2001).

There are three black arrows. With some groups we can go from 'talking nice' directly to 'generative dialogue'. These are usually the people who are like us, with similar values and aspirations. But the challenge for facilitators is to create, identify or adapt the best ways of getting there in groups composed of individuals with disparate values, cultures and ways of being in and viewing the world.

During a workshop a group may move in and out of these fields of conversation. It is possible to move from 'talking nice' to the other modes.

Four fields of listening

If there are four fields of conversation, it may be useful to consider four different ways of listening to complement the ways of conversing. The Chinese character for 'listen' contains the subcharacters for a heart, eye and ear (see my website, www.hogans.id.au). We need to activate all these organs to listen actively and authentically. Listening is the first step in making dialogue effective. During the 'talking nice' stage, people listen with their eyes and ears: only just enough to know when to nod their head or affirm what is being said (and sometimes not even that much!). During the 'talking tough' stage, eyes, ears and minds are involved, as people have to listen in order to work out what to disagree with and how they will phrase their disagreement. In the 'reflecting' stage, people start to listen with their eyes, ears, minds and hearts. Feelings are stirred and they can empathize with the person. During the generative dialogue stage, people start to listen in a very much deeper way, using eyes, ears, minds and hearts, and engage with their hands in a metaphorical sense: that is, they are geared to transformative action. (See the visual and oral processes used to move participants from their heads to their hearts and hands in Aboriginal issues later in this chapter.)

The following stories illustrate elements related to types of dialogue; how they are obtained or not obtained, an analysis of what happened, and questions to reflect upon.

Reflective and generative dialogue

Adam Kahane states that he has spent over 20 years trying to understand how to change the world. As part of that journey he developed the four-stage process for talking and listening based on the work of Otto Scharmer of the Massachusetts Institute of Technology and his own observations of the peace-building process in postwar Guatemala (see Ochaeta's story, below). This country suffered one of the worst civil wars in Latin America between 1962 and 1996, yet observing the 'process of dialogue' during scenario planning workshops of the Visión Guatemala project from 1997 to 2001, Kahane noticed how the level of dialogue changed everyone from surface to deep thinking.

Story: Ochaeta's story

Ochaeta [director of the Guatemalan Archdiocesan Human Rights Office, which was documenting the atrocities of the civil war] said he had a story that he wanted to tell … [He] had gone to a Mayan village to witness the exhumation of a mass grave – one of many – from a massacre. When the earth had been removed, he noticed a number of small bones. He asked the forensics team if people had had their bones broken during the massacre. No, the grave contained the corpses of women who had been pregnant. The small bones belonged to their foetuses. When Ochaeta finished telling his story, the team was completely silent … I looked around the circle and caught the eye of an old man, who simply nodded at me slowly. The silence lasted a long time, perhaps five minutes. I was leading this session and had never experienced a silence like this; I was dumbstruck and had no idea what to say or do, so I did nothing. The silence lasted a long time, perhaps five minutes. When it ended, we took a break, and then continued with the workshop.

This silence had an enormous impact on the group and on me. Then it ended. The five minutes that followed Ochaeta's story, was in Generative Dialogue. One person spoke after another, but at times it was as if they were completing each other's thoughts. The normal sense of separation between people seemed lessened; two participants referred to the experience as one of 'communion.' As they moved from appreciating each other's different perspectives (as in Reflective Dialogue) to being, for a while, a whole collective 'I'. In Generative Dialogue, each story is like a hologram that contains the whole picture and connects us to the human condition.

There is no doubt that during and after this story people were listening with all their senses: minds, ears, eyes, hearts and this led to the joint determination to act. In interviews years later, many members of the team referred to it. In the words of one member:

> The group gained the possibility of speaking frankly. Things could be said without upsetting the other party. I believe this helped to create a favourable atmosphere in which to express, if not the truth, certainly each person's truth … In the end, and particularly after listening to Ochaeta's story, I understood and felt in my heart all that had happened. And there was a feeling that we must struggle to prevent this from happening again.

At the end of that session, I made an uncharacteristic observation: 'I felt that there was spirit in the room.'

Source: Kahane (2004: 116–17).

This story illustrates that a facilitator needs to get everyone in the frame of mind to be motivated to explore an issue together. When in dialogue mode, group members explore an issue as if it is a reflective mirror ball of the kind suspended from the ceiling in ballrooms and discos. That is, a facilitator is helping everyone to look at the issue 'from every which way' (not just a helicopter view from above). In dialogue we want to help participants to become observers of their own thinking (Senge, 1990). (This is where the ladder of assumptions or inference is useful: see Figure 7.4, page 227.)

This story also illustrates the wonders of silence, which signifies a 'point of change' or mindshift taking place. If we bulldoze that silence because of our own tensions, then we may lose rare and precious opportunities (as Gill Baxter commented to me, 2006). (See also uses of silence in Chapter 9.)

Background needed by facilitators

The taxonomy shown in Table 7.1 (on pages 222–23) is to give facilitators a summary of modes of talking and listening, facilitation roles and possible impact.

Each of the four modes of conversation is legitimate and useful, but if we want participants to create new social realities, the conversation needs to include reflective dialogue and generative dialogue. For example, the sacred book of the Mayan Q'iche people is called the *Popol Vuh*. It contains the following text: 'We did not put our ideas together. We put our purposes together. And we agreed, and then we decided' (Kahane, 2004).

In generative dialogue, participants discuss how to achieve a deeper and united purpose. So the question is, in how many different ways can facilitators enable participants to move through these stages of dialogue? The concept of 'dialogue' is sometimes mistaken as 'consultation', where other stakeholders are asked for their input, but remain outside the core decision-making process. Generative dialogue involves a higher level of power sharing (see Arnstein's model in Chapter 3). Generative dialogue is especially difficult when culturally diverse stakeholders have different ways of speaking (abrupt and to the point, versus circuitous extended story telling) and a facilitator needs to alert the group to this and work out some sort of way of honouring both within the time available.

Resources on dialogue

The GDP Support Team Publication *Dialogic Approaches to Global Challenges: Moving from 'dialogue fatigue' to dialogic change processes: a working paper* is available at www.generativedialogue.org/resources

See also Otto Scharmer's website (www.ottoscharmer.com) and forthcoming book *Theory U: Leading profound innovation by presencing emerging futures*.

Facilitating dialogue in culturally diverse groups

The following activities relate to the issues raised in the mindscape (Figures 7.1 and 7.2). Initially there are many processes documented for setting the scene and building trust (Schwarz, 2002; Hogan, 2003; Keating, 2003). It is a hallmark of a professional facilitator who spends a great deal of time choosing or adapting processes for culturally diverse groups. I have included the following exercise because I witnessed its expert use in a very large culturally diverse group, and it was memorable!

Warm-up activity to identify sources of conflict

This activity was demonstrated by Gilbert Brenson-Lazán, a North American who has lived and worked in Latin America for 35 years, at a facilitators' conference in Taipei in 2003. It can be used with groups of any size.

Stages

1. Ask everyone to stand and join hands in a circle.
2. Explain that the only rule is that once their hands are joined they cannot let go of their two neighbours' hands.
3. Round One: While moving your hands in the same way, tell them: 'Hands up! Hands down! Hands up! Hands down! (repeat three or four more times).' Tell them how well they did it, and that they just passed the first exam in their postgraduate degree in hand-raising!
4. Round Two: Repeat the same, but this time you should say one thing and do another thing (you raise your hands and tell them 'Hands down!' to see if they are listening or just following). Also you should do it faster. Congratulate them again for passing the second exam in their postgraduate degree.
5. Round Three: 'Hands up! Hands down! Hands up! Hands down! Right hand up!' Almost all of them will enter into some form of conflict as they look for different ways to resolve the conflict. Stop them and ask them to share their ideas on what is happening and how to resolve it. Give them a few minutes and then repeat Round Three.
6. Participants return to their tables to talk about how similar things happen in real life.

Table 7.1 Taxonomy of talking, listening, facilitation and impact

Modes of talking	Modes of listening	Facilitator role	Impact
Generative dialogue The least common; the most precious; allows a group to discover its larger and deeper shared purpose; vital for the success of deep change initiatives; deeply personal stories are told which connect with everyone to energize a shift in the group.	**Deep listening** **with head, open heart and hands** **(ie motivation to work towards a** **positive change)** Participants are tuned in to the potential of the whole system and what is being born amidst and through us.	*The facilitator uses strategies to* *help participants to decentre* Most of us feel we live at the centre of our own universe. Speaking from the heart: thoughts, feelings and dreams. Scenario planning: good and bad futures. Planning desirable futures. Dreaming. The facilitator encourages the use of metaphors. Everyone prepared to engage with respect even those with totally opposite views (stretch comfort zone). Everyone listens to how they are talking and listening, to how they express categories and stereotype. Everyone eats and walks together over a period of time with no outside distractions. Hold silences as they indicate shifts of thinking. Suggest periods of silence.	A deep story is told which resonates in everyone; ie whole collective 'I'; meaning emerges not from any one person, but from the centre of the circle, as if there was a spirit in the room. Creative energy comes from a personal connection with the whole. Individuals give up their positions in order to generate innovative solutions. Listening to the whole to develop frameworks for the greater good.

Reflective dialogue *Inquiry* Allows us to participate in the future/s that is/are emerging. Participants start to give their perspective openly.	**Empathic listening with the head and heart** Participants listen with empathy and respect. They are not processing rebuttal arguments but letting in the ideas of others who think very differently from themselves, so they hear issues from a different perspective	The facilitator holds the space so that people listen with respect and empathy. Invite someone you know will speak from the heart or demonstrate by offering a story.	Authentic storytelling from the heart, ie people tell the stories behind their positions. Role reversal occurs; move outside of ourselves; standing in their shoes, seeing through their eyes; listen self-reflectively to them, and hear them and others. They inquire into how things came to be as they are and envision how they might be. 'What is personal is most universal' (Carl Rogers).
Talking tough *Debating mode* Say what they are really thinking; authentic and speech, a step towards greater authenticity. Nothing new is created. 'I think ...' 'Your view isn't valid because ...'	**Win–lose listening** Participants listen to things that confirm their point of view. Think in debate mode and make quick judgements. Defensiveness if our view is attacked. Hear opposing ideas; create nothing new; search for alternative facts, perspectives, and options, to back up our point of view or to challenge the argument of others.	Facilitator channels opinions for and against an idea using PMI or arguments for and against, or SWOT. Six thinking hats, force field analysis. Facilitator gets everyone to think from each side rather than just their side.	Participants start to think in debate mode. Then start to look at other points of view. Everyone gets their 'cards on the table'. Difference is recognized. If you don't know all the positions it is hard to move on.
Talking nice Downloading. Politeness mode 'How are you?' 'I'm fine.' 'Good weather for the time of year.' Safe sports news. Safe TV programmes.	**Half listening** Maintains the status quo, re-enacts the patterns of the past.	Facilitator models genuine listening, contracts for desirable group norms, and asks participants to describe authentic behaviours. Introduces appropriate warm-up activities to enable participants to get to know one another, build trust in each other and the facilitator.	Polite talk; participants say what they are expected to say according to the rules; they download their thoughts and feelings onto the world; it is predictable and efficient; constrained by politics or politeness; being stuck here leads to oppression or collapse. No real listening.

Source: adapted from Scharmer (2001), Kahane (2004).

Debrief

In the debrief be sure to cover the:

- first impulse to struggle and try to overpower (or give in) to the person alongside;
- mistaken assumption: the leader did NOT say participants could NOT also raise their left hands;
- conclusions regarding interdependence;
- way conflicts begin and the different ways they evolve.

Raising awareness of assumptions and stereotypes

The following exercise enables a facilitator to draw out participants to being open about their assumptions about the facilitator.

Exercise: Look at me and what do you see?

'Look at me and what do you see?' is a non-threatening activity which can raise awareness of the assumptions, stereotypes and mistakes we make about others. It was developed by Lindy Stirling, a facilitator in Perth, Australia who runs workshops for teachers to raise awareness about human rights issues in schools.

Stage 1

Say, 'As a whole group please look at me [the facilitator] and tell me what you see.' In societies where there is very high respect for authority figures, it may be regarded as impolite to make personal observations about a facilitator, so it might be necessary to give some examples to warm the participants to the task, for example, 'You could say, "You've got short hair."'

Stage 2

This is an example of possible dialogue between facilitator and participants:

Participant: You've got dark hair and dark eyes.
Facilitator: Yes, what else?
Participant: You wear glasses.
Facilitator: Well I've got a pair of glasses in my top blouse pocket, but I could have picked them up and put them there for safe keeping till I find the owner.

Participant: You are married.

Facilitator: Are you saying I am married because I'm wearing a ring on the fourth finger of my left hand? You CAN say 'You are wearing jewellery', or 'You are wearing a ring on your fourth finger', but you don't know that I am married. (In South America and other cultures a woman's wedding ring is worn on the right hand. In India, gold necklaces are worn by married women.) What else did you SEE?

(Do not unpack assumptions at this stage, just try to get the participants to describe exactly what they see.)

Participant: You must be well educated. You speak well, you have a wide vocabulary.

Facilitator: Thank you, but does this mean I am educated? Do some people who are not well educated speak well, and have a wide vocabulary?

Participant: Yes.

Facilitator: OK, so we can't make an assumption based on that. How do you define educated?

Participant: Well, it means ...

Facilitator: That's interesting because I define it this way. [...] What else can you SEE?

Now divide the participants into small groups, and say something on the lines of 'From your observations so far, discuss what you THINK about me, my family, my values, my life, who I am, what I do and so on. Don't worry as it is very hard to offend me.' (Be prepared to honour this comment!)

This could lead to a dialogue on these lines:

Participant: You are from Malta or Greece.

Facilitator: That's interesting. Why do you think that?

Participant: Because you have dark hair.

Facilitator: And why did you link dark hair to Malta or Greece?

Participant: Because I have two girl friends, one is from Malta and the other is from Greece, and they both have dark hair like you.

Facilitator: Do all people from Malta and Greece have dark hair?

Participant: No.

Facilitator: Do people from other countries have dark hair?

Participant: Yes.

Facilitator: Any other thoughts?

Participant: You have three kids ...

Facilitator: So this exercise shows us how often our assumptions
are based on our previous experiences, on very little
information, on the stereotypes and assumptions we
make in life every day. And it shows that we are often as
spectacularly wrong as we originally believe ourselves to
be right! It shows how fallible we all are (how able to make
mistakes).

Confronting assumptions about others

In workshops participants (and facilitators for that matter) sometimes
make sweeping statements or generalizations about other individuals or
groups. We all do it: it is a natural part of being human, as our brains
process what we see, hear and experience. Generalizations in themselves
are not necessarily bad, as they help us to deal with the complexities of
the world around us. We would go mad if we tried to process each piece
of data or external stimulus; our brains just would not be able to cope.
Stereotypes too are not bad in themselves, and some may be positive,
though others are negative. Stereotypes become unhelpful when they
limit our understanding to the stereotype and restrict other perceptions
that may be more accurate. A stereotype is *one* perception only, and can
stop us from thinking.

The main thing is that facilitators should have strategies to help themselves and participants to recognize preconceived ideas.

The ladder of assumptions or inference

The 'ladder of assumptions or inference' is useful to give to participants
as a handout during a debriefing discussion of the exercise above. The
metaphor of the ladder is easy to remember. It is also called the 'process
of abstraction model' and gives us a useful framework to enable us to
study how we 'jump to conclusions'. The more experience we have, the
more likely we are to fall into this trap. Our thinking processes are so fast
that we go through many stages subconsciously, from observing reality to
making a decision to act (stay and talk it through or stay and remain quiet,
fight or flight, and so on). The ladder of assumptions (see Figure 7.4) could
be used in a training situation to raise awareness of participants to their
internal thinking processes in a non-threatening way.

Starting at the bottom, on rung one, a real incident occurs. It might be
recorded by an imaginary all-seeing camera from all angles. We 'see' and
hear selected data and make meaning of it based on our past biases (some
of which were generated by our families and community). From that we
build up assumptions and conclusions. Over time we build up a series
of beliefs which not only lead to actions, but also help us to make short
cuts and influence what we choose to select from reality. In other words

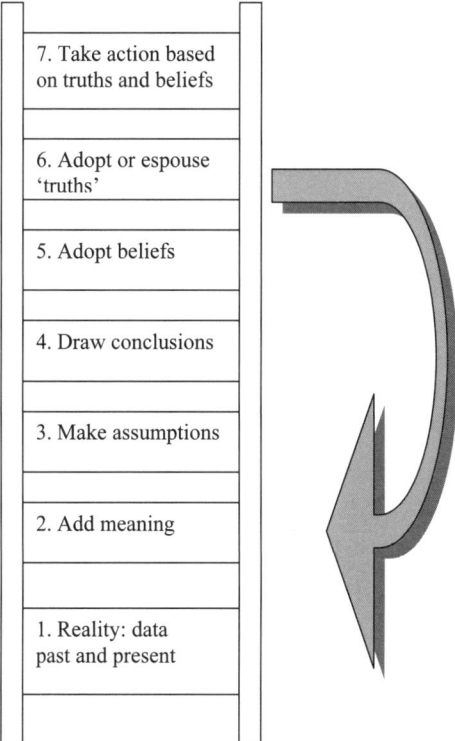

Figure 7.4 Ladder of assumptions

Sources: based on Argyris, Putnam and Smith (1985) and Margulies and Valenza (2005).

our beliefs and assumptions become 'self-fulfilling prophecies'. Often we are unaware of how our prejudices impact on what we see and how we act. Like actors, we forget we are playing a role and become trapped in the theatre of our minds (Senge, 1990). Read Table 7.2 from bottom to the top.

Continued negative assumptions may lead to prejudice, and people may avoid one another or ostracize others. At worst, negative assumptions could lead to harassment in the form of being disrespectful, bullying, name calling, and ultimately, but not always thank goodness, ethnic violence and war.

In workshops we can only observe what goes on in front of us in the whole group. There are all sorts of issues that may occur in small groups or at breaks.

Table 7.2   Thoughts behind the ladder of assumptions

8. Add meaning:	The next time Juan laughs, I will assume that he is laughing at me again.
7. Take action:	Never join a group with Juan, exclude him from our group.
6. The truth is:	Juan is a bad person.
5. Adopt beliefs:	Our group should avoid Juan.
4. Draw conclusions:	Juan is a nasty person.
3. Make assumptions:	Juan does not like me or Juan thinks I'm stupid.
2. Add meaning:	Juan laughed at me.
1. Reality: data past and present coloured by past biases	Present: Juan walks past you and laughs. Past: your parents told you to be wary about people who look like Juan.

Questions are best

If the facilitator or other participants 'jump' on a generalization or the person making the generalization, he or she can feel cornered, embarrassed or angry, and could lose face. We need ways to enable people to 'unpack' their thoughts and assumptions, and to broaden their perspective to show there are other ways of interpreting events, without knocking the ladder from under them. We need some questions to enable people to:

● sit on the top rung for a moment and slow down the thinking process;
● observe what they have said;
● analyse the thought processes that led to those conclusions without feeling threatened;
● climb down the rungs of the ladder if they choose (people need somewhere to go: like animals, they often fight to get out if they are cornered (metaphorically or literally).

Using the ladder

You could say:

Let's stop for a minute and explore where that idea comes from. Can you see where you are on the ladder?
Is this the right conclusion?
Is it the only possible conclusion?
Is it based on facts?
What are you thinking?
Why are you thinking that?
How did you come to that thought?

To explore the source of assumptions

Where does this opinion come from?
How do you know that?
Can you tell me what are your thoughts are based on?
What data is that based on?

If someone generalizes from a database of one example

Does that example follow for all others (women, the other group)?
In this example this is so. Have any of the others in the room had a similar or different experience to this?
If people overseas used you to generalize about all Australians, what might they say? How would you feel?
How real is that?
What is being left out here?
How do you feel about your culture being described by outsiders?

Bring in the wider group to broaden the discussion

That's one point of view. What do the others think?

If two people seem to be misunderstanding each other

Say to person A, 'Where did your thought come from?' or 'What do you mean by this term?' And to person B, 'Where did your thought come from?' or 'What do you mean by this term?'

Generalizations based on 'all' and 'never'

All people from x group are …

The facilitator could ask, 'All?'

People from X group *never* work.

The facilitator could ask, 'Never?'

The ladder can be used to help participants understand other people's actions, or inaction, including other participants, family and friends; the actions of people from other cultural groups and the actions of entire governments.

An example of assumptions made about those wearing a veil

Currently there is focus on the issue of the *hijab* or veil worn by some Muslim women in their own countries, and as migrants or refugees. I have heard comments like, 'Those people coming here wearing strange headgear: if they want to come here, they should dress like us.' In this statement there is no evidence of curiosity, or inclusivity, or any attempt to understand or bridge across separate groups. Some facilitation questions might include:

- Can you tell me why that headgear is important to these women? (role reversal)
- Where does it come from?
- Do we have the right to say it's wrong to wear a veil?
- Are the women choosing to wear the veil? If the answer is 'yes', what is its purpose from their perspective? How can we find out more?
- Is having individual choice important to them?
- Do people in other cultures wear head covering? (The answer has to be 'Yes', as with some Christian nuns, some women in Italy and South America who wear a lace mantilla, and some married orthodox Jewish women who wear a wig, veil or hat in public. Some Indian men and Sikhs wear turbans; some Arabs wear a *keffiyeh*, a square of white or chequered cotton cloth, folded and wrapped in various styles around the head and sometimes held in place by a rope circlet, or *agal*.)
- What does this clothing mean to these groups?
- What does the term 'identity' mean to you? How many different groups do you identify with? What things do you wear to identify with a group, for example at work or in your leisure activities?
- What does the term 'identity' mean to others?

In this way the facilitator is neither defending nor attacking the clothing practice of different groups wearing various types of clothing, but the questions invite the participants to think about the issues from a broader perspective and to find out more information.

We need to acknowledge degrees of racism in all of us

Often issues of racism are described as 'out there' and we do not realize that things we think, say or do may be profoundly hurtful to others, as the following story illustrates.

STORY: OWNING RACISM

I was in a session in Canada where we were focusing on racism and there had been many comments about endemic racism between American Blacks and Whites. Then a small elderly woman began to speak. She talked of being from Quebec in French-speaking Canada, and the pain of arriving at a conference in another part of her own country and being expected to speak in English, which was for her a foreign language. She was profoundly hurt when her compatriots could not pronounce her name, and joked and suggested she should change the pronunciation so it would be easier to spell.

Suddenly in a way that had not been clear to all before, the racial cultural divide was apparent. From that moment on we spoke of the racism in all of us, how I am living and how I own this issue as my own in my daily life.

Lawrence Philbrook, an Anglo-American facilitator working in Taiwan

Process assumptions

Process and content assumptions happen in any group, but facilitators have to be even more aware of these possibilities in cross-cultural groups. When there is a dissonance between facilitator and participants this may lead to a breakdown in communication.

Lane, DiStefano and Maznevski (1997) describe 'process assumptions' which are made about a communication or interaction. If they are not accurate, not conscious and not clarified, they may undermine communication. John Gabarro (1983, cited by Lane *et al*, 1997) gives the following examples of assuming that the:

- other person sees the situation the same way as you do;
- other person is making the same assumptions as you are;
- other person is or should be experiencing the same feelings as you are;
- communication situation has no relationships to past events;
- other person's understanding is or should be based on your logic, not his or her feelings.

Lane *et al* (1997: 26) add:

- The other person is seen as the one who has the 'problem' or does not understand the logic of the situation.
- People from the dominant culture in the group assume their culture is superior, and assume that people from minority groups want to become more like them.

Perception and content assumptions and misunderstandings

Sometimes misunderstandings arise from misperceptions or miscommunication. Sandy Schuman (2000) wrote:

> Professor Russel Martin drilled into me as an undergraduate, 'meanings are in people not in words.' When there is conflict ascertain if it is genuine, or based on miscommunication. If the conflict involves the use of a particular word or phrase, define it; to avoid the misconceptions that are created when multiple meanings are inferred from the same word, stop using the word and instead use its longer definitions.

The following story illustrates this point.

STORY: THE MEANING OF 'WILDERNESS'

The debate in New York's Adirondack Mountains region had become increasingly polarized; interpersonal and interorganizational relationships had deteriorated. The 'Public Conversations Project' convened a group of about 20 environmentalists, developers, forest industry people, sportsmen and others with diverse views. The aim of the dialogue was to have individuals, however polarized their viewpoints, come together for two days as people, rather than as parties or positions, and understand each other. People were to attend voluntarily as individuals, not as representatives of organizations or constituencies. Given the potential volatility of the meeting they were asked to agree explicitly to a set of ground rules detailed in the invitational letter. One of the ground rules stated, '... avoid making negative attributions not only about those in the room, but also those not present'. This was especially important in this case because some attendees at previous dialogues in this region had verbally attacked others.

Well into the meeting, the conversation turned to the topic of wilderness and its implications for the future of the region. Some participants expressed the view that wilderness areas did not contribute to the regional economy and were not valued by residents. Others felt that wilderness areas were essential to maintaining the environmental and economic character of the region. One individual, Jeff, asserted, 'The people who support wilderness areas are outsiders, they don't live here; local residents who have to make their living here don't see any value in wilderness.' In response, Betty claimed, 'I know hundreds of friends who support wilderness!' To which Jeff snapped, 'I don't think you even have a hundred friends!'

As facilitator I interrupted abruptly and alerted the group to this violation of ground rules. I physically turned to John, who was sitting away from the fray, and asked him, 'What comes to mind when you think of wilderness?' He replied, 'Pristine, untouched lands where one can observe nature on its own terms.' I asked if anyone had a different interpretation. From across the room another participant said, 'I had in mind what it says in the Adirondack Park Agency law, that a wilderness area is a designated area in which motor vehicles are not permitted; there can be trails and lean-tos, just no motor vehicles.'

I turned back to Betty and asked her which definition she had in mind when she said she knew hundreds of residents who supported wilderness. 'The definition in the law,' she replied. Then I asked Jeff, and he replied, 'The pristine wilderness.' I followed up with him and asked, 'Do you think that residents support the designation of areas in which no motor vehicles are allowed?' 'Yes,' he replied. I paused and then remarked, 'So hurtful words were spoken because there were different meanings in use for the same term.' I paused for a long time, resisting the temptation to ask Jeff if he wanted to apologize, and hoping that he would, but none was forthcoming.

Sandy Schuman, US facilitator in New York, 2000

Sandy Schuman later commented:

I felt good that I intervened immediately before there was any escalation in this potentially volatile situation. Also, I felt I had done an outstanding job in diagnosing a potential source of miscommunication, the meaning attached to the word *wilderness*, and I turned out to be correct. Nonetheless I felt that I failed to address adequately the basic violation of the ground rule, nor did I help the group deal with it emotionally. In a way, by dealing with the conflict substantively I undermined the ability of the group to deal with it interpersonally.

(Schuman, 2000)

This story illustrates the 'talking tough', argumentative type of dialogue, and the fine line between adhering to the ground rules and addressing the feelings level, of how sharp retaliatory comments can hurt and potentially lead to a breakdown in communication. The participants at this stage did not reach empathy for each other and the stage of reflective dialogue. Schuman reflected that he prevented the group from dealing with their deeper interpersonal issues. From my perspective this depends on the purpose of the group, which also defines the boundaries and depth of discussion.

When dialogue stops, learning stops

The following story graphically illustrates the hurt and frustration which occurred when dialogue stopped. A clash of belief systems occurred between students and a visiting lecturer regarding female circumcision (infibulation).

STORY: WHEN BELIEF SYSTEMS CLASH AND DIALOGUE STOPS

This story is set in 1998 in a school of social work in a university in Australia. The school emphasized the importance for social workers of being able to work within and between different cultural groups. The university also has a mandate to enhance cross-cultural understanding.

A Muslim guest speaker was invited to speak on aspects of Islamic culture. Both local Australian and international undergraduate students were present in the class. There was no resident university lecturer present. An unintended outcome was the discomfort and distress experienced by participants when their beliefs and values were challenged, and some local students walked out as a protest against the guest speaker's defence of infibulation. Afterwards the staff held focus groups with local and international students separately to learn from this incident. Both sets of students said that when their values, ideas and certainties were challenged, the natural response was to disengage with difference that discomforts, and seek likeness that affirms. The stand made by some students against infibulation by walking out on the guest speaker illustrated that 'withdrawal' in some circumstances may be a blunt instrument for change and 'learning ceased'.

These were among the initial student comments:

> ... the subject of female circumcision came up and that is basically where the conversation and learning process stopped because there was a backlash from the classroom as to how bad that practice is.
>
> (local student)

> Some students like you know, they didn't agree with what she was saying. And they really walk out! On her! It was so embarrassing. Even though you not agree with other peoples' culture or religion, you don't do that sort of thing! They don't agree with what she is saying so ... I was really, really feeling frustrated and upset. And then they asking you, 'Did you do that sort of thing? You are a Muslim; did you do that sort of thing?' You know! I couldn't believe that, you know, what they say ... I feel really upset when they sort of look at you, like whispering you know.
>
> (international student)

> I mean I walked out of the lecture. I think it came after she tried to convince us that female circumcision stops venereal disease. She was really justifying ...
>
> (local student)

Later, a lecturer/researcher commented:

> There was general agreement that a social work lecturer should have been there to mediate. Beyond this there were no suggestions on how with hindsight students might have acted differently. As researchers

we mentioned the story in the final joint session but the subject was quickly changed.

Obviously this incident emotionally impacted on those who experienced it and indeed even on those who experienced its telling. In many ways telling this tale reproduces the bizarre 'othering' that can take place when we talk of culture. 'Radical Feminists' and 'Mutilating Muslims' are easy targets to demonise. Such categorisation into a stereotyped 'other' was played out in a classroom designed to develop cultural sensitivity. Students carried from the experience distrust, anger, confusion and a confirmation of a cultural chasm.

The full version of this story can be found at lsn.curtin.edu.au/tlf/tlf1998/chandra ratna.html

We need to set up workshops that involve discussions of fundamental beliefs carefully. They need more time and 'cultural safety' than ordinary workshops. In examining this story perhaps it is useful to think about necessary prior groundwork.

The lecturer could have prepared the class for the speaker beforehand by asking the students to discuss how they could get the most out of the session, for example by discussing questions they might like to ask the guest about areas that puzzled them. It would have been useful to brief the visitor about these issues, and to discuss jointly how these issues could be handled. A visitor has a right to hear the ground rules of the group. The class lecturer should have been present to ensure that the visitor was treated with respect, and that students from different cultural groups treated each other with respect: that is, there was a need to refer to the ground rules of the class.

Guest speakers are often regarded as representatives of very large groups. As individuals they will not be stereotypical and will have many different individual belief systems. Normally when there is a visitor to a group the participants tend to become more restrained with a stranger in their midst. Dissent is often stifled and a lecturer has to work hard to facilitate useful discussion. Frequently, the inclusion of a stranger in a group sends the participants back to the 'forming' stage of group development. Students don't know what questions to ask for fear they might appear stupid, or that the guest 'expert' may ridicule or humiliate them in front of their peers. The room has to be culturally safe for everyone.

But what happens when you get to emotive topics like clitoral circumcision? Was it appropriate to get to that level of intimate questions on a first visit? Clitoral circumcision is a culturally ingrained practice in parts of Africa. As social workers these students needed to be trained to work with peoples from diverse backgrounds, both in the Australian context and overseas. Getting angry would merely invoke anger and defensiveness, or at best a debate and win–lose style argument.

If the speaker had agreed to discuss this topic, what questions could the students have asked to understand this cultural practice more fully? Obviously there was lack of information regarding the research into this practice. If the lecturer had been there, how could she have led those present into reflective and generative dialogue? Then after the visitor had left and after research into the topic, how could the lecturer have led the students to consider how they would handle this situation in the communities in which they would work in the future?

But what happens when the lives of others are made miserable and unhealthy by practices which are given valence by the elders of both sexes in these cultures, especially when the rights of both males and females to a healthy and productive sexual life are violated? As David Maybury-Lewis (1992) said, values need to be constantly reviewed in the light of new evidence.

The authors raised very pertinent questions:

● How do we realize the learning opportunities inherent in such events?
● How do we work with conflicting belief systems as they emerge?

From this case story I would add that as facilitators we need to:

● ensure that students and visiting speakers are in alignment regarding the purposes of the session together;
● brief a group to welcome a visitor and treat him/her with respect (remembering that 'respect' is different in dissimilar cultures);
● design processes to engender reflective thinking (such as role reversal to appreciate the pressures of cultural norms);
● think of ways of developing generative dialogue during the speaker's visit or after the speaker has left;
● involve local and international Muslim students in the room as additional cultural informants when appropriate;
● consider very carefully when it is permissible to leave the room when a guest (who is not a lecturer) visits a group;
● consider ways of helping participants to listen even when they hear things that are contradictory to their values.

Some possible facilitative questions might be:

What delights/pleases you about xxx culture?
What puzzles/confuses you about xxx culture?
What annoys or frustrates you about xxx culture?
What is different from your culture?
What is the same as your culture?
What additional research needs to be done on xxx issue?

What other speakers might it be appropriate to invite in order to hear 'other sides' of the issue?

If there are tensions between culture xxx and the host culture, what strategies could participants suggest which would still honour and value all parties?

Opening eyes and windows

See also the wonderful work by Windows for Peace, an NGO of Palestinians and Jews from both sides of the Green Line working together to promote acquaintance, understanding and reconciliation between both peoples through educational programmes, the media and art. *Windows* is a bilingual Hebrew-Arabic youth magazine written by and for the youth of both peoples, reflecting the daily life in the region and serving as a base for a new educational programme to help junior high school students cope with the conflict and its implications on their lives. See the website www.win-peace.org

Use of superordinate goals to unite disparate groups

> Visions and dreams pull us together, issues separate us.
>
> Flo Frank

According to the management literature (Vecchio, Hearn and Southey, 1992), 'superordinate goals' are higher-level goals or those that cannot be achieved by one group alone. Setting these large goals for disparate or antagonistic groups (in theory) gives them opportunities to work together, breaks down barriers, encourages people to see each other as just people, and can help overcome differences. In order to achieve these goals, individuals or teams are invited to unite to achieve a common objective, instead of seeing each other as 'us' and 'them' or 'the other' and 'the other'. The theory is that the barriers that divide people may be weakened, as the drive for cooperation is potentially greater than the internal conflict.

However, this only occurs if everyone not only has a clear vision of the goal, but also shares in developing it. Even then disparate groups may have trouble coming together if there is not proper attention to the process or processes required to achieve the goal. Sometimes differences may be driven underground for a while, only to resurface before or after the goal has been achieved. In other words, a vision and charismatic leadership are often not enough. Conversely, differences may be aired in a constructive way in order to be utilized collaboratively to shape and modify the goal.

The idea in any group project is that individuals give up ownership of ideas to the common good. This of course is not always easy, especially in groups or cultures that are highly individualistic and competitive, or where participants are passionate about their particular beliefs or ideas.

The following two case stories concern the superordinate goals of creating first, a joint 'multicultural tapestry' to represent Australia and its diverse cultures with their different religious beliefs, and second, a 'silk curtain' to represent the boundary on entering a Quaker meeting and the design of pictures representing what is to be a Quaker.

STORY: THE MULTICULTURAL TAPESTRY

Over the years the characteristics of migrants have changed in Australia. Eight years ago we had many from Serbia and Bosnia, now we are getting many from Africa. Most cultural groups who use our services seldom mix with each other and appear to have negative stereotypes about each other's cultures, methods of worship, dietary practices and the roles of women. Sometimes there is inter-group jealousy; sometimes when people meet from different cultures they do not even want to look at each other.

A project was formed and received some government funds to bring different groups of women together: that is, Aboriginal women, Anglo-Australian, Baha'i, Hindu, Jewish, Muslim, Russian Orthodox and a Sahaj-Marg yoga meditation group. At first, some groups hesitated to join, making excuses: 'My religious group xxx won't allow it.' Sometimes we used gentle persuasion and then pulled back to give them time to reflect; it's a skill. But eventually they came along, especially when they realized the project was going ahead and they didn't want to be left out.

The grant covered two project coordinators, a project artist, materials and refreshments. The artist did not have facilitation experience. The aim of the project was to honour the uniqueness of Australia and its people from diverse cultural backgrounds. The women were invited to illustrate the essence of their religion or beliefs in a multicultural tapestry.

At first they worked on separate tasks at separate tables. There were some-times 80 or 90 people as participants brought along their family and friends. Usually there were around 50 people. It was very noisy. Each group had a bilingual worker who would meet with the project coordinators and artist each week. Then after a few weeks they visited one another's tables to see what each was creating. Then some suggested that they should rotate the responsibility of bringing food and drink and providing examples of their songs and dances. Some shared stories of migration, settlement and citizenship.

We thought things were going well. They had agreed early on that the back-ground piece of canvas which was 3 metres by 3 metres should represent the indigenous Aboriginal dreamtime in Kimberley red with traditional dot patterns. The Anglo-Australians said, 'We don't have a strong religious faith', and they decided to create small separate pieces representing the flora and fauna of Australia.

Then the time came to put the pieces together. All those involved had by that time developed ownership and pride in their work. But they could not come to any agreement on where to place their pieces. There was conflict over the prime position at the top. Some said, 'If ours goes at the bottom it will be below eye level', and 'We will lose our uniqueness.' Others said, 'Our culture is better than yours' or 'Our religion is older than yours.'

Everyone seemed tired and energy levels dropped. Time quickly passed and the date came closer for the launch. Over 100 people had been invited, including the minister whose department had provided the funding and other dignitaries. There were meant to be cultural presentations from each group in front of the minister. But the group was falling apart. The artist was so stressed he had to go to bed with a bad stomach. He had offered to do the layout himself, but that was not appropriate as it was a community project and the decision had to be a consensus from the group. The Anglo-Australian group felt the whole thing was tokenistic and walked out in frustration and said they would boycott the launch.

The day of the launch arrived and we quickly Velcroed the pieces onto the backcloth. We were relieved when the Anglo-Australian group turned up unexpectedly and sang 'Waltzing Matilda'. We watched nervously as the Velcro was coming undone. Even the minister noticed it and suggested that we should sew the pieces on more securely.

The project had 'finished' on a sad note. We packed the quilt away in a cupboard and got on with other work projects. Three to four weeks went by. Then I received a phone call from a representative from one group. 'We need to finish the tapestry.' I said we would not longer be involved, it was up to them.

Some of the women came back because they felt trust in what we are trying to do. We didn't force them, it came from them. There was a ripple effect: when one group came back, so did the others. The Anglo-Australian group embroidered all the edging. They decided to change the canvas backing cloth (which was difficult to sew on) to a heavy material. They discussed it and some suggested, 'Make it lighter, the red is too dominant.' The Aboriginal participants quietly said, 'No, that is Kimberly red, and that's it.' Some said, 'We don't mind where our piece of work goes on the tapestry.' Some natural leaders had emerged from within.

I think we should have discussed layout earlier on, agreeing the whole picture perhaps by halfway through the project. It got so intense; maybe we should have gone out one week together, just to relax. We didn't foresee the argument but we should have done. But by going through it everyone learnt a great deal.

In hindsight, what could have been done differently? The numbers involved here were huge and it must have been hard to ensure communication if different people turned up for different sessions. Discussions might have helped near the beginning and during the project to ensure that the key players were involved in describing the overall vision and goals, to try to achieve some consensus early on. I wondered what the ground rules were to ensure that mixing and interaction would evolve early on.

The high numbers of attendees must have made communication difficult. Perhaps at each session a meeting with the representatives from each group would have been useful, plus the development of methods to ensure that issues and agreements were communicated back to the others.

Community artists need some training in facilitation work. I really admired the organizers for being able to shelve the project at the end, and as a result allowing the emergent empowerment of the group to finalize the quilt. It is hard for organizers not to take over ownership of a group task, and to let their own egos become bound up with the success or failure of a project.

I found this an inspiring project, and then heard another teaching story where a superordinate goal led to increased harmony and a shared and deeper understanding of Quaker beliefs, between youth from a wide range of ages and backgrounds.

STORY: THE SILK CURTAIN

A group of children and young people of different age groups (from 5 to 16) and from different backgrounds were attending a Quaker children's meeting every fortnight in a city in Australia. The reality of weekly family life was that while most of the children attended the children's meeting regularly, some did not. The programme was very formal, with a set sequence of activities led by one of the parents, and the children either behaved badly or were increasingly reluctant to attend.

Parents, children and other concerned adults met for a one-day 'dreaming' exercise. A vision for the children's meeting grew from the discussions. What was needed was a more relaxed, informative and inspiring programme where friendships could grow and children would feel they belonged to a Quaker community. Parents wanted their children to learn about being a Quaker through stories, participation in the Quaker community, and through Quaker service to the wider community.

Three adults (with a facilitation background) who did not have young children offered to take over the 45-minute children's meeting. The structure of these sessions was loosened. Each session included a few minutes' silence in the Quaker tradition, introductions of people in the group, reflections on the last session (in which some or none of the children present at this meeting may have participated), activities which enabled everyone in the children's meeting to explore a particular idea, a few minutes' discussion to create a summary, and a few minutes' silence to conclude. The children then rejoined the larger Meeting for Worship to participate in the last minutes of the worship and to share their own experiences in the children's meeting.

The project began with children discussing their perceptions of 'boundaries'. People have real and visible, but also invisible boundaries that help them determine how to behave.

The children and adults explored the local environment together, noticing physical boundaries such as fences, curbs, footpaths, roads and clothes, as well as boundaries between people. They were asked to represent these boundaries with playdough, construction materials and in drawings.

Some members of the meeting suggested that the children might create a curtain for the doorway into the Meeting Room. This doorway is a kind of boundary which signals to people who enter into the meeting space what they may do and what they may not do. It is both a visible and an invisible boundary, marking the boundary between the outside world and a shared place of worship.

The children had their own perceptions and understandings of this space. They were puzzled by adults' willingness to sit in silence for an hour, and challenged by the expectation that they would participate in this silence for 15 minutes. From the children's perspective, meeting for worship was boring and the adults were overly serious.

The children decided that the adults and the room needed livening up, and created a silk curtain with a realistic picture that was symbolic: a sky of hope, a landscape of generosity and kindness, a shoreline of perseverance and a sea of peace.

The challenges for the facilitators in this project were many:

● Different parents wanted varying degrees of formality in the children's meeting.
● Different children wanted varying degrees of overt Quaker philosophy.
● Different children attended each meeting, so the facilitators needed to carry forward the ideas from one group to the next.
● Children had never built upon their own and each other's ideas in a long project, so were not used to listening to each other within the meeting, let alone listening to voices that had been heard in another meeting when they were not there.
● Adults were not sure that the children were capable of the deep and philosophical thinking they were doing.
● Adults were concerned that their children might be bored with a repetitive process, since their own experience in leading the previous formal process of the children's meeting had been so negative.

Below are some of the facilitative questions and responses by one of the facilitators who is a qualified community artist (F = facilitator, *Ch* = child).

F: What is a boundary and why do boundaries exist?
Ch: Boundaries show where one thing starts and another thing ends. A boundary marks places we can't go. Boundaries keep things in or out. Boundaries have different purposes. Sometimes they are for protecting people, keeping people safe or just having fun. We are boundaries because we can stop people. Some people see boundaries that other people don't because they have different personalities. Sometimes, it is more fun to go over the boundary or find ways around the boundary.
F: How close do we let people come? Describe the space between people.
Ch: We saw how people react to the closeness between each other. Some people don't mind but some can be very protective.
F: What do people think about in Meeting for Worship?
Ch: Things we like doing like football and soccer. Nature. Friends. When are we going out? What are we doing after Meeting?
F: What do people do in Meeting for Worship?
Ch: Nothing, they are trying to clear their mind. Wait, wonder when it will be my turn to speak. Sleep.
F: Why do people come to Meeting for Worship?
Ch: To see their friends. To be part of a community. Security. I feel safe here.
F: What colour is silence?
Ch: Silence is white, prayer is blue.
F: What might we put on a curtain to the Meeting Room that would signal to those who enter the space that this is a Quaker space?

Ch: *Quaker ideas. Godly things. Magic, mystery , riddles. Peacefulness and sim-*
      plicity. Laughter, fun, comical fun. Welcome. Hope. Humbleness. Kindness,
      Perseverance.
F: How can we represent these ideas?
Ch: *It needs to be something stylish that incorporates everyone's ideas. It*
      should be a picture of things God has given us. Stars, butterflies, bright
      colours with the light shining through. People. A sky of hope, a land of
      generosity and kindness, a beach of perseverance and a sea of peace.
F: How can we represent hope, kindness, perseverance and peace?
Ch: *A peace symbol, a dove and olive branch and a dolphin are images of peace.*
      Stars, the sun, the moon, flowers, fish, swirls and spirals are images of
      hope. People, koalas, dogs and giraffes are images of kindness. Waves,
      caterpillars, ladybirds, bees and ants are images of perseverance. Riding a
      bike requires perseverance. Babies and parents persevere!
F: How are you going to divide the four main spaces for each idea? How much
      space do you need for the ideas of peace? (Shows a line about a quarter of
      the way up the length of paper.) More than this, less than this?
F: For the edge of the sea, what kind of line do we need? What does that look
      like?
Ch: *A wavy line. A swirly line.*
F: Do you have ideas about how this will look? (Two children nod.)
F: Why don't you have a go on a scrap piece of paper drawing your lines? (The
      children have two very different ideas.)
F: Have you two talked about what you have in mind? How can you make your
      ideas work together? Can I leave that in your capable hands?

Eventually lots of draft drawings were drawn and redrawn on pieces of paper.
Flipchart paper was stuck together and the small drawings were laid out, moved
around or redrawn until everyone was happy.
The drawn picture or cartoon was too large to paint in one length.

F: We have some choices. We can cut off a bit of our picture so we can make
      just one panel. We could cut the picture in half and make two panels. You
      wanted this to be a realistic picture? What do you think we should do?
Ch: *I don't think we should cut people's drawings off the picture.*
F: Well, we could put the drawings we cut off back into the picture at different
      places.
Ch: *But the curtain wouldn't hang properly if it was too narrow.*
F: We could put some fabric around it like the frame of a picture.
Ch: *It would nice to have people walk through our picture into the Meeting*
      Room.
F: So do we cut it down the middle?
Ch: *And have a frame on each part.*
F: We need to draw the picture onto the silk with the resist. Are we going to
      try and draw our own pictures or just everyone's pictures?
Ch: *Not everyone is here. It will be easier if we just draw the pictures in one*
      area.

Six children worked on drawing and then painting on the silk simultaneously.
They checked with each other about colour choices, and added images in spaces
they felt were too large and blank. The first part of the curtain took six hours to

complete. The second part only two hours, since many decisions had been made already.

The resulting curtain is hanging in the Meeting Room. Adults who have heard some of this story are so excited about it. They have asked for articles for the Quaker newsletter, a story of the curtain's making to be made and a plaque describing the curtain to be placed beside the doorway.

In this story, the facilitators were committed to the group for the long term. They volunteered to change the behaviours of the children at the Quaker meeting by involving the children in generating the solution and their superordinate goal. Long before the children decided on the curtain they were involved in active dialogue where their ideas and contributions were honoured. Their creativity was encouraged and supported, and as a result their confidence grew. There were behaviour boundaries too. There was a commitment to consensus decision making right from the start, so there was no power play for dominance of pictures or ideas.

Facilitating cultural inclusivity

One of the key skills needed by facilitators is how to work with dominators: individuals or groups who dominate the air space. We need to be able to use a number of equalizing processes.

The next two stories and strategies describe the difficulties that many teams face with the inequities of power and ownership in development projects. Frequently 'expatriates' (who are seen as the power holders) dominate the 'air space' in culturally diverse meetings while complaining outside the meeting that the 'locals' do not participate. The 'locals' on their part realize that speaking out might be risky, as they are usually employed on a contract basis, have families to maintain, and they could be penalized when their contracts come up for renewal. They are in their countries for the long term, while expatriates come and go.

The second story then illustrates a case where a local power holder refuses to let others participate, and where an expatriate facilitator has to draw a workshop to an early close and use other strategies.

STORY: CREATING SPACE FOR THE UNSPOKEN

This story was written by William Savage, organizational and community development facilitator who is based in Bangkok, Thailand.

In late 1997, I was contracted to conduct a strategic planning workshop for an INGO's country office in Cambodia, which was managed by the organization's affiliate in Australia. The workshop was one of a series across the organization's country offices in Asia and the world. The participants were Khmer 'national staff' from Cambodia and 'international staff' from Australia and the United States.

This workshop was part of a global strategic planning process that was starting with 'the field'. Each of the country-level facilitators was provided with a manual and package of materials which contained everything needed to run the workshops, from an agenda to activities and methods, sheets of coloured dots, and a set of prescribed outputs which were to be synthesized regionally and then globally. Ultimately the outcomes of the worldwide workshops would find their way to the organization's headquarters in Australia, where a global strategic plan would be drafted.

While the detailed workshop manual prepared by the person coordinating the planning process was appreciated, a couple of us who had been contracted to facilitate various country-level workshops discussed and agreed with her that while we would each 'deliver' the required outputs, we would use our own experience-learned methods to produce them. One of these outputs was a SWOT analysis – strengths, weaknesses, opportunities and threats – of the organization's country office.

One of the principles that informs my facilitation practice is that I tend not to make too many decisions in advance about how any one session or activity will be run. I like to wait until I've met the group and have worked through previous activities, learning how to make each subsequent one most relevant for the purpose and process we're engaged in together. Another way of saying this is being aware of 'where the group is at' and working with them there.

Another principle is that any sort of organizational-level event can provide opportunities to bring to the surface and deal with interpersonal issues which may be affecting the workplace, and I look out for these, the issues and the opportunities. In several pre-workshop discussions with individuals, both 'international' and 'national' senior and junior staff, I became aware that there were serious difficulties being faced by the Khmer staff in their relationships with the senior non-Khmer management. While I wasn't sure what these were, I sensed that there was an opportunity for them to be communicated through the SWOT analysis.

When we got to that session in the workshop timetable, I suggested that the whole group (about 30 people) should divide into several smaller groups, with the Khmer staff in their own groups, and the non-Khmers in theirs. The first reaction to this grouping suggestion was a comment that, 'In [our organization] we always work together.' I responded that for this activity it would be beneficial if our Cambodian colleagues could work in Khmer, knowing that segregation of the groups was the only way they would be able to speak freely.

When the groups came together to report back their versions of the SWOT analysis, I suggested that the final SWOT table should contain only statements with which everyone in the room agreed. This was phrased in terms of building consensus on the state of the organization's country office. We covered one wall of the room with the SWOT flipcharts, all the strengths together, the weaknesses, the opportunities and the threats, some written in Khmer and some in English. In turn, a spokesperson for each of the groups read out their entries, with interpretation across both languages.

Once this was done, I began pointing out and marking the entries that were common across the groups, and then those that seemed uncontroversial but that were not mentioned by all or most groups, seeking comment and then agreement from the whole group at each step. For the entries that were easily agreed, we found wording that was acceptable to everyone. Most of the strengths and opportunities, some of the threats and a few of the weaknesses were dealt with in this way.

This left a set of entries, mostly weaknesses, which were clearly going to be controversial, and at the heart of the difficulties facing the Khmer staff. So we took these one by one. One statement of weakness written by a Khmer group was 'inequity between "national" and "international" staff'. When they were asked to give an example of this, we heard how when Khmer and non-Khmer staff travelled to the same location, to do the same work and to live in the same accommodation, the daily allowance for the 'international' staff was still higher than that for the 'national' staff.

I asked that we take comments on the issue of inequity from anyone who wanted to contribute. These ranged from other examples, to an observation that all that was being asked for was fairness, to a statement about how 'that's the way it is', to the country director (an outside 'international' person) suggesting that the statement on inequity be removed. It was then written up on a sheet called 'left-overs' along with a couple other entries on which consensus had not been reached, and that was how we ended the day.

Another of the required outputs for the strategic planning process was a set of core values, the session for which took place towards the end of the final workshop day. Once we had worked through that activity, we ended up with words like 'fairness' and 'equity'. Another principle of mine is always trying to use participants' own words, the language they have been using to talk about the work and the task at hand.

So it wasn't much of a stretch at that point to go back to the SWOT analysis and to ask people to come up with suggestions about how to reword the 'left-over' entries so that they reflected the core values they had just agreed they shared. They decided that since the SWOT would be a public document they would need to word the comment about inequity more discreetly, and they then agreed (including the country director) on some steps to begin working on their internal staff issues.

I learnt towards the end of the workshop that following the session on the SWOT analysis, the country director had met with one of the Khmer women who spoke up most strongly about the inequity issue. He gave her a hard time and told her she should not have talked about such matters in the workshop. Although she was quite upset about this, I tried to reassure her that we needed to get through the workshop and that there was a chance that some change could take place. I also told her that expatriates come and go and that she would still be there, if she could just stick with it.

A few years later, on another trip to Cambodia, I met the Khmer woman. She was still with the organization, with a lot more responsibility and satisfaction with her work. That country director was long gone. She recalled the circumstances during the strategic planning workshop and the reassurances I had given her when she spoke up.

The facilitator clearly observed the lack of inclusivity in the behaviour of the country director and the inequities between local and expatriate staff. He took steps to redress the balance of power by splitting the groups to enable individuals to speak more freely. The 'left-over' or parking lot enabled issues to be noted and returned to. The payback for being outspoken is an issue that all facilitators need to be aware of. Since local staff are frequently on contract conditions, their country directors wield a great deal of power.

STORY: ENCOURAGING CULTURAL INCLUSIVITY

This story was told by Abigayle Carmody, an Irish-Australian facilitator working in Papua New Guinea.

I was called in to facilitate a workshop to enable a team on an aid development project in Papua New Guinea to work more effectively. There were six expatriates and eight local team members. They had been working together for a year. The local team members seemed ill at ease at the outset. The culturally diverse expatriate team dominated all discussions, and would get started on issues before we had got to this stage. When an older local woman did speak she would speak on behalf of her group. Other members of the local team would tell her what they wanted to say, and she would in turn tell the whole group. The expatriate members interrupted and assertively disagreed with what was being said: they wanted to get to the 'real issues'. I felt I had to revise the agenda (which had been handed to me by the project director, a problem in itself) and start again. I called a break.

I asked the older local woman how she would like to recommence the meeting. She said she would like to say a prayer. This is how her people liked to start meetings, she said. We did just that, it took just a couple of minutes and brought a certain calm into the room.

Next, I asked what each member knew about each other's cultures; very little, as it turned out. We redid the introductions using people's names and their meanings as a way of learning a little about the cultures represented. Everyone had slowed down and really listened to each other's stories. The atmosphere in the room had changed. I then introduced a 'talking stick' (an example of facilitators needing to have things up our sleeves) and explained that the person who held it had permission to speak and was not to be on visuals). The local team responded very positively to this, and each one of the team members requested the stick, one after the other. The expatriate team members then had their turn. We just talked about what we wanted from the three days, what the strengths in the team were, and how we could use them to move forward.

In this story the facilitator modelled how to be culturally inclusive and opened the doors for the enhancement of mutual cross-cultural under-standing. Learning was around power distance (hierarchy) and collectivism and how this impacted on the communication process, that trust building takes time, that the expatriate team needed to honour the ritual of starting meetings, and most importantly, that everyone has a story to tell.

STORY: USING INDIRECT STRATEGIES TO GIVE VOICE TO THOSE LESS POWERFUL

There are times when a participatory approach is simply not appropriate.

I was working as a consultant in conjunction with the heads of two government departments in a country in Asia called Xxx. I'll call one Mr Tham, a powerful senior official who was close to retirement, and the other, the head of an organization representing women's interests, Mrs Maniphan. Each of them had two younger staff members, all of whom who were keen to learn.

I worked alongside a Xxx counterpart who also acted as interpreter (I'll call him Kanya). Before a workshop, I discussed with Kanya the goals of the session, which were to enable Mr Tham and Mrs Maniphan to review their community training workshops which we had observed in the rural towns, identifying the things that went well and those areas that might need improvement. I was trying to put into practice the ideas of 'appreciative inquiry': to enable participants to focus on what was going well (see Chapter 2).

The meeting comprised only eight people. Kanya and I made notes on flipcharts in Xxx and English respectively as Mr Tham spoke at length on the benefits of his lectures to country-based staff. Mrs Maniphan, who had used some interactive exercises and role play, then gave her feedback.

All appeared to be going well until we reached the stage for ideas for improvements. Mr Tham kept speaking, covering old ground. I waited for a pause and suggested that perhaps we could use the round robin process to go around the group. I invited to Mrs Maniphan to speak.

Mr Tham interrupted. Because of his seniority it was culturally not appropriate to confront him directly. I again waited until he had finished.

Mrs Maniphan said to Mr Tham, 'We have to encourage our younger team members to give their ideas.' I suggested writing down ideas on cards. Mr Tham interrupted again. 'I am old, and I will not live much longer, so I deserve to be able to speak.' Indeed he made it very clear that he was not going to let anyone else speak. I felt my hackles rising, but realized there was absolutely nothing I could do. I drew the workshop to a close somewhat early, saying, 'Mr Tham, I know how busy you are. Perhaps I could go around to each person in turn and gather ideas for you, which Kanya will put into a list.' Mr Tham agreed.

At lunchtime Kanya was so frustrated. We held a debriefing discussion and I had to admit that there are times when shuttle diplomacy (working one on one) is the only way, and that there are times 'when a participatory approach does not work'.

This story illustrates the need for power holders in developing countries genuinely to want to have input or facilitation work from overseas advisers. It is an interesting example of dominance, and one that I have heard repeated in hierarchical societies.

Few of us would appreciate a foreigner imposed on us to improve our work without our consent and motivation. Mr Tham was used to working autocratically and did not see the need for staff participation or participatory learning and evaluation. He said repeatedly about his lectures, 'If I have told them, they know it.' He was in a powerful position and had friends in high places. There was no reason for him to change what he was doing. His department wanted overseas funding, and with that came a responsibility to use the funding to change and make improvements regarding the project, but that didn't mean it would happen. In this instance shuttle diplomacy was the most appropriate strategy to encourage some equity of engagement with ideas.

Holding up a mirror to the 'others'

Sometimes we have blind spots and cannot imagine how we are perceived by people from other cultures. The following is a useful and equitable two- or three-way communication process to illuminate blind spots and develop strategies for better communication and team work.

The mirroring process between cultural groups

The mirroring process is a useful multisensory exercise including role play, drawing and singing, for bicultural groups that have been working together for some time, but who are keen to improve communication between them. It is based on the work of Virginia Satir (1983). Participants from 'culture A' are asked to hold up a metaphorical mirror to the participants from 'culture B' (and vice versa) so that everyone can learn more about how they behave and communicate. There need to be high levels of trust for this exercise.

It is important to focus participants on issues, not people. Participants are asked to form groups of four or five people of homogeneous cultures. Provide them with flipchart paper, felt-tip pens and masking tape. Props like scarves, local cloth, and musical instruments such as drums, rattles and shakers are useful to encourage a light-hearted sense of fun and creativity. Beware of wooden pipes and flutes for hygiene reasons.

Explain that each group will be asked to illustrate the characteristics of the 'other' culture using role play, skits, drawings, poems, storytelling, songs, chants or even rap. Among the things to illustrate are aspects of the 'other' culture that they like, appreciate and admire, and those they find difficult to understand and/or 'puzzling'. Participants are also asked to offer suggestions for improving communication between members of the different cultures, ie 'bridges'.

Allow groups at least 20 minutes for preparation and five minutes to show each skit to represent the other culture. Allow at least one hour for debriefing and discussion.

This activity leads to increased awareness of the 'other' and each other's 'blind spots', and may take a group to a new level of understanding. This process helps to open up communication between cultural groups, to raise issues to the surface in a playful way.

Where role play is used, the facilitator later asks each group to state verbally the points they were trying to get across to check for accuracy. From these issues, the group generates a list of 'Hints for improved communication between culture A and culture B'.

The process could lead to polarizing the two groups into 'them' and 'us' if time is not spent in debriefing to highlight how the information gained can be used to enable participants to work better as a team. (For a more detailed example of this process used in Nepal between development workers, see Hogan, 2003.)

Mirroring process between organizations or polarized groups

The purpose of this process is to heighten awareness of perceptions and assumptions we make about other organizations, their representatives, and vice versa (Kettle and Saul, 2004). The relationships between people from different organizations often impact on the type, rate and quality of communications between them. Often we stereotype others: 'Oo, they're from the government, so of course they're ...' A similar exercise was developed by Dr Chasin (1986) of the Public Conversations Project to raise awareness of groups whose values and opinions are polarized to learn how hurtful their stereotyping can be. Some of their debriefing questions have been incorporated below.

Introduction

An introduction might include: 'Misunderstandings and conflict may be fuelled by distorted perceptions that people hold of one another; and assumptions people make about others who don't share their views or their culture or their experiences. Many people would like to feel less stereotyped by others. We would like to lead you through an exercise that will allow you to communicate how you feel stereotyped, and to indicate which of those stereotypes are most inaccurate or hurtful.'

Stage 1   Generation of lists

Each subgroup completes flipcharts 1 and 2 about themselves and flipchart 3 about 'the other' group/s (see Table 7.3).

Table 7.3   Perceptions of self and as seen by others

1. How you perceive your own organization	2. How you think people from other organizations perceive you	3. How others actually see your organization (to be filled in later by other participants)

Stage 2   Groups exchange their perceptions of each other

Flipchart 3 is given to the group it describes.

Stage 3   Reflection on the stereotypes

Say 'Now we'd like to give you an opportunity to reflect on the stereotypes about your group on flipchart 3 and to think about which seem most inaccurate in your view. Please discuss:

● Which is most *painful or hurts*? Then put a 'P' next to the stereotype that is most *painful* or offensive.
● Which do you feel are the most *inaccurate*? Put an 'I' next to the three stereotypes you feel are most inaccurate
● Which are the most understandable? Put a 'U' next to the stereotype or stereotypes that you think are most *understandable*. By doing this you're not saying it's true of you; you could be saying only that this is a stereotype your group does too little to correct. This category is an option; we'd like to encourage you to give it some thought.

Continue, 'Before any of you approach the flipcharts, please take a minute to think. Then go up when you are ready. When you have finished marking the lists, chose a recorder to report to the other group/s on what you marked, and if you wish you can say something about how the process went.'

Group reports (8–10 minutes each to the full group)

Now is the time for each group to report to the other. Each group has been invited to share not only the lists and the markings, but also something about the process.

Give these instructions: 'We'd like to have each person take the opportunity to speak, if you'd like to say something about the stereotype that you marked as most *painful*. Again you can pass if you prefer. Perhaps you could say what it is about the way you understand yourself, the way you know yourself, what is it about your experience that makes the stereotype that you marked the most painful. We'd like you to share just a couple of sentences, whatever you feel comfortable with. Again, what is it about how you understand yourself, know yourself, and understand your experience that makes one of these judgements or distorted perceptions so painful?'

Debrief: observations of participants

These are some typical observations:

> When we think of ourselves we tend to think positively; when we look at other organizations we tend to be critical.
> We work for the government and we often get flack from others, but we are doing our best.
> We cannot ignore the negative feedback we got.
> It's not Asian to speak out, but this exercise gave us an opportunity to write what we really think.
> We are not our organization, yet in a way we are.
> There are so many truths and realities; my truth is only one of many.
> Oh, but the third column is so negative!
> We must be careful of generalizations, otherwise it destroys relationships.
> The main thing is we should not be defensive, we can use this information as triggers for action.
> When I meet someone from another organization I have to map who they are and look for bridges.

Once awareness has been raised, the facilitator must be ready to help groups move on, to identify how they can interact more productively and or build bridges in the future. This may also happen on an individual level, as the following story illustrates.

STORY: AN ASSUMPTION

I met someone at a function and he said 'Oh you're from xxx, that defunct organization ...' So I continued talking to him and tried to see how I could build bridges and perhaps change his assumptions about me and the organization I currently work for. Now we are good friends.

Kevin Kettle, Irish facilitator, Bangkok

Simulation: role reversal

Another way of enabling groups of participants to 'walk in each other's moccasins' is to provide a simple problem-solving simulation story in which they are all stakeholders.

Stages

1. Divide up the participants into their work groupings: for instance NGOs, INGOs, government, private sector.
2. Allocate a change of role for each group. For example, the participants from NGOs take on the role of government officials and the participants from INGOs take on the role of the indigenous people.
3. Distribute a story. (I have not included one here as it is best to write one specific to the workshop topic and background of the participants.) Allow everyone time to read and discuss it, and note down the issues from the perspective of their new roles.
4. Encourage the groups to work out strategies to resolve the situation. Ask them to note down what happens and what it would be useful to have happen.
5. Debrief facilitative questions include 'What have you learnt?', 'What will you do differently as a result?', 'What new strategies might work better?' (Ask each group to tutor another.)

8

Facilitating reconciliation

Introduction

Reconciliation is required to enable people to move on after conflict. Many countries are struggling with the aftermath of colonization, despotic rule, unjust governance and conflict. This chapter contains:

- processes to engender understanding of the impact of colonization on indigenous groups in Australia;
- strategies to take participants from their heads to their hearts to their hands, to take action to enhance equity and healing;
- the power of storytelling in reconciliation work;
- reconciliation strategies in South Africa;
- use of scenario planning to develop sustainable and equitable governance in South Africa.

Reconciliation and healing between cultures within a country: Australia

Facilitation work often involves us in motivating others to take action for social change. There are many types of reconciliation: political, economic, educational and personal. This section focuses on aspects of all four areas.

Workshops to lessen health inequities in Australia

The history of colonial rule and the collision of cultures in Australia left indigenous groups disadvantaged. To our shame the health statistics for Aboriginal people are similar to those in developing countries. The causes are complex, but one of the many strategies to enhance the health and well-being of indigenous groups is to involve them actively in efforts to improve health care.

In order to change people's mindsets and to stir them into action, a number of stages are involved. These are outlined in Figure 8.1. The stages were developed for a project targeting medical practitioners in Australia to be more proactive in 'Working Better in Aboriginal and Torres Strait Islander Health' in their communities. The workshop stages were carefully developed and tested by a culturally diverse team comprising medical practitioners, indigenous and Anglo-Australian facilitators (Hogan, 2005).

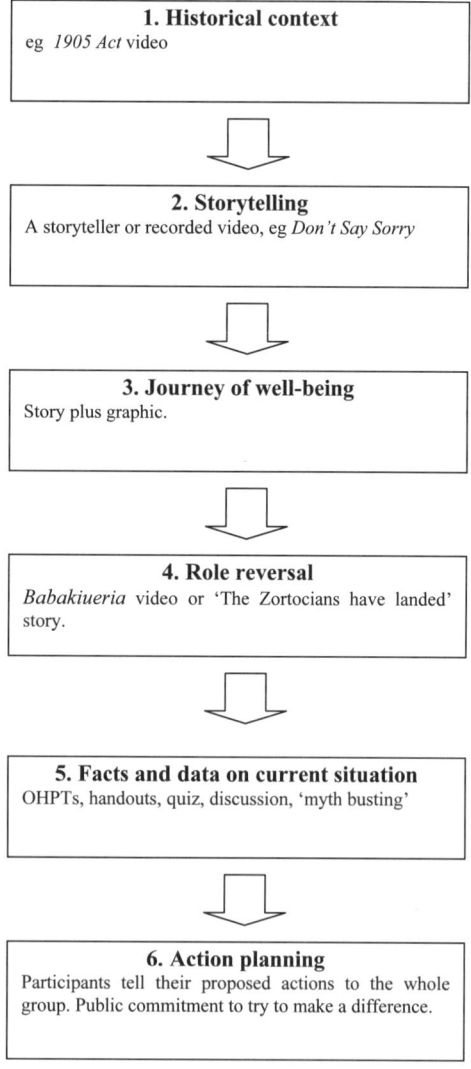

Figure 8.1 Processes to move participants from thinking and feeling to action

Stage 1   The historical context

Doctors and health workers were shown a short factual video entitled *1905 Act* (Graham, 1989). This video gives an historical account of the impact of the 1905 Act and white settlement on the Aboriginal people in Western Australia. Using photos and archival film footage, it graphically details the government regulations on indigenous peoples and the impact on the stolen generation, whereby children were taken from their families in order to be educated in mission schools as domestic and farm labourers. At this stage it is easy for participants to view a video dispassionately and to remain in their 'heads'.

Stage 2   Storytelling: Heads and hearts

Intellectual argument will not change people's way of being and interacting; often only a moving experience will change that. We need people to feel. We invited a wonderful indigenous storyteller, Christine Jacobs, who was taken from her family at a very young age. As well as talking about her experiences of being part of the 'stolen generation', she gave us valuable advice on working with storytellers. She has taught us to appreciate the power of story and the courage of those who tell their stories.

Christine had a message for those who were prepared to listen to her:

> Although I had all this happen to me, I don't feel bitter and I don't hate white people any more or blame the government. I have forgiven all my abusers and I have thanked all of those people who helped me. Don't say 'sorry' to me. I don't need your sorry. I am getting on with my life. I just want to look after my family and tell my story and all I ask is for you to listen.

Christine was recognized for her work for reconciliation by being invited to open parliament only weeks before her death, and in her invitation to open the Reconciliation Conference in Canberra on 24 April 2005. Tragically she died in a car accident only a day prior to opening the National Day of Healing 2005 and before meeting the prime minister, John Howard. Christine's 14-year-old daughter Tamara bravely gave Christine's prepared speech in Canberra the day after Christine died. Christine's message is summed up in a video she made with the Film and TV Institute entitled *Don't Say Sorry* (Jacobs, 2005).

Please note that the 'think–feel–act' sequence has cultural underpinnings, and it may be necessary to change the sequence in some cultures, particularly Latino ones, to 'feel–think–act'.

Using and debriefing stories

> The most important journey you'll ever make is from your head to your heart.
>
> A Coorong indigenous Australian man

In many cultural awareness workshops, Aboriginal and/or Torres Strait Islander people are invited to tell 'their story'. Storytelling is an art, and telling someone an intimate story about yourself is a gift. Telling that story to strangers is a risk. This can be a very emotional experience for the storyteller as well as the participants. Some storytellers use the story as a form of healing for both themselves and others. The story can re-traumatize the teller and/or the listeners. Facilitators need to prepare carefully to ensure that is it is a positive experience for the storyteller, and to help everyone to gain the most from the experience.

Be very careful to consider beforehand what you want to achieve from the storytelling activity. Tim Muirhead, an Anglo-Australian facilitator, commented, 'There should no blame, no shame. Just acknowledgement. We are only guilty if we turn away from it. The ultimate privilege is if you ignore it – and get away with it.'

All stories have 'hooks' which act at various levels to connect into our many and varied previous experiences, so one story which is well debriefed is often enough to get your points across. One indigenous storyteller commented, 'It feels like voyeurism, like white fellas are watching our pain, but not helping us to deal with it.' We need to be mindful that storytelling can re-trigger the trauma. Christine Jacobs said, 'Every time I tell my story I feel energized. I get a high from it because I have helped someone know what I've been through and that we can move on. I just want people to acknowledge our story.'

Interacting with the guest storyteller beforehand

Preferably meet the storyteller face to face beforehand. Explain the purpose of the session carefully and how it fits into the context of your workshop. Ask storytellers:

- what they would like to know about the participants (some story-tellers like to know a lot, others find it less nerve-racking if they do not know that important people are present);
- what they need: a glass of water, chair, overhead projector, white-board;
- how they would like to be introduced;
- what they would like to happen if they and/or the participants become distressed during the story;
- how they will keep track of time and how they can be reminded gently if they are running out of time;

- how much time they have afterwards: would they like to join the group for tea and/or lunch to meet the participants informally?
- how they would like the debrief to be handled: for example, perhaps with the facilitator next to them to help to explain questions from the participants if necessary.

It is normal for some participants to be shy of a new person and perhaps more formal than they had been in earlier parts of the workshop, so it may help if the storyteller can join everyone for tea/coffee first.

Timing

Timing is important as often the main message, for example about reconciliation, is at the end. There also needs to be time for questions and discussion. The storytelling part is the most important in the whole workshop day. Figure 8.2 suggests a timeline.

Make sure you allow adequate timing for the storyteller and then debrief with participants. Christine Jacobs commented, 'Once I had to go to a school assembly and tell my story of the stolen generation in 10 minutes.'

Once you have invited people to 'speak from the heart' you may wish to return to the 'head'. For example, in relation to Christine's talk it could be useful to have some statistics about the impact of the stolen generation, and some background knowledge of the history of government policy in relation to the stolen generation. Questions we asked the participants in our workshop were:

- What are the implications of this story and statistics for your practice as a GP?
- What sort of things do you need to know about as a result of this experience?
- What would you do differently as a result of this experience?
- In how many ways can you share power with your Aboriginal and Torres Strait Islander patients?

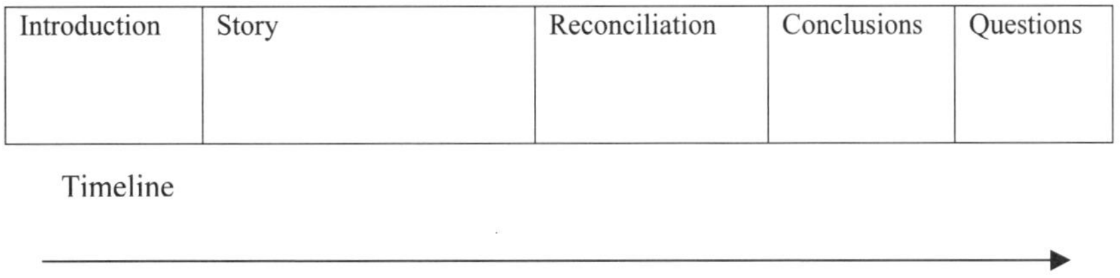

Introduction	Story	Reconciliation	Conclusions	Questions

Timeline

Figure 8.2 Suggested division of time in a reconcilation workshop

After the story

The speaker and participants will be in a very different 'emotional space'. Often this is when shifts in the attitudes and/or stereotypes of the participants take place. There are no hard and fast rules for how to debrief these events. Four stages help:

- Allow a few minutes for individual silent reflection.
- Small group discussion of the first two stages of the ORID process with one person noting ideas. Prompts could be, 'During the story, what went on in your head?' (objective question) and 'During the story, what went on in your heart?' (reflective question). Please note that we left the interpretative and decisional questions to the end of the day.
- A volunteer from each small group notes everyone's ideas on a flipchart (see Table 8.1).
- A representative from each group reports back to the whole group, showing the flipchart ideas.

Table 8.1   Objective and reflective questions

During the story, what went on in your head?	*During the story, what went on in your heart?*
●	●
●	●

Alternative strategies

Alternatively you can play a video recording of an Aboriginal or Torres Strait Islander person telling her/his story and debrief in the same way. However, a video is not as powerful as a real storyteller.

Stage 3   Journey of well-being

The 'journey of well-being' was developed by Tim Muirhead in Perth (see Figure 8.3). The diagram has far more impact if you draw it slowly from left to right on the white board describing the stages as you go. Of course it has a different impact if it is drawn by an Indigenous facilitator. The 'journey' can be adapted to any country which has experienced colonization by another group. The story telling might include:

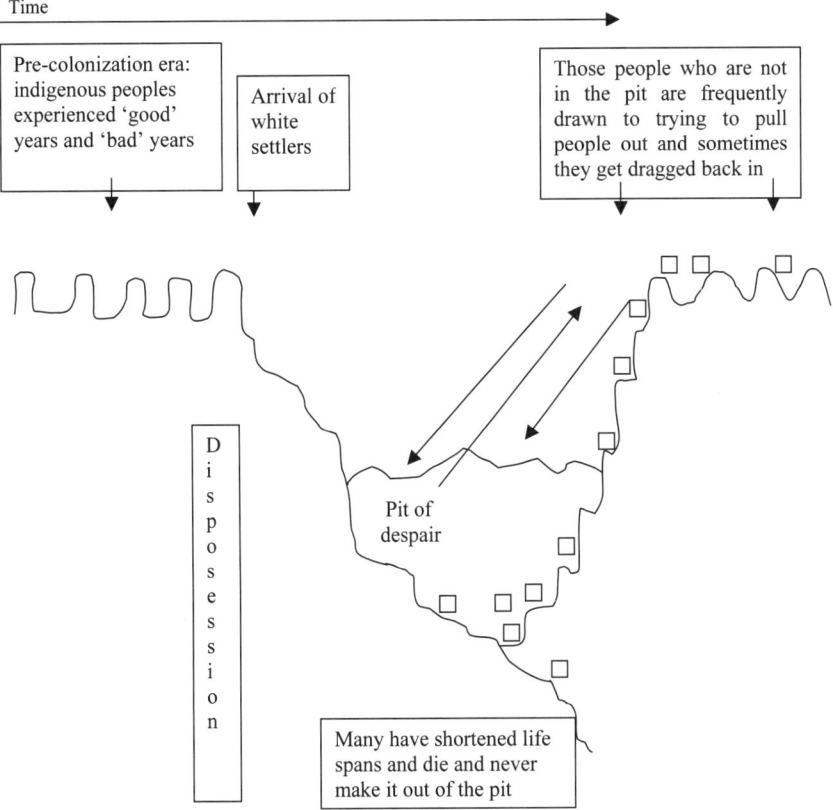

Key
Pit of despair = poverty, substance abuse, high levels
of violence, imprisonment. Some Aboriginal children
born into this pit believe that is the way things are for
Aboriginal people.

☐ Aboriginal people

Figure 8.3 The journey of well-being

Source: Tim Muirhead.

In the pre-colonization era people lived their lives with its ups and downs,
good years, bad years, rituals, gatherings and festivals, disagreements
and peacemaking. When the colonizers arrived there was total disruption
of previous ways of life, hunting and gathering areas. There was fighting
and land theft. Additionally there was the spread of disease (sometimes
purposefully) and social disruptions as children were separated from their
families. The Aboriginal culture, language and customs were suppressed.
As a result, many sank into a 'pit of despair' involving alcohol and drug
abuse and domestic violence. Some children grew up thinking that that
was how life was meant to be for Aboriginal people. Some managed to

ride these traumas, adapt and succeed in the new system, and have tried to help extended family members 'out of the pit'. At times the enormity of the problems means they also get pulled back in.

Acknowledge, work with and look beyond current realities

This session aims to explore how non-Aboriginal participants – in this case, general practitioners and health workers – can be assisted to challenge and move beyond *their own* mindset in relation to Aboriginal people, patients and communities. It was followed by presentation of data to debunk misconceptions. For instance, many people think that Aboriginal people are given extraordinary extra funding, but in reality they are not.

There is also a need to acknowledge participants' own negative experiences, especially those that have involved Aboriginal people. Facilitators need to be able to allow people to feel aggrieved by these experiences *and* explore how to move beyond them.

Stage 4   Role reversal

Role reversal is another useful strategy to raise awareness and develop empathy. A well-chosen video can help participants to view life from the point of view of 'the other'.

Babakiueria video

Babakiueria is an alternative view of Australian history since 1788 (Featherstone, 1987). It is a satire that reverses the roles, imagining what it would be like if a fleet of ships arrived to try and settle an area inhabited by white natives. What would it be like to be white if the Aboriginal peoples were the colonizing and later the dominant cultural group in Australia? It exposes the racism inherent in much of mainstream Australian history and the media via role reversal in documentary style.

The absurdity and traumas of colonialism and racism are highlighted in this fake documentary, which envisions a world in which the Aboriginal people are the discoverers of white middle-class Australia, and make simplistic and patronizing judgements and assumptions about the people and their culture. Aspects of white culture are shown by a well-meaning, but naïve, Aboriginal researcher who lives with a white family for six months. Cultural values explored include religion, the betting office, violence, the ritual of football matches, and marches to honour death, sacrifice and killing millions in wars. It illustrates the government policy of removing children from white families to work, resulting in the disillusionment and anger of white youth. It ends with the resettlement of families to a totally new environment, their shock, and the authorities saying it will help them to learn new skills. While the context of the video is Australian, the video helps to generate discussion in other cultural contexts also.

In order to help group discussion Gill Baxter, a colleague in Perth, split her multicultural group of postgraduate counselling students into two groups: one to watch and empathize with the point of view of the white family, the other to watch and empathize with the point of view of the Aboriginal family in the video. She commented (2006):

> At the end everyone was so shocked and it was hard to get them to talk, but eventually I couldn't shut them up. I asked two very well-off white women on purpose to take the part of the white family ... at the end the thought of being shunted into the bush and told to learn new skills shocked them to their foundations. The most learning seemed to be about the levels of anger that were expressed by the young boy against his parents. Nobody had seen that perspective before. It was a great exercise for learning to be in another's shoes.

In order to maximize the use of video interactively facilitators may like to consider the following.

Making video viewing interactive

We watch television at home for relaxation. We automatically 'switch off'. If you want to get the most out of a video as a learning tool, you must actively engage participants in 'observational learning'.

Preview

Always ask yourself when choosing a video or teaching aid:

- What am I trying to teach and/or what I am trying to get participants to think about?
- Is this the most useful tool to use for what I'm trying to achieve?

Setting the scene

Set the scene for the video by telling participants:

- why you chose to use this particular video;
- who made it;
- the date it was made (the context may impact on the presentation of ideas);
- how long it is (or the segment being used);
- why you will stop and start the video for discussion (invite participants to call a halt if they wish to discuss or question anything);
- any terms that they may not understand.

Cultural warning

If the video contains footage of Aboriginal and/or Torres Strait Islander peoples, please warn indigenous participants beforehand, particularly if the video contains pictures of people who may now be deceased.

Some general hints

You do not have to show all the video: be selective. Be prepared to use the remote control 'pause' button and stimulate interaction on topics as they arise. Ask if everyone can see and hear properly, and if not, ask them to rearrange the seating.

After the video

Invite everyone to stand and stretch. Sometimes people are sleepy after a video. If participants are slow to respond, invite them to talk about the video in pairs first, before a whole group discussion.

Debriefing the video and transference of learning back to the workplace

- Use the ORID process (see Chapter 1) with the whole group or in pairs.
- Use all your senses while you are watching this video: what do you see, hear, and feel?
- What delights you?
- What annoys you?
- What surprises you?
- What puzzles you?
- What cultural biases or assumptions were you aware of (in yourself and/or in the video)?
- Would you recommend this to your colleagues? If 'yes', why? If 'no', why?

Stage 5 Facts and data on the current situation

It is crucial *not* to deny realities: for example, there is statistically much more 'dysfunctional' behaviour in Aboriginal communities than non-Aboriginal communities. Some Aboriginal and non-Aboriginal people respond with mistrust and hostility to each other. So participants will need to be able to safely explore what is reality and what is myth, and what are the *causes* of those realities. Then they can also explore how GPs and health workers can respond to this effectively to be part of the solution.

In doing this it is crucial not to be *overwhelmed* by realities. We used stories of hope and strength that help participants know that working positively can reap great rewards.

Stage 6   Action planning

Who is going to do what, by when and with what resources? What are the ways in which success can be monitored?

Getting caught in the headlights

In developing the workshop we knew that there might be some medical staff with racist attitudes. We did not want to close off their comments, but we did feel the need to equip the trainee facilitators with some strategies to handle generalizations about Aboriginal people. The following strategies were developed by Nina Boydell (Hogan, 2005) from an initial idea by Scott Fatnowna.

Most of the time, most participants do not actively try to sabotage facilitators, but prior thought and preparation pay off. There are a variety of ways in which comments from participants can floor a facilitator, because they 'press buttons' or the comment momentarily means you are 'caught in the headlights like a kangaroo'. You may freeze, feel angry, go blank and/or not know what to do. There are some generic ways of dealing with this.

- Bring in the other participants. Ask participants what they make of the comment. 'Are there any other views?' Keep cool and note all ideas on flipchart paper (use this to divert any negative energies through you to the paper). Note all the differing ideas.
- Use a continuum. Ask participants to form a continuum from 'agree' to 'disagree' (and variations in between), and invite each to speak and give reasons for his or her stance. Ask the people at the extremes, 'What made you go to this point?' When everyone has finished speaking, ask, 'In the light of new ideas/evidence and now everyone has spoken, would anyone like to shift position? Where are you now? How does it feel when you move from one position to another?'
- Gain 'think time': use the parking lot. If you do not want to get caught up and diverted off the main aim of the session, say, 'That's interesting, let's minute it and come back to it later.' That gives you 'think time'.
- Gain 'think time' by inviting in the other facilitator. 'Perhaps xxx would like to comment on this?'
- Go back to the ground rules. Refer back to the ground rules, especially those regarding respect between participants and respect between facilitator and participants.
- Call a break. If the participant/s are repeatedly not willing to keep to the ground rules, call a break or 'time out'. Speak to them separately. Offer alternatives: stay but adhere to the ground rules, or leave.
- Stop the workshop. It may be better to stop than to carry on.

See also 'Difficult situations', Chapter 6 in Hogan (2003).

Reconciliation among refugees

Hurt and pain know no boundaries. Refugees may escape to safer places, but the results of atrocities sometimes take generations to heal. There are no quick or easy methods to aid healing. The healing process may also re-trigger pain. The first step however is for the 'other' to listen to the 'other', without interruption or discussion, to bear witness to their story. The following story relates an incident between African refugees in Australia.

STORY: A SERENDIPITOUS MOMENT OF RECONCILIATION AMONGST REFUGEES

A talk about cultural patterns of communication and family structures was co-originated by Anna, an Anglo facilitator who works with an agency that provides support and counselling for refugees in an Australian city. Three African bicultural workers were invited to be part of a session on cultural awareness. However, 15 participants from different African countries turned up unexpectedly.

Anna explains:

> As people were arriving I noticed more and more migrants coming into the room who I had never met before. A number of the newcomers came in and sat up front with the bicultural workers. This felt really strange – about 14 of them.
>
> The discussion started. A couple of the newcomers gave me a prod when they wanted to speak. Flomo [a man from the Congo, one of the leaders in the group] went first . . . . Grace [a Tutsi woman from Rwanda] said it was in conditioning that a male should speak first. She went on to describe the terrible problems she had to bear in Rwanda and the difficulties of settling in Australia. One African woman rather abruptly told her to just get on with her life in Australia, and Grace answered, 'How can I do that?' The discussion started to focus on the political events in Rwanda between the Hutu and the Tutsis [many atrocities were committed in 1994].
>
> I didn't feel comfortable to intervene. I was very conscious of the fact that I was the only white person on the panel, and that a powerful discussion was taking place that I felt I didn't have the right to stop just because it wasn't on the agenda. As the convening facilitator I could have gone back to the ground rules. It was turning into a heated debate. The audience just watched dumbfounded. I was feeling anxious about how to verbally respond to the situation, so to make myself more physically present I leant forward on my seat.
>
> Another member of the panel was Peter [a Hutu man from the Congo]. French was his mother tongue. He suddenly spoke, and wanted to speak in his own language, French. (As always with these groups there were so many bilingual speakers.) Grace, who was still upset, volunteered to translate. I was so surprised and moved as he launched into a passionate apology to the Tutsi people for the atrocities

that were committed by his people. And it was Grace who was saying his words in English. There was such powerful energy in the room. Suddenly the racial tension within the group ended and shifted into a deeply moving silence.

So following my instincts worked. I am so glad that I didn't do the ground rules thing as that would have capped a most extraordinary moment.

At the end I thanked everyone for attending.

This story illustrates the need for 'holding space' and 'listening to intuition' versus intervention; going to the ground rules and control versus *laissez-faire*. A curious and respectful attitude when working with multicultural groups is more important than vast amounts of cultural knowledge; however a background and awareness of communication and values across cultures is vital. Somehow in this group everyone listened to Grace's tragic story, ie 'reflective dialogue'. Even though some were not empathic and suggested she should move on, somehow it triggered empathy in Peter and he had the courage to speak out and apologize. He was not the perpetrator, but as with restorative justice processes, an apology from a representative may be a major contributor to the healing process.

Reconciliation and healing between cultures within a country: African examples

You'd better eat the bitterness before it eats you.

Chinese saying

As mentioned above, there are many types of reconciliation: political, economic, educational and personal. But for each type, injustices and violations need to be acknowledged, feelings vented, heard and honoured, so that healing and reconciliation may be enhanced. Processes are needed for managing the guilt, saying and being sorry, healing of memories (though not forgetting) and moving on from 'us' and 'them' to become just 'us'; moving from 'human wrongs' to 'human rights and responsibilities'.

The journey of encounter with the 'other' is also an encounter with oneself which can teach us a great deal.

Father Michael Lapsley, Cape Town

Some say that we all hold within us the powers to be wonderfully loving and compassionate and the powers to be incredibly evil. Certainly the Milgram experiments indicated this (Milgram, 1963). Luckily for us all, for most of the time the former is most likely. Many countries, however, have a history of institutionalized oppression, racism and violence of some sectors of the population, including Australia, the United States, the United Kingdom, South Africa, Tibet and Brazil, while others have experienced genocide of certain ethnic groups, as happened in Rwanda.

Below I describe a workshop developed by, and two films which focus on the work of, the Truth and Reconciliation Commission (TRC) in South Africa. To set the scene and give context to the remarkable healing work in South Africa, I recommend the following films, which made a profound impact on me around the time I visited South Africa.

Documentary video: *Long Night's Journey into Day*

The documentary *Long Night's Journey into Day* describes post-Apartheid South Africa, and gives an intimate look at a country's attempts to heal itself with truth (rather than vengeance) as the balm. It shows the country trying to forge a lasting peace after 40 years of notorious racial segregation. The documentary studies the TRC set up by the post-apartheid, democratic government to consider amnesty for perpetrators of crimes committed under the Apartheid regime. It tracks the story of just a handful of the 10,000 requests for amnesty that came before the TRC. In exchange for absolute truth about their activities and human rights abuses, perpetrators could earn amnesty for the crimes they committed before Apartheid collapsed in 1994. It shows hearings where murderers met the surviving family members of their victims in four cases. The stories in the documentary illustrate the universal themes of conflict, forgiveness and renewal. The TRC raised some of the most profound moral and ethical questions facing the world today: questions about justice, truth, forgiveness, redemption, and the ability of brutalized and brutalizing individuals to subsequently coexist in harmony.

> History despite its wrenching pain cannot be unlived, but if faced with courage cannot be lived again … We have to face it because we can't let it happen again.
>
> Tobia Ungely

See www.irisfilms.org/longnight/index.htm

Film: *Red Dust*

The film *Red Dust* is based on a novel by Gillian Slovo (2002) and directed by Tom Hooper (2005), and goes a long way towards explaining the healing philosophy and methodology behind the TRC. It illustrates the ground rules of the commission: total disclosure, complete honesty, no holds barred. It solves a murder mystery, but leaves open and raw the wounds suffered by its victims, and shows how the hurt suffered under apartheid may be forgiven, but never truly 'resolved.' See www.infilm. com.au/reviews/reddust.htm

Other resources

California newsreel produces a variety of videos on diversity training, multiculturalism and social change. See www.newsreel.org/

Other feature movies which touch on the theme of racism include *The Rabbit-Proof Fence, Cry Freedom, Mississippi Burning, Malcolm X, The Color Purple* and *A Dry White Season.*

Reconciliation in South Africa

Perhaps the country that has led the way for the world in reconciliation work is South Africa. I visited Johannesburg and Cape Town for the first time in 2005, and was immediately impressed by the spirit of the people I met who worked in the area of HIV/AIDS (see my website, www.hogans. id.au) and those who worked for reconciliation to build a safer and more equitable 'Rainbow Nation'. Dr Frans Cilliers and his colleagues in the Department of Industrial and Organizational Psychology of the University of South Africa have facilitated the Robben Island Diversity Experience (RIDE), based around the old prison where Nelson Mandela was held. This has been presented six times over the last few years (Pretorius, 2004) and has been attended by organizational development consultants, psychologists and facilitators. It is based on a model developed by the Tavistock Institute in the United Kingdom, called a 'group relations working conference'. For more information see Cilliers (2004).

Scenario planning on a country-wide basis

> The best metaphors are often the ones participants create themselves.
>
> (Deal and Masman, 2003: 16)

The purpose of scenario planning is to identify possible futures or scenarios, both good and bad. It differs from the search conference process which invites participants only to plan for 'desirable futures' (Hogan, 2003). The scenario planning process was developed by Royal Dutch/Shell in the 1970s to enable managers to develop strategies towards desirable futures, and plan to avoid undesirable futures, or at least have contingency plans in case the latter occur.

The process was used to plan on a country-wide basis for the first time by Adam Kahane, the then head of scenario planning with Royal

Dutch/Shell, at the now famous Mont Fleur workshops held in Cape Town, South Africa in 1991 after the collapse of the apartheid regime. Participants comprised a microcosm of South Africa's cultural diversity and political extremes – 'a microcosm of the future South Africa' (Kahane, 2002) – and at the time people who literally hated each other. They told stories of left-wing revolution, right-wing revolts and free market utopias which were reported as 'fabulously liberating'. The first brainstorming exercise generated 30 stories, which were narrowed down to four over a period of months. The first three were negative scenarios to avoid, and the last was cited as most desirable (Kahane, 2004: 23):

● 'The ostrich', illustrating a non-representative white government sticking its head in the sand to try to avoid a negotiated settlement with the black majority.
● 'The lame duck', representing a prolonged transition with a weak government that satisfies no one.
● 'Icarus', where radical, left-wing and dangerous overspending on social welfare would bankrupt the economy.
● 'The flight of the flamingos', in which the transition is successful because all the key building blocks are put in place so that all members of the society rise slowly and together.

The catchy scenario metaphor titles were easy to remember, and were used subsequently by politicians and economists. In this context they made a significant contribution to the development of governance in South Africa. I believe it is significant for the facilitation profession that the processes we use are transferable to country-wide situations, and as a result may contribute significantly to solving 'tough problems' and ending conflict. The scenario planning process was not as successful in Colombia, the Basque area of Spain and Ecuador. But then the timing of these workshops within the history of the conflict may have been very different.

What are the critical factors for success? Adam Kahane, the facilitator of the Mont Fleur workshops, commented, 'We have to choose an open way over a closed way' (2004: 129–30), and made 10 suggestions which are useful for facilitators and participants alike:

1. Pay attention to your state of being and to how you are talking and listening. Notice your own assumptions, reasons, contradictions anxieties, prejudices and projections.
2. Speak up. Notice and say what you are thinking, feeling and wanting.
3. Remember that you don't know the truth about anything. When you think that you are absolutely certain about the ways things are, add 'in my opinion' to your sentence. Don't take yourself too seriously.

4. Engage with and listen to others who have a stake in the system. Seek out people who have different, even opposing, perspectives from yours. Stretch beyond your comfort zone.
5. Reflect on your own role in the system. Examine how what you are doing or not doing is contributing to things being the way they are.
6. Listen with empathy. Look at the system through the eyes of the other. Imagine yourself in the shoes of the other.
7. Listen to what is being said not just by yourself and others, but through all of you. Listen to what is emerging in the system as a whole. Listen with your heart. Speak from your heart.
8. Stop talking. Camp out beside the questions and let answers come to you.
9. Relax and be fully present. Open up your mind and heart and will. Open yourself up to being touched and transformed.
10. Try out these suggestions and notice what happens. Sense what shifts in your relationships with others, with yourself, and with the world. Keep on practising.

The suggestions are not easy to follow all the time, but are useful for facilitators and participants to practise every day. Quakers suggest that we should bring our prejudices against those we violently disagree with to the forefront of our brains, then mentally 'bathe them in light' and cast a space of respect and love around them. In that way we can listen and act from the best side of ourselves.

Memories of fear, distrust and humiliation are alive and well in many groups. As facilitators we have to plough the ground to create neutral common ground that is safe to walk on. We need to listen to pain, suffering and anger with the fullest attention of our being.

I believe the use of facilitation methods on a country-wide basis is a significant shift in the development of the facilitation profession. Our democracies are in trouble, and we need to develop different ways of 'doing democracy'. This movement is well under way, and the facilitation profession has a great deal to offer. For more ideas see *Deliberative Democracy Handbook* (Gastil and Levine, 2005) and *Working Together* (Government of Western Australia, 2006).

9

Language and silence

Introduction

> 'When I use a word, it means just what I choose it to mean ... neither more nor less,' Humpty Dumpty said in rather a scornful tone.
>
> Lewis Carroll, *Through the Looking Glass*

An awareness and understanding of language and the place that silence plays in communication is important when facilitating cross-culturally. This chapter discusses:

- the relationship between language and culture;
- concepts that do not always translate well across cultures;
- speech patterns;
- different interpretations of concepts across cultures;
- different meanings and uses of silence;
- communicating with interpreters and translators.

> Meanings are in people not in words.
>
> Professor Russel Martin, www.storiesatwork.com

The relationship between language and culture

Edward Sapir and Benjamin Whorf first wrote about the connections between language and culture over half a century ago when they proposed the 'linguistic relativity hypothesis'. They suggested that people's habitual thought patterns and ways of perceiving the environment and the world are conditioned by the structures, categories and distinctions available to them in their native language. As a result when people from different cultures meet, their world views will vary according to how differently their languages are semantically and grammatically structured (Trudgill, 2003).

UNESCO reported in 2006 that more than half of the some 6,000 languages spoken in the world today may disappear by the end of the century. The organization announced its efforts to safeguard languages by aiming at ensuring greater diversity on the Internet and in official texts.

> When a language dies it is a vision of the world that disappears ... Language is much more than an instrument, considerably more than a tool. In structuring our thoughts, in coordinating our social relations and in building our relationship with reality, it constitutes a fundamental dimension of the human being.
>
> UNESCO Director-General Koichiro Matsuura, speech on International Mother Language Day, 22 February 2006

Code switching

Code switching is a term in linguistics referring to alternating between one or more languages or dialects in mid-sentence between people who have more than one language in common. Sometimes the switch lasts only for a few sentences, or even a single phrase. The switch is commonly made according to the subject of discourse, but may be for a variety of other reasons such as the mood of the speaker. (For example, a person might swear only in French.) Code switching often occurs in bilingual communities or families: for instance, Spanish-speaking migrant families in the United States might speak a mixture of Spanish and English words known as 'Spanglish'.

Code switching also occurs within a particular language. For instance, people would probably not use the same words or phrases when speaking to a superior (an elder, teacher, advisor or supervisor) as they would use when speaking to their friends in an informal atmosphere (encyclopedia. laborlawtalk.com/Code-switching).

The term is also now used to describe the ability to change behaviour patterns so that they are congruent with the people and context you are in. For example, a teenager might be very able to code switch between the acceptable behaviours with his family, his peer group and school. Those who are not adept at this may be seen as rude or deviant.

Understanding

If English is the dominant language of a workshop, the participants with better English (but whose first language/s are not English) have greater status and often wish to show their skills to the rest of the group. However, if you are working through interpreters this may become confusing for them and you. The less linguistically able may feel embarrassed to show their lack of understanding. You cannot tell whether participants understand by their body language (as this may be ambiguous). Closed questions like 'Do you understand?' invariably get nods of agreement. We need to provide participants with safe opportunities for clarification and requests for repetition or elaboration. Say, for instance, 'Are there any areas you would like me to repeat?' or 'Are there any areas you would like me to explain again?' Note that simple constructions are easiest to translate. Try to avoid questions like 'Would you like me to repeat or clarify anything?'

Place the participants in a knowing position by saying things like, 'I am relatively new to xxx culture. Can you tell me from your perspective on …?' and 'Can you help me by …?' For small group work it is important to reinforce the practicality for participants to speak in their common mother tongue (if there is one) as it is more inclusive.

Need for lexicons

There is a need for bilingual and or multilingual lexicons (the vocabulary of a branch of knowledge) to help interpreters. For example, common words and phrases in the world of facilitation and development include:

being present or centred, holding space, ownership, empowerment, accountability, partnership, participation and transparency, consultation, process(es), outcomes, commitment, collaboration, dysfunctional, sustainable

If there are many facilitators it is important that they are consistent in their use of terminology. Table 9.1 shows a template for a bilingual lexicon.

Table 9.1 Example of an English–Lao lexicon

English term	English definition	Lao term in Lao language	Lao definition in Lao language

Some technical words do not have a direct translation, so in many countries the English term is becoming internationally used. For instance in Nepali a 'theodolite' is called a 'theodolite'. Still include these words in the lexicon.

Language is constantly changing, and new words are devised to express new concepts which can and do change the way we think and behave.

Sound volume

It is important that people can hear one another clearly in workshops. External distracters like fans and air conditioners can seriously impede understanding. In large groups (over 40 people) it is necessary to use a microphone. It is important to have a number of cordless or radio microphones to pass around the participants.

Proverbs

Proverbs are phrases which contain some teaching or advice. They are one way in which values are passed from one generation to another. Professional interpreters are often taught proverbs as part of their language training, but untrained interpreters may not know sayings or proverbs from your culture. In some workshops you can ask participants for local proverbs as a way of stimulating discussion about issues that are pertinent to the workshop.

> We asked people to give us examples of lots of Myanmar proverbs or stories. This works well because local people like to tell us these. Especially during gender workshops we use the list of proverbs they generate to show how they are discriminatory against women, such as 'the sun does not rise if the hen crows'. So we joke and say, 'Well even if the cock crows at 2.00 am the sun does not rise,' and we all laugh.
>
> Myanmar gender development worker

A collection of local proverbs in workshops can be very illuminating and used as discussion triggers about cultural similarities and differences. For example,

> 'No need to know the person, only the family' is a Chinese saying implying the importance of family over the individual.

> 'It takes a whole village to raise a child' is an African expression.

> 'The nail that stands out gets hit' is an Asian saying illustrating that nonconformity and individualism are not tolerated.

Resources

See Lonely Planet (2004) and Howard (2003).

Use of slang

Generally speaking it is important for facilitators to avoid the use of slang words and expressions, as the interpreter is unlikely to have a vocabulary of slang words. However, for bilingual facilitators it can be a useful way of gaining entry into a group. In Myanmar facilitators from Yangon, the capital, may feel just as alien when visiting ethnic groups as foreign development workers from outside:

> The trouble with working with minority groups in Myanmar is that they see a division between 'them' and 'us'. They don't like strangers and we are strangers to them. We are mainstream Myanmar and they blame us for some of the things that have been done to them. So we have to work around and find our common problems, but tactfully … we must not use any English words … that makes them feel very uncomfortable indeed. We have to be so careful when we speak regarding intonation and tone … we have to be so much more polite in our language (they find people like me from the city of Yangon sound very brash).
>
> Development worker in Kachin state, Myanmar

Talking about emotions

In many cultures it is not culturally acceptable to cry or show emotion. However, in Latino cultures emotions are very open. If I want to tap into feelings about a topic I find it useful to use pictures of emotions, like *The Bears*, *Koala Company* and S*tones Have Feelings Too* from Innovative Resources (see page Chapter 6). These act as legitimate conversation triggers and the interpreter can then fill in the fine details.

Concepts do not always translate across cultures

One key issue is that the field of 'management' is only about 50 years old, and facilitation only 25 years old. New terms have been developed, often in English, to describe new concepts and ideas: for example 'the web' and 'the internet'. These words do not exist in other languages. Indeed a concept itself may be alien: for example 'customer service' is neither understood nor valued in some countries (this is explained later); 'liberal' and 'dictatorial' have no direct equivalent in Bahasa Malaysia.

Words and phrases have different meaning in different cultural contexts. If there are no similarities of context between the world of the facilitator and that of participants, communication and mutual understanding may be a problem. One example is an article in the 17 July 1997 issue of the *St Paul Pioneer Press* (from Minnesota, USA), entitled 'Translating cancer'.

One of the frustrating obstacles that oncologists have long faced when trying to help St Paul's large Hmong community is that there is no word for cancer in Hmong, or even a concept of it in their homeland of Lao PDR. The Hmong immigrants had also had little or no access to Western medicine, and cancer deaths or incidences were often attributed to other causes. Many Hmong patients refused treatment. The physicians later discovered to their surprise and horror that interpreters were struggling with ways to describe unfamiliar concepts (germs, viruses and so on) and as a result they often told patients things like, 'We'd like to put fire in you' when trying to persuade a patient to undergo radiation therapy (www. health-exchange.net/translation_meaning.html).

Self 'I' and 'we'

In a collectivist society, people are taught from an early age to put the good of the group first, and 'group rights and responsibilities' are more important than 'individual rights'. The concept of 'self' as a separate entity is different from the concept of 'self' in more individualistic societies, where being different is rewarded. This has a significant impact on the ways in which:

- facilitators introduce themselves;
- facilitators ask participants to introduce themselves;
- participants view one another as they introduce themselves.

In collective societies people do not like to be singled out for extra praise, nor do they wish to 'boast' about their achievements.

> At school we were not taught to be individuals. It was not proper to talk about our achievements. For example, currently we are conducting interviews with high-achieving women who are alumni of the most prestigious girls' school in Malaysia. We will have to interview 'significant others' because they will not speak about their own achievements.
>
> Asma Abdullah, Malaysian facilitator, Kuala Lumpur

This is why it is better in collective cultures to use introductions about the naming or meaning of names, family connections and place of birth rather than achievements.

Thank you

In the United Kingdom one of the first things I remember being instilled into me by my mother was the need to say 'please' and 'thank you'. If these golden words were not said, I was regarded as being rude. However, in many countries, such as Nepal, India and Iraq, the word 'thank you' is not used as frequently. For example, if shop assistants serve you, they are paid to do this service, so you do not have to say 'please' and 'thank you'. You only use these words in circumstances of a large gift or very special service. In Myanmar, someone said, 'If I do you a favour I do not expect you to say thank you, but you owe me a favour at a later date. We often think Westerners are so superficial the way you keep saying "thank you" for everything.'

It is important how much these basic differences in actions can cause offence. It is useful for facilitators to know about language constructions and usage.

Health concepts

Concepts of 'health', 'illness', 'depression' and 'mental health' vary from culture to culture. Some indigenous groups do not have words for or understand issues of germs and viruses. Likewise concepts of appropriate treatment vary. It may include rituals for appeasing the spirits or ancestors. It is useful to invite interpreters to help find appropriate words for terms like HIV and AIDS. Some examples of specific terms I have encountered that that have caused difficulties follow.

Customer service

A survey revealed that government staff in an Asian country not surprisingly had a different interpretation of the concepts of 'customer', 'client' and 'service' than the Australian development workers in the country. The idea that government workers 'serve' the people is a concept at the heart of democracy. In an oligarchic and hierarchical society, government officials have intrinsically higher status than the rest of the community. As a result of a superior mindset they see themselves as doing villagers a favour rather than providing a service. This may impact negatively on the way in which some government officials interact with villagers. It would be impossible to change mindsets, but it might be possible to influence behaviours. For example, helping behaviours can be developed by:

- the provision of prompt, up-to-date, accurate and consistent information about the project;
- ensuring that all project staff in all locations and at all levels *and* village authorities give consistent answers to the common questions of villagers;
- ensuring that the attitude and behaviour of project staff show that they care about helping villagers participate in the project.

Land owner

In English the term 'land owner' is used for someone who has bought some land. Even though that land is regarded as 'belonging' to the person, in fact in probably all countries the land belongs to the state (or crown) and may be reclaimed if necessary. In some countries the term 'land owner' is replaced by the term 'land user'.

Time orientation

The Quechua language of Peru uses orientations of time differently from English speakers. The Quechua speakers visualize the future as being behind, as it cannot be seen, and the past as in front, as it can be seen (Samovar and Porter, 2004).

Speech patterns

It is best not to use:

- long complex sentences with multiple clauses;
- technical or scientific jargon without explanation;
- slang such as 'You must be joking' or 'See yeh later';
- metaphors unless you explain them;
- idioms such as 'It's raining cats and dogs';
- euphemisms like 'Where is the loo?';
- sports terminology such as 'We need to get some runs on the board';
- contractions like 'comin', 'bye' and 'oughta';
- abbreviations without explaining what they stand for;
- acronyms such as 'I'm going to finish ASAP' (Axtell, 1995).

One facilitator used many colloquialisms, for example, 'This organization needs to identify "windows of opportunity".' The interpreter had never heard the phrase before, and translated, 'This organization needs more windows.'

Rephrase clichés. For example:

- instead of 'at this moment in time' use 'now';
- instead of 'window of opportunity' use 'good chance' or simply 'opportunity';
- instead of 'level playing field' use 'everyone has the same opportunities'.

Use simple vocabulary and short sentences; break your sequence at logical points, at the end of a phrase, clause or sentence. There is a happy medium. If you stop after very short phrases, the interpreter may not be able to gauge the full meaning.

Put inflection into your voice. Even if participants cannot understand your words they can pick up your feelings such as enthusiasm and concern.

If you ramble and use a very long sentence, go back and say, 'In summary what I am trying to say is ...' To make a specific point, slow down, stress the key words, or repeat. 'This point is important, so I'll say it again' or 'Let me just repeat this point.'

Discourse or sentence markers

Use discourse or sentence markers to signal that you are moving to a different stage in your talk. For example:

> At this stage I would like to introduce you to a process called ...
> I must repeat this as this point is so important.
> In summary ...
> The reasons for XXX are as follows. First, ...
> Let us look at the situation from both sides, first of all from the perspective of the villagers, then from the perspective of the administrators.
> This process is divided into two stages. First, ... Second, ...
> Now we have finished part one of the workshop, let us move on to part two.

Opening the space for questions

Participants often have to feel safe before asking questions or offering opinions. Asking a question can be embarrassing. People are reluctant to show their ignorance or to feel stupid. In some cultures questioning is actively discouraged at school. Orchestrate the generation of questions. Signal at the beginning that you welcome questions, by saying, 'All questions are useful', or 'There is no such thing as a stupid question.' This gives participants permission to ask basic questions.

Check understanding

Watch the body language of participants (and the interpreter) all the time. If the interpreter does not understand something, simplify. Look for synonyms and explain your idea in a different way. Repeating the same words louder does not work. Remember, 'Only a fool keeps doing the same thing expecting different results.'

Be careful not to make assumptions. Closed questions (that require a 'yes' or 'no' answer) like 'Do you understand?' are likely to be greeted with silence. Nobody wants to feel stupid. More importantly, in some cultures it is the participants' responsibility to understand, and it is regarded as their fault if they do not. To point out to a teacher that they do not understand indicates that the teacher is at fault and did not explain something properly, and results in the teacher losing face.

Alternatives include paired discussions or 'buzz' groups: ask participants to talk to a partner for three minutes to generate questions. Then invite each pair to put a question forward. Or ask each pair to write down questions on Post-it notes. Explain that you will shuffle them so they will remain anonymous.

Another idea is to ask the group to summarize the main points. 'Can you summarize what you have to do? Let's hear one idea from each volunteer.'

Ask the interpreter to repeat questions from the participants (if necessary in both languages) to ensure they have heard correctly, and to ensure that everyone is tuned in to listening to the answer. During question and answer time, allow only one person to speak at a time, as background noise will be distracting for all concerned.

Facilitator questions

Keep questions simple and straightforward. Don't say 'You've done it, haven't you?' but 'Have you done it yet?' It is better to ask many short questions than one convoluted one. At times you may find that some participants side-step questions by giving obtuse answers. If this happens, repeat, 'My question was ...' or 'My point was ...' Or think for a moment and ask yourself if you need to ask the same question in private, or of someone else. The 'side-stepper' may be sending you a message or might just be being obstructive. (See Strachan, 2006.)

Negative questions

Do not use negative questions such as 'Is this not true?', 'You didn't complete the questionnaire, did you?' or 'Does anyone *not* understand?'

Commands and requests

In some countries where there have been authoritarian governments, the language structures people use may cause offence. Under certain regimes, people only hear commands, such as those from a boss to a worker, or from a teacher to a student, implying that there is no choice. If such people go to other countries to study and say 'You must give me this book', a facilitator is likely to assume the person is being rude. So inductions are required to re-teach them how to make polite requests as opposed to imperatives.

Use of idioms in English

Table 9.2 is a dialogue written by Ian Gordon, New Zealand (unpublished) to illustrate the many ways in which English speakers use the verb 'to give' colloquially. On the left is the imaginary dialogue and on the right is the explanation of the meaning. Where possible, do not use colloquialisms.

Table 9.2   The word 'give'

	Dialogue using verb to give	Explanation
Alan	They tell me you give a lot of time to gardening.	They tell me you like gardening.
Mary	Now don't give me that.	Are you joking?
Alan	You haven't given it up, surely?	Have you stopped?
Mary	I gave it away last year.	I stopped last year.
Alan	You just gave up?	You just stopped.
Mary	Give over, will you! I gave in.	Listen to me, will you! I stopped.
Alan	What gives in the garden?	What does your garden contain?
Mary	It's all given over now to lawns and shrubs.	It's all covered now by lawns and shrubs.
Alan	And yet I hear it given out that you used to give out vegetables to everyone.	And I hear it being said that you used to distribute vegetables to everyone.
Mary	That was last year, my enthusiasm gave out and the garden just had to give way.	That was last year, my enthusiasm diminished and the garden just had to make room (for other things).
Alan	And what gives now?	What's happening now?
Mary	I'm giving all my spare time to the house.	I'm spending all my spare time working on the house.

Numbers

Long numbers can be confusing. Repeat them or write them on a whiteboard.

Use of tones in English

We tend to think that English is not a tonal language in the same way that Chinese is, but we use tones for expression, and they can give a totally different meaning. Try out the different tones to accompany the verb 'to see'.

I'll *see* you tomorrow (declarative statement of fact)
I'll *see* you tomorrow? (question)
I'll *see* you tomorrow! (excitement)

I'll *see* you tomorrow (demandingly)
I'll *see* you tomorrow (resignedly)
I'll *see* you tomorrow (conspiratorially)
I'll *see* you tomorrow (invitingly)
I'll *see* you tomorrow (sexually)
I will *see* you tomorrow (evenly spaced words, flat intonation like a machine)

Assumptions

Even if you do not hear English being spoken, do not assume people around you cannot understand. So be careful of aside comments to interpreters.

Summaries

Summarize and repeat what you have been saying using different terms. Be diplomatic, saying for instance, 'I know I sometimes speak very fast, so perhaps it would be helpful if I repeat the five main points' (Axtell, 1995).

Different cultural interpretations of concepts

English and Chinese interpretation of 'crisis'

I like to use the different concepts of crisis as a teaching tool. Sometimes we experience a 'crisis' during group work or during transitions. In the English language the term 'crisis' has totally negative connotations. (In Bahasa Indonesia 'krisis' and in Vietnamese 'khunghoang' also have negative interpretations.) The Chinese see 'crisis' as offering two meanings. It is written with two symbols which represent 'opportunity' and 'danger' (see my website: www.hogans.id.au), so for them crisis is like a two-sided coin. We can choose how to respond. For example, in danger mode: 'Oh, this is awful! How could they make me redundant? This is the end of everything for me. I can't do anything about this.' But in opportunity mode: 'Well, this feels horrible. I cannot believe it. I'm angry and hurt. But, maybe there is a chance here to try out something different. I've always wanted to try ... but I didn't want to give up my secure job because of my family commitments. Now may be I could give it a try.'

Different meanings and uses of silence

Silence is used differently across cultures in its duration, frequency, meaning and intent. There are different types, degrees and textures to silence. It is a very complex concept. We need to be careful how we use it and how we interpret it. Silence is not simply a lack of speech; it replaces words and invites turn taking, reflection, or termination of communication. Silence may be used as a means of encouraging discourse or freezing someone out.

Many of the books written on facilitation describe silence in participants as a negative, as 'not participating', having nothing to say and not 'playing the game'. The literature is full of topics like 'How to get silent participants to talk'.

Nurturance of silence by facilitators: silence is golden

In Filipino culture (Goldberger *et al*, 1996), there are two sayings:

> Speech is silver, but silence is golden.
> Silent waters run deep.

These sayings are not trying to keep individuals quiet. What they are saying is that silence reflects wisdom and strength. The practice of keeping silence is known in Sanskrit as *Moana* or *Mouna*, and is actually a yoga practice in its own right. Again in this context it is linked to strength.

For facilitators, silence in participants can indicate that there is a psychological shift taking place, Gill Baxter pointed out to me (in 2006). As facilitators we need to honour it, allow it to grow. We must not kill it by our own need to fill the silent space. It takes facilitation strength to 'hold the silence'.

Linguistic uses of silence by facilitators

Linguistically, silence is a major necessity at the end of sentences for mental processing and 'catch up' by listeners whose major languages are other than English. We often forget the complicated mental processes that are happening for speakers, listeners and interpreters. At the end of process instructions a prolonged silence can give participants time to reflect on what has been said, and to think of clarifying questions.

Silence exercise: Stimulating discussion about silence

Robert Chambers suggested a 'Silence exercise' (2002: 178–79) to enable facilitators and participants to discuss silence by experiencing it. It may need a little courage and determination for some, and takes less than five minutes.

Stages

1. The facilitator introduces the subject of talking and silence, and how in workshop situations facilitators can inadvertently disempower participants by their felt need to keep talking, to fill in silences with words. Empowerment means learning to 'sit down and shut up'.
2. The facilitator sits down and says nothing for one minute. Often participants are embarrassed and may show this by giggling. Some may talk to a partner, or some may encourage the facilitator to stand up again. But the speech and initiative are passed to them.

For a more structured exercise on silence see Rifkin (1999).

Tapping into the 'great silence'

> Meditation is as natural to the spirit as breathing is to the body.
>
> John Main, Benedictine monk

Meditation has been part of many different spiritual traditions across the world. The Native American Ohiyesa, a Santee Dakota physician, has been quoted as saying of traditional Native American culture, 'Each soul must meet the morning sun, the new sweet earth and the Great Silence, alone …' (quoted in Kaplan, 2002: 188). The stillness and silence of meditation can be so useful for all age groups. I was impressed in Lao PDR when I watched children at a local community centre, where among many other activities we trained children to be clowns. We would facilitate the noisiest clowning activities with them, but before they left to go to their homes, the Lao staff always invited them to sit and meditate to calm down. I admit I used to open my eyes to see what was happening, but I always saw them quietly and peacefully sitting with eyes firmly closed, even the tiny four-year-olds.

Gathered silence

The Religious Society of Friends or Quakers use the power of 'gathered silence', where people sit in stillness to attend to their inner deeper knowledge. When they speak it is said to be out of the spirit.

Story: Quaker silence, the night after 11 September 2001

I recall 12 September 2001, the day after '9/11', lecturers were standing talking in corridors, and no one could concentrate on work. There was also the issue of how to discuss what had happened with students. I was scheduled to teach a postgraduate facilitation class that night. All day I was wondering what to do. Some postgraduate facilitation students were due to demonstrate some processes as part of their assessment. I knew this would not be possible or appropriate.

At the last minute I decided to play the CD of John Lennon's 'Give peace a chance'. (I always had some form of music playing when they arrived.) There were many very strong women in the group who were dedicated to peace and environmental movements. Many were clearly distressed. I suggested we should sit in a circle, and that individuals might like to speak only when and if they felt moved to speak, as in the Quaker tradition. I waited for a response, and they readily agreed to the process.

I noted everyone placed their chairs very closely together. For some time we sat in silence. Then slowly people spoke. I was struck by the many different levels of interpretations and responses to the event. There was no judgement or discussion. There were long periods of productive silence too. The group was brought so much closer together that night.

Margo, a student, later wrote:

> The realization of the impact of the planes crashing into the Twin Towers was enormous. I had been involved in the peace movement and working for social justice for years. I am also married to someone from Israel and had visited countries in the Middle East, so the impact was great. It was as though 'innocence and hope' died with this event. I walked into the classroom and 'Give peace a chance' was playing. I became very angry. I wanted to call out, 'Peace has just been killed, why are you playing this song!' It seemed to trivialize the event, though I could see what Chris was trying to do. Chris suggested we sit in a circle of silence. It was very powerful.
>
> It probably took an age for anyone to speak, but sitting together in silence allowed us to sit together in grief. It allowed each of us to 'drop down' into what we were feeling and then gradually each person had something to say. I remember expressing my sadness that everyone who had worked so hard to achieve peace in the Middle East would be back to where they started.
>
> Each person had something different to share. One of the class members was not there because her brother worked in the Twin Towers and she was still trying to contact him (thankfully he was alive and well). As a process, it was totally appropriate. I think it could be used in any 'shock, change, grief' situation. It seemed like a privilege to have this opportunity to 'process' the event in a safe place. It did contribute to the 'closeness' of the group.

In hindsight, calmer instrumental music would have been more appropriate. Taking a last-minute decision on such a night was a risk. 'Give peace a chance' is a song of hope, and I was praying that a war would not break out as a result of knee-jerk reactions by the West at that time.

Breaking the 'culture of silence' and conscientization

Paulo Freire (1972) revolutionized education systems not just to teach literacy and numeracy, but to enable the poor to use these skills to look critically at their world and to break out of their 'culture of silence', imposed by their oppressors. They could take control of their own destinies by finding their voices and developing their minds to raise awareness of the abuses of power. Goldberger *et al* (1996: 4) cite the 'structural silence' imposed on some women as 'a position of *not knowing* in which a person feels voiceless, powerless and mindless'.

Silence may be chosen and used strategically as a tactic for protection from dangerous authority, or it may be imposed. As facilitators we need to be mindful of this, and consider whether or not workshops and open discussions are appropriate in some circumstances.

There is often avoidance silence in groups and communities regarding sexual abuse, domestic violence and HIV/AIDS. There is also the avoidance silence after extreme trauma, as in cases like the Holocaust victims and the Korean 'comfort women' whose stories were not told for half a century. It is logical to train long-term resident migrants in facilitation skills to help new arrivals from their own country to overcome problems that are unmentionable, or even not perceived as a 'problem' in that culture. Teams of 'insider' and 'outsider' co-facilitators can achieve a great deal where there is collaboration, rapport and synergy.

We spent a lot of time coming to a definition of domestic violence, and again, the women reflected on their own life experiences to come up with the following: hitting, punching, hurling abusive language, unreasonable jealousy that imprisons a woman in the house, refusal to share money so women could not go out, violent rages where the man hits something else, abusing the children or using them in the violence against women, and so on.

Susan Ferguson, Australian facilitator, domestic violence project
in Brisbane, Australia, 2005

Use of silence by participants

I have noticed that some facilitators from Western countries make assumptions and sometimes unfair judgements about those who stay silent in workshops. This is partly due, I believe, to a mistaken belief that 'participation' requires verbal contributions. However, participants may be participating by actively listening and thinking.

The following ideas are a blend of ideas from my own experiences, and those of Terence Wong (2005) and Colma Keating (in discussions with me in 2006).

Initial contact

When we meet a person for the first time there is often an awkward 'pregnant pause' after the initial 'hello'. So, it is useful if the facilitator can bridge this gap with a simple question (see 'Talking nice', in Chapter 7).

At the beginning of workshops, some participants stay silent out of embarrassment, respect, fear, or a well-learnt strategy to observe the context first before jumping in. The 'wait and see' strategy can be very useful also for foreigners in another country.

Thinking and reflecting

Silence can indicate deep reflection and thought. People need time to think, especially if their first language is not English and that is the language of the workshop. We often pressure people to reply too quickly, and they become 'lost for words' through embarrassment. I met one facilitator who said she helped herself to be comfortable with silence by keeping her hands behind her back and counting with her fingers up to eight before speaking.

In one programme for unemployed youth in Western Australia, a young woman remained almost silent for most of the course. Some weeks after it had finished the coordinator rang me and showed me a detailed letter from the young woman, thanking her for the programme and describing over four well-written pages what she had learnt from being part of the group.

Many people prefer to think in silence, without verbal fill-ins, and become confused if you throw in another question or comment before they have had time to think about an answer to the previous one. Some people's preferred learning style is 'reflector' as opposed to 'activist', 'theorist' or 'pragmatist' (Honey and Mumford, 1992). Participants with a more activist preference will almost always want to process idea aloud.

Experiencing emotion

People often stay quiet when they sink deep into their feelings. If a person is upset or crying, a facilitator needs to be careful about touch. Sitting beside a person or a hand on the shoulder might be appreciated (depending on the cultural context and gender codes of behaviour). Just sitting and politely 'listening' to the person's silence honours the importance of their feelings.

Only speak if you have something new or useful to say

Some cultures teach that you only speak if you have something new or useful, worthwhile or pithy to say. Some individuals prefer to wait and watch.

STORY: A QUIET PARTICIPANT

A university lecturer who claimed to have a facilitative approach went up to one quiet man in a class of postgraduate diploma in adult education students, and stood over him, saying, 'And when are we going to hear from you?' What she did not know was the man in question was extremely bright and articulate, and had high status in the group. He was known and respected by his peers for his thoughtful and provocative comments. Also the class was a cohesive group of mature-age professionals who had studied together for one year. A classmate intervened and said, 'He'll talk when he's got something useful to say.' The class laughed. The lecturer backed off, but had lost face by her top-down confrontational approach.

Steve Hogan, Anglo-Australian postgraduate student

Speak to make your presence felt

In some Western cultures you are almost expected to speak in a group to make your presence felt. If you do not speak you may be perceived as lacking, or even be distrusted.

Gender and status

In some cultures women are taught to stay silent in order to give the men status or 'face'. An African migrant woman in Perth said, 'Even though I feel strong now I still cannot bring myself to speak before the men have spoken.'

Silence as respect

People of lower levels in the hierarchy, or lower class or caste, may be expected to remain silent as a sign of respect to those higher than themselves.

Silence as a meeting norm

In countries like Japan, team members may not discuss an issue in front of a whole meeting group, as the issue has already been thoroughly discussed and decided upon beforehand. The meeting might be being held to publicly ratify the agreement.

Likewise in some Aboriginal groups in Australia, only leaders will speak at meetings and others are required to be present but silent. Decisions may have been made already.

Silence to let others speak

When I worked with a group of Aboriginal people in the north-west of Western Australia, I facilitated a search conference for a group of unemployed youth so that they could have input into the design of their course. The community leader, Vince, stayed silent for the whole time at the back of the room. This really surprised me as he had been so enthusiastic about the project. Afterwards I asked him why he remained silent, and he said 'I was afraid that if I spoke our young people would not speak out. I was trying to help you, Chris.'

Voice as dominance

Some people speak in groups as a way of dominating and showing their power in the group and indirectly silencing others.

Evaluating

Participants may be evaluating what has been said and linking it to their previous experiences. They may decide that the topic is not worth pursuing, or regard the topic as not suitable or safe for open conversation in a group.

Pedagogical silence

The rules of academic writing often stultify students' voices. They are allowed to research and quote from the literature *ad nauseam* but heaven forbid those who might have the audacity to write 'I think ...' Is it any wonder that lecturers complain that it is sometimes hard to get students engaged in discussion? As a result they punish 'silence' by giving marks for participation: saying anything as long as you speak. (Why they do this and how they keep records of it is an anathema to me.) Some lecturers know little about how to encourage dialogue of itself, and are stuck in modes of debate.

Stuck silence

Sometimes a participant may use silence to wait for the facilitator to answer a problem, saying perhaps, 'I don't know how to tell you' or 'I don't know what to do', followed by silence. After an extended pause it may be useful to ask, 'What would you say if you did know?' Follow this by another pause, and wait and let the participants use the silence to think. Or if a more humorous approach is appropriate to lift the person out of their contemplative silence, try, 'Does it start with a, b, c or d?' or 'What would you do if you knew you could not fail?'

Avoidance silence

Avoidance silence is used to defer talking about issues that may be painful, embarrassing or shameful. A participant might keep their voice lowered or ignore the facilitator, or their body language might mean, 'I don't know, I'm not here, please don't ask me.'

The 'Memory box' work in Africa has made a major impact in breaking the silence about HIV/AIDS between family members in a supportive environment. It enables the capturing of the stories of people who are HIV positive as a means of healing trauma and to build resilience in children (Morgan, 2003; Nsitmane, 2005; Lewis, 2006; see also 'Health and Wellbeing' on my website, www.hogans.id.au).

I read a story on the web of a facilitator who had not been properly briefed about the level of conflict in a group. Everyone sat in silence. Eventually the facilitator took a candle from his box, lit it and placed it in the centre of the group. After 20 minutes when the candle died down he suggested that the group had ended and the participants left. Sometimes groups are just not ready to talk. The anger, hurt or pain might be too great, or the environment deemed to be unsafe.

There may be silence in families about ethnicity, as described by Sally Morgan in *My Place* (1988). She was raised by her family in Perth, Western Australia, thinking she was of Indian descent; in the book she describes her search for her Aboriginal identity.

Dutiful, polite attention

A group of participants may be politely listening and giving the facilitator 'respectful attention'. I heard of one facilitator who completely misinterpreted the participants' silent body language and said in a confronting tone, 'Are you listening to me?' As a result he insulted his audience and they were very confused.

Electronic silence

In electronic discussion groups there may be those who remain silent. E-loafers do not do any conversation work and e-lurkers may be seen as peeping toms. E-facilitators need to be aware of them as their silence may lead to distrust, since they are not contributing to the work of the group.

Termination silence

When a facilitator asks 'Is there anything more anyone would like to add?' a silent response may indicate 'No, let's finish this topic and move on' or 'We are tired and are ready for a break.'

Ritual silence

There is the use of ritual silence at funerals and reflexive eulogies. At the beginning of workshops a period of silence may be held to honour someone or some event. In Quaker meetings silence is purposefully used for eventually allowing the spirit to speak.

Assent or dissent

Silence can mean assent or dissent. That is why activists are always urging people to speak up on issues that matter to them. During negotiations, Japanese use silence to consider a proposal carefully. Westerners often assume this means disagreement or rejection, and start to argue or make concessions (Adler, 1997). Silence can also mean dissent, but if overridden by fear it prevents speech in an open forum.

Punitive silence

I recall at primary school, silence was used as a form of punishment. The nuns knew well how to use the 'stony silence' of disapproval. As a result, we did not enjoy it.

Hints for facilitators to 'facilitate or hold silence'

There are times when a facilitator needs to use silence purposefully, but some find it hard to facilitate silence, so here are some strategies:

- Hold one hand behind your back and count to 10 on your fingers.
- Put your forefinger on your mouth and stand very still while you wait for someone to speak.
- Write ideas on a flipchart. There is usually silence while you do this and it slows down conversation and enables everyone to think.
- Pass around a talking stick. The travel time gives silence.
- I ask, 'Are there any questions?' Silence does not mean there are no questions. I wait and wait – and wait. Eventually I play around. I turn my head from side to side and ask the group with my eyes for the same response from each one. This induces laughter and breaks the 'tension of silence' for some. After the laughter, often a question emerges.
- Sit and wait, smile and wait, wait and sit, wait and smile.

Build in time for silent sessions

- One hour's solo walk at lunchtime in beautiful surroundings.
- Fifteen minutes of guided meditation focusing on breathing while sitting in chairs, or sitting/lying on the floor if that is appropriate. For example, you can start by saying slowly and quietly, 'Breathe in, slowly and out and re-lax.'

Remember not to switch modes suddenly. If people have calmed down, do not suddenly switch on loud music, as happened at a workshop I attended. When I felt silent and calm the music was so jarring.

10

Facilitating with interpreters and translators

Introduction

This chapter is important for facilitators who are working with and through interpreters and translators. It includes discussion of:

- the mental processing involved in interpreting;
- choosing and working with an interpreter, the roles and responsibilities of interpreters and facilitators, and ethical issues;
- debriefing experiential learning activities;
- the mutual misunderstanding zone;
- translating documents, accuracy, back translation and readability of handouts.

Types of interpreting

An interpreter is a person who translates the meaning of speech from one language to another verbally, from a 'source' language to a 'target' language. There are two types. In consecutive interpreting, the speaker says a few sentences, pauses, and then the interpreter speaks. With simultaneous interpreting, the interpreter speaks almost at the same time as the speaker.

A translator is a person who translates written work from one language into another. 'No translation is ever perfect because cultures and languages are different' (Nolan, 2005: 3).

Interpreters, translators and facilitators have to concentrate and work very hard. The process is not easy. Some interpreters and translators have had formal training, but many have not. Likewise many facilitators and presenters have little idea of the complexities involved in interpreting. Misunderstandings in communication between people are normal. It is what we do to prevent, intervene where necessary and counteract miscommunication that is important. It helps facilitators, trainers, writers, interpreters and translators if they understand:

- the mental processes involved in interpreting and translating (see Figure 10.1);
- each other's roles and responsibilities and contexts;
- ethical issues;
- that some concepts are not easily translated;
- language and speech patterns.

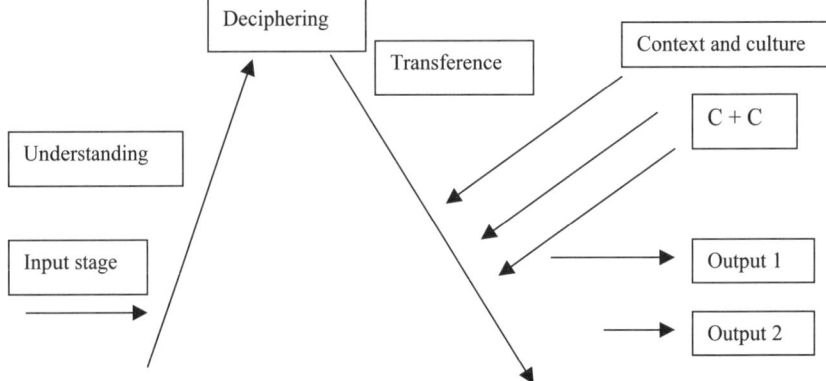

Stages	Explanation
The input stage	The interpreter must have excellent hearing and receive the message preferably without interference from external visual distractions and noise
Understanding	This is the most important stage of the interpreting triangle. Not understanding or misunderstanding will result in a breakdown of communication. It may be avoided to some extent by a thorough briefing beforehand.
Deciphering	At this stage the interpreter gets rid of all the words, retaining the concept, the idea
Transference	The concept or idea is now transferred into the other language
Context & culture	During the transfer stage the meaning (which may be complicated and constrained by cultural context) is clarified by cultural and contextual considerations for the participants
Output 1	The interpreter finds an equivalent idiomatic expression or if no exact word is available must explain in a number of sentences
Output 2	The interpreter transfers the meaning to the participants

Figure 10.1   The interpreting process

Source: adapted from a handout from Auckland Institute of Technology: Centre for the Training of Translators and Interpreters.

Choosing an interpreter

When choosing an interpreter there are a number of things to check (Samovar and Porter, 2004).

Compatibility

There needs to be three-way rapport between the facilitator, the interpreter and the participants. The interpreter may have his/her own way of building rapport which is culturally appropriate and may be different to that of the facilitator. There needs to be compatibility between the facilitator and interpreter. The interpreter needs to have confidence but is not likely to attempt to dominate proceedings (unless you are training him/her to co-facilitate or to take over the facilitation role).

You need to feel comfortable with the interpreter as a person. If you are interviewing interpreters for a job, it is useful to give them a mock role play whereby you invite participants who can speak both languages and who are familiar with the vocabulary in question, for example, on gender issues. Brief the participants to speak only their mother tongue in the role play. At the end, ask participants and the interview panel to complete a checklist regarding interpretation skills and vocabulary (the rational side of decision making). Additionally, give each individual a separate piece of paper on which to write which applicant they are most comfortable with based purely on instinct.

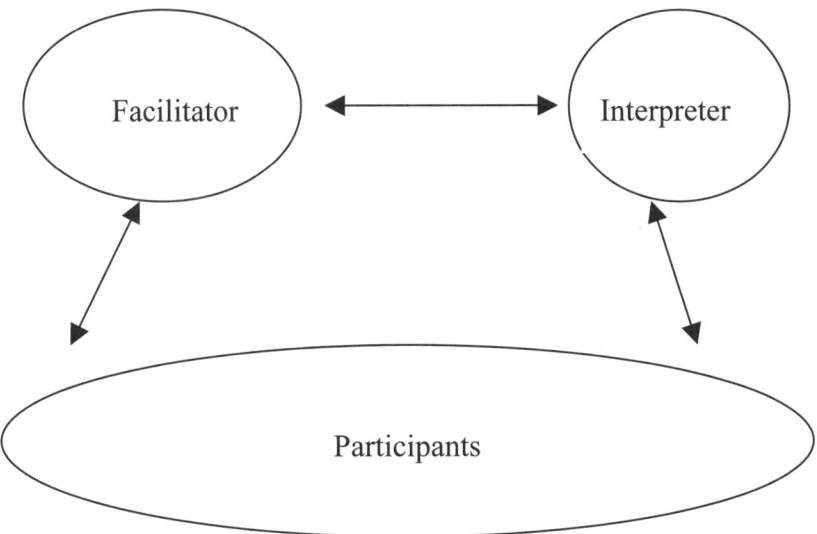

Figure 10.2   Rapport in three directions

Ethnic compatibility

The interpreter preferably needs to be of the same ethnic background as the participants.

Dialect

The interpreter should speak the same dialect/s as the participants.

Specialist knowledge and experience

The interpreter should have some specialized experience in the field under discussion, but should not be over-confident and intervene in ways that detract from his/her main role as interpreter. It may not be possible to find an interpreter with specialist knowledge, but any interpreter needs to be motivated to learn about the field in question, and could work with the facilitator to develop a lexicon of key phrases.

Roles and responsibilities of interpreters

The roles of interpreters are often not as clear-cut as one might expect. Apart from interpreting and translating duties, they often:

- are ambassadors for their countries or ethnic group;
- act as cultural translators;
- have a prior history with many members of the local group, which is very useful (but also may bring hidden obligations);
- have a future with many members of the local group.

Local interpreters not only live in the community, but also are part of it, with their own status, family, employment and political positions. Therefore they may have some personal agenda (whether you like it or not). The impact of this can be minimized by adhering to professional guidelines and duty statements.

   The amount that each interpreter can remember varies enormously, so it is useful if the interpreter if necessary signals the speaker to stop by raising a hand. The interpreter needs to use the first person (direct speech). This means speaking the originator's words as if he/she was saying them; for example, say 'Do you have any questions?', not 'She said, do you have any questions?' The aim is to communicate as directly as possible.

   Interpreters move around the world and meanwhile usage of their mother tongue at home changes. As a result it is important that they admit if they do not understand a new word or a different use of an old term.

   Interpreters may also act as mediators during times of misunderstandings between an individual or groups of foreigners and local organizations. Multilingual mediators, however, like all mediators, should be neutral and not aligned to either group. Mediation is a highly specialized skill.

Roles and responsibilities of facilitators

There is an obligation for facilitators to find out before a workshop whether some participants may need the help of an interpreter and whether a suitably skilled interpreter is available. This ensures a measure of language equity during the workshop.

The facilitator needs to take time to get to know the interpreter and his/her preferred ways of working (and vice versa). Facilitators in foreign countries need to remember that local interpreters/translators will be living in the country or community long after they themselves leave, and therefore they should never be put in a compromising or awkward position. It is important wherever possible for facilitators and interpreters to work as a team and to respect one another's skills and knowledge.

Likewise facilitators may have many roles. They:

- are ambassadors for their countries/cultures;
- act as cultural translators;
- are there to make sure there is cultural safety;
- are process experts.

It is important for facilitators to use simply constructed, compact sentences with one idea per sentence.

> It is important to see the interpreter as your ally, not someone who impedes your facilitation. Most facilitators undermine the importance of building rapport with the interpreter and merely see him/her as a 'tool' to translate whatever they say. Facilitators should first communicate with the interpreter and share with him/her their facilitation style/philosophy, and see the interpreter as an extension of themselves, bridging the communication gap between the facilitator and the group. In this way, remarkable outcomes can be achieved.
>
> Vivienne Teo, Chinese/Eurasian facilitator in Singapore

See the discussion of pre-workshop meetings later on in this chapter.

Interpreters as facilitators

I have found, working alongside local counterparts who are also interpreters, that in the long term it is beneficial to build up their facilitation skills (if they are motivated to do so). This means that after capacity building and experience, provided you have mutual trust and have thoroughly discussed and agreed upon the purpose of the workshop and processes, they can then facilitate in the local language. You can observe and the local facilitator can brief you at breaks on what is happening, and consult with you if things get difficult.

STORY: INTERPRETERS WHO ARE TRAINING AS FACILITATORS IN E. TIMOR

I have found that working with interpreters is marvellous when the interpreter is one of the students of the facilitation course that I conduct with a variety of local NGOs. Then they have an overview of the methodology and are very helpful with understanding what is going on and what should be going on. In these instances I consider them to be co-facilitators. In any case I would go over the procedures with the interpreter beforehand so that he/she can know something of what to expect. With ICA methodologies the most difficult thing for interpreters is to interpret at the level of consciousness we are at. All our processes go through four levels of questioning: objective, reflective, interpretive and then decisional. If the interpretation is not done at the level of reflection, it does not work as well. It is hard when not knowing the language to know if the wording is at the correct level. We can only get the translations back and forth between English and the local language (Tetun, Bahasa Indonesian or Portuguese) and judge as best we can.

Carol Borovic, Anglo-Australian facilitator in East Timor

Roles and responsibilities of the employer

It is important that there is a clear duty statement for the interpreter. This may need to be adjusted as the role or work changes. It is useful to monitor progress and ethical issues if they arise. Inexperienced bilingual staff may take over sessions or not have adequate English vocabulary (see the comments on lexicons above). It is important to use professionally trained interpreters in health areas as there may be dangerous health consequences and legal risks if mistakes are made.

Ethical issues in interpreting

There is a traditional code of ethics used in the training of interpreters which includes the following basic principles:

- Interpret/translate accurately and honestly to the best of your ability, adding and omitting nothing.
- Maintain absolute confidentiality (on private, heath, legal and other issues).
- Be impartial and objective (do not allow feelings and bias to influence translations).
- Maintain personal professional honesty and integrity (and do not take any personal advantage of knowledge gained).
- Undertake only work for which you are qualified (work involving many unfamiliar specialist terms, for example, in the health or legal field, may make interpreting impossible).

- Act always with professional dignity and independence (for example preparing thoroughly, reading beforehand, seeking advice where needed, saying if you do not understand, giving full attention to the work in hand, turning off your mobile phone, and being punctual) (Roberts-Smith, Frey and Bessell-Browne, 1990: 70).

It is important that the interpreter always translates the meaning and intention of the speaker, and everything that is said by the facilitator and the participants. Interpreters should not purposefully omit or add material which changes the meaning of what has been said. One interpreter commented, 'If the speech is very long, I interpret only some of it. After all, the participants want to eat and break for lunch soon!' The interpreter should not omit information. But on the other hand, the facilitator should be in tune with energy levels and should allow time to eat!

Interpreting takes immense concentration and is very tiring. You should not ask an interpreter to interpret for more than 90 minutes to two hours at a time. Interpreters need a proper break time, so do not enlist their help with informal interpreting with participants during a coffee break.

Do not assume your interpreter can work overtime. He/she may have many family commitments.

The following stories illustrate some of these points.

STORY: LAUGH PLEASE

The interpreter told the participants that the facilitator had told a joke which he (the interpreter) did not understand. Instead of asking the speaker to explain again, the interpreter said to the audience, 'The speaker just told a joke and I do not understand it. Please would you help me and laugh now.' The audience broke up into laughter.

The interpreter may have acted in good faith to save the facilitator from losing face. This story is amusing; however, the interpreter had aligned himself with the audience and was not being totally ethical. He knowingly colluded with the participants to deceive the speaker. Again this story emphasizes the need for pre-briefing the interpreter.

STORY: FOOD FOR THOUGHT

A foreign ambassador went to the south of Lao PDR and visited a village. The headman was very honoured, but was somewhat embarrassed by what he regarded as lack of warning to enable adequate food preparations for such a high-ranking visitor. The interpreter with the ambassador recounted the following story:

> The village headman gave a farewell speech saying, 'Ambassador, thank you for visiting our village. We hope you have enjoyed your stay, but next time, please stay longer. We would like to be able to take you to visit our waterfall a few kilometres away. It is so beautiful, the finest in the province. We would also like to be able to prepare for you a big feast of local delicacies like bear paws, giant cat paws and so on.' (He reeled off a long list of delicacies from endangered species.) Knowing the attitude of many foreigners to eating endangered animals, the interpreter changed the headman's words, thinking that the ambassador might be shocked and react inappropriately. He said, 'On your next visit we will prepare many traditional delicacies for you.'

Again the interpreter did not interpret accurately. Perhaps he was worried that the ambassador might not be able to mask his revulsion: controlling body language is one of the most difficult things to do. We cannot *not* communicate! However, the interpreter's job is to interpret the real meaning.

It depends on the circumstances, but interpreters should not:

- pass on confidential information;
- reply to or answer a question (this is the job of the facilitator);
- give any personal opinion on a topic of the workshop (interpreters are not participants).

Pre-workshop briefing meeting

Pre-reading

Your participants (and interpreters) will appreciate a handout with the title of your workshop, your name, role and organization, and your key headings. If possible give interpreters materials at least one week prior to your workshop. Do not assume that it has all been read and understood. Interpreters are often very overworked in organizations. Do not expect your interpreter to make up for your lack of preparation. Prepare before a meeting; listen to their advice and be prepared to adapt.

Pre-workshop meetings

Meet with interpreters to discuss and agree on some ground rules of communication. Never walk into a workshop without preparation; it is unfair to everyone, including the participants. Give interpreters an overview of the purpose and desired outcomes of your workshop, and show them the main headings. Discuss:

- the characteristics of the participants;
- the names of important participants, appropriate titles, honorifics and other ways of showing respect;

● greetings and ways of introducing people in the cultures which will be represented: for example, will participants nod, bow, shake hands or put palms together?
● who will introduce who, and in what language;
● the tone and degree of formality required;
● potential cultural, political or gender issues which could divide rather than unite a group.

If there is a range of speaking abilities in the group, ensure that everything is translated to help the participants who are less skilled linguistically. Discuss and agree on signals between one another so there are no surprises during your workshop. For example, an interpreter could frown to signal non-understanding or raise a hand to signal to you to slow down.

Explain idioms and metaphors you want to use, and check that they are culturally suitable. Ask the interpreter to suggest useful metaphors. Discuss technical words and phrases which might not have a direct translation, such as 'empowerment'. You may need to discuss how to explain them.

Raise any contentious or potentially embarrassing issues you will be addressing that may need extra-careful phraseology or explanation. Discuss with the interpreter the usage (or non-usage) of sensitive words and local pseudonyms for (for example) contraception, sex, gender, virginity, menstruation, circumcision and HIV/AIDS.

During your conversation interpreters have an opportunity to listen to your personal way of speaking, intonation, emphasis and volume (and vice versa). All speakers have their own particular way of speaking. Also there are many dialects: Australian, American, Canadian, South African and Singaporean English are all dialects of English.

Prepare examples and case studies that are relevant to your participants. If necessary check these with your interpreter, or ask for examples and case stories from participants in advance. (See Chapter 5 for further discussion of metaphors, stories and so on.)

If you wish to show a film, PowerPoint slides or overhead projector transparencies in a foreign language, show them to the interpreter beforehand. If possible ensure that diagrams are bilingual, and that the interpreter understands the diagrams. Visual literacy varies tremendously from one individual to another, and you may have to teach participants how to read a diagram (see Chapter 6).

Plan varieties of interaction such as paired discussions early in your workshops to enable participants to speak in their own language (if necessary), generate examples, complete short exercises, and think of issues and solutions. Keep people actively involved.

> ## STORY: NEED FOR AGREEMENT BEFOREHAND
>
> In one NGO in Vientiane, Lao PDR, I asked a staff member whom I did not know very well to translate during my forthcoming workshop. I grinned. 'The manager said you were the best person for the job, and he said you are the most fluent English and Lao speaker in the group.' The staff member said, 'Oh, but they (the Lao staff) don't need translations.' I replied that some did not, but translation would make it easier for a small minority to follow what was happening in the workshop. I added I was concerned as I would be using some abstract terms. She agreed to be the interpreter.
>
> During the workshop she stopped interpreting and it was a little embarrassing. She even sat down, so every time I explained something abstract I looked at her and said, 'Please interpret', which she did. But her heart did not seem to be in it. I sensed there was some passive resistance on her part. I could not confront her in front of the group, as it would have been very embarrassing. I felt I could not ask the group members directly whether they wanted her to interpret, as the minority with lesser English might feel embarrassed to admit they needed help. (Often I have had private thanks from individuals saying they appreciated having an interpreter.)
>
> Later, I asked her why she had stopped translating. She replied, 'Oh, I looked at the group and they looked as if they understood.' I was very surprised and pointed out that by looking at faces you could not make the assumption that all of them did understand, and that indeed in the room there were people with a broad spread of linguistic ability.

I did not feel I really got to the bottom of her reasoning. Perhaps she thought I was putting the Lao staff down by suggesting that their English was not good enough. My intentions were to help the Lao staff to learn something new. Workshops can be tiring at the best of times. Workshops that are conducted totally in a foreign language are even more tiring. Also the translation process helps to slow communication down. It aids assimilation of new ideas and gives people think time.

I learnt later from the experience that there has to be total understanding and trust between speaker and interpreter. Again this story illustrates the importance of adequate preparation time and a chance for both parties to list all the issues involved.

At the beginning of a workshop

The role of the interpreters should be explained to the participants. In development work in many instances a local counterpart or programme officer may perform an administrative role with a group as well as an interpreting role. If possible it is better to split the roles of programme officer and interpreter; however this is rarely financially feasible. In other instances a local counterpart who is multilingual may become the front facilitator, with you 'backstopping' where necessary.

During the workshop: body language

Remember you are on show all the time. Watch your body language. Always treat people with respect. Do not start speaking to others whilst your interpreter is speaking to the group.

It is important that both facilitators and interpreters look at the whole of the audience and maintain eye contact (not with each other) in order to engage their listeners. Both interpreters and facilitators may be drawn to look towards the most powerful people in the room, and forget to maintain contact with all participants. It is important to keep looking around the room, to make eye contact with as many people as possible.

Look at Figure 10.1 to gain an overview of the stages that an interpreter must go through in comprehending your words and converting them into a meaningful translation. It is a complicated and often underestimated process. Be comfortable with silences at the end of your statements, and allow the interpreter time to compute what you have said.

Use the active voice unless the identity of the actors is not clear or you are trying to depersonalize a contentious issue. Avoid humour that puts down or discounts members or that can be misinterpreted. Choose words that give equal recognition to all participants: for example, do not always use 'he'; use 'they' wherever possible, or 'he/she'. Indeed it is clearer to use proper nouns or other nouns rather than pronouns.

Managing energy levels

Make sure there is water available for the interpreter, facilitator and participants. Interpreting is very tiring, so have stand-up two-minute stretch breaks if possible every 30 minutes and proper breaks every hour. Do not engage the interpreter in further interpreting during the breaks.

Use of local language

It is always useful to learn a few words of the local language. Even 'hello' in the local language and a smile will help to make contact with your participants.

In contrast to the above, some facilitators wish to develop empathy by speaking a few words of the local language to the audience, in the middle of a workshop, thereby showing that at least they know a few words. While this may help the facilitator and the participants, it can be quite disconcerting for the interpreter who is expecting the speaker to use English exclusively. Also there is a quandary. Should the local words be translated or not? It breaks up the sequence of the sentences for the interpreter. Again this issue should be discussed at the briefing meeting.

Debriefing experiential learning activities

Since experiential learning takes some participants out of their comfort zone, it helps if you ensure that the debriefing comments are clear. When I was working in Lao PDR with government officials, the facilitator scribed in English and the Lao Polytechnic staff took turns to scribe in the Lao language. The same two alternating colours were used so that participants could read either the English or the Lao versions. Many participants took notes in both English and Lao, and reported that this helped them to develop their English vocabulary. (See photo on my website, www. hogans.id.au)

The mutual misunderstanding zone

Body language

Watch the body language of participants carefully. Listen to your intuition. If you see eyes changing focus or eyebrows frowning, stop and go back.

Misunderstandings: critical incident

In a workshop in Australia a participant turned to some Aboriginal parti-cipants and said, 'All you indigenous mob are communists'. When the facilitator probed, it turned out that what the person meant was, 'You have group or collectivist values: your family and members of your kinship group and mutual sharing are so important to you.'

There will be times when communication breaks down. This is nor-mal, and is sometimes called the 'mutual misunderstanding zone'. It is important not to seek a quick-fix solution, but to try to delve into the causes of the misunderstanding. (Some of the stories later in the chapter illustrate this point.) If necessary call for a break, as it is hard to unravel meaning sometimes in front of the group. You may feel frustrated and even exasperated, but watch your body language (see Table 10.1).

Table 10.1   The mutual misunderstanding zone

Common feelings	*Underlying problems*	*Desirable behaviours*	*Desired state*
frustration	different	patience	shared perspectives
confusion	perspectives	perseverance	shared framework of
perplexity	competing frames	tolerance	understanding
anxiety	of reference	sense of humour	
exasperation	tiredness		
	overload of new		
	data		

Do not show annoyance or lose your temper, or you will lose face. Stay calm, and above all keep a sense of humour. Never become irritated with interpreters, as you don't know what it is like to be in the middle.

> You cannot always rely *totally* on interpreters, that they have understood and conveyed your message and back again, so it is vital that you keep watching the body language of the participants … indeed in one workshop a man in the group watched the confusion and spotted the communication breakdown before we did … so he became a kind of 'emergent interpreter.'

Development worker working with
minority groups in northern Myanmar

STORY: SEMANTICS

In one workshop I was asked to teach lecturers about writing objectives. I asked the interpreter to translate a handout into Lao about the types of verbs to use and those to avoid. I also indicated that it was useful to use a lead-in sentence, along the lines of, 'At the end of this session, participants will be able to: …'

The teaching point was that when writing objectives it is desirable to use 'action verbs' like 'describe', 'compare' and 'evaluate' rather than vague verbs like 'know' 'understand' and 'appreciate'. The workshop was going well, until we reached the stage of useful and non-useful verbs. I emphasized the need to use action verbs and avoid verbs like 'to know' A long discussion ensued. I sat down, thinking that the interpreter knew what she was doing and understood the material – and she did. After a while I was puzzled: it seemed like the participants were really unhappy about something. The interpreter told me that the participants insisted that you had to be able to use the verb 'to know'. I was very puzzled and didn't know what question to ask to clarify the issue.

It was close to lunchtime, and everyone was getting tired, so I called for a break. We were in the 'misunderstanding zone'. During lunch I sat with the interpreter and asked what was going on. It materialized that in the Lao language, in order to make sense the lead-in sentence had to be phrased as 'At the end of this session participants *will be able to know how to:*' . Of course this language construction was fine, but the interpreter had been following my directive exactly, and assumed she could not use the verb 'to know'. After lunch the situation was clarified immediately. The Lao lecturers proceeded with their lead-in sentence and were happy not to use the verb 'to know' as the infinitive after the lead-in sentence.

STORY: SOME CONFUSING TIMES IN THE SHAN AND THAI LANGUAGES

The Shan tribe in Myanmar cannot speak Myanmar, so as Shan is similar to Thai, Thai interpreters are called in. But sometimes closeness can be a problem. There are so many different subtribes that sometimes it is impossible to avoid confusion.

You know there are big problems of identity. They see me as 'them'. I tried to do research and it was hopeless until I employed five local staff. They do not like outsiders. I am from the city, so I am so different from them. Villagers feel uncomfortable and excluded if we use English words. We have to be much more polite with our body language and tone in how we greet people, especially elders. We have to sit with them for a long time to establish our credibility. We always watch the body language of the locals so carefully, even with interpreters.

Nilar Myaing, Myanmar development worker in Yangon

Visual aids

Introduce a visual aid, saying for example, 'This is a plan (or a cross-section or side view) of ...' to help the interpreter and participants to read the visual aid. Explain the axes on graphs before talking about content. Explain units of measurement. If you are planning to have graphics in two languages, remember to allow plenty of space for information, as the translation may take up more than double the space of the English explanation.

Stopping to draw on flipcharts helps your participants. It gives a breathing space in the mass of language people are trying to digest.

Remember there will be some people in the group who learn more by seeing visuals than by hearing words. (See also Chapter 6.)

At the end of a workshop

Thank the interpreter in front of the group, and afterwards ask him/her for feedback and advice. Ask the audience to complete an evaluation with questions relating to the interpreting process, such as:

- Were you encouraged to ask questions?
- What did the interpreter do well?
- Do you have any suggestions for improvement for the interpreter?
- What did the facilitator do well?
- Do you have any suggestions for improvement for the facilitator?

Translating documents

Test questionnaires

It is always important to check translated documents and pre-test questionnaires.

> When I worked in Singapore I was involved in quite a few survey translations for the Asian region. The first time I used a translator for an Indonesian survey, I asked one of my Indonesian colleagues in Jakarta to test run the translated survey. Fortunately we discovered that some words in Bahasa Indonesia were no longer in use, and that new words had entered the language in a very short period of time: you almost had to live in the country to keep track of the changes. My (Indonesian) translator had moved to Singapore 10 years before, and she was also new to the jargon of an organizational survey company. So what actually happened? We designed a question in the survey about rating the organizational climate in our client organization. This was a key concept as we were trying to establish employees' perceptions about the corporate culture of the international organization across the globe, and how it was perceived in a recently acquired subsidiary in Jakarta. Apparently my Indonesian translator was not very familiar with the concept of 'Organizational Climate' and translated it as 'Environmental issues': a translation that my Indonesian colleague found very funny!
>
> (Thissen, 2005)

Back-translation

Translation is costly and needs to be built into budget planning. 'Back translation' is the process of a new translator translating a document that has already been translated into a foreign language back into the original language. This is essential when translating raw data from workshops and focus group discussions. (Focus group discussions (FGDs) are held with small groups of up to eight people. They are particularly useful for obtaining data on social norms and cultural expectations on various issues.) All the good work of a focus group facilitator in not 'interpreting' verbatim comments can be wiped out by a careless translator.

Back translation involves two separate translators. One translates a document from language A to language B. Another translates the output from language B back to language A. Because of its high cost, back translation is not very common, but in very high-risk areas it is well worth the investment. Back translation can improve the reliability and validity of research in different languages. In one story about voting instructions, 'Put an x in the square' which had supposedly been translated into Italian, was back translated 'put a crucifix in each piazza'.

Second translation

For important documents that are being translated into your own language, it may be necessary to allocate time and funds for a second translation by another translator. The outputs from each can then be compared and outstanding discrepancies in translation analysed.

Auto-translation

Auto-translation is increasing, with packages available on the internet. Their usage is not yet common as the meaning of certain words is often misunderstood by the translation program. The software tends to translate word by word, frequently resulting in gibberish, especially between dissimilar languages. For translation of short paragraphs see Babelfish at www.babelfish.altavista.com

Readability of handouts

Do not produce two physically separate handouts (one in English, and one in the other language) as it is very difficult to cross-reference. Type English on one page of A4 and the other language on the facing page. Number corresponding paragraphs identically in each language, so that the speaker can easily direct the attention of the participants to particular areas.

Keep paragraphs aligned with one another for easy comparison. Some languages need more space than English, so it helps to even things up by using for example, size 13 font for English and size 12 font for the other longer language version. Alternatively use one-and-a-half line spacing for the English and single spacing for the longer language.

For short documents such as a bilingual fire drill which contains short numbered commands, you could use landscape format, and a table with English and the other language side by side.

Text should be 12 point minimum and well spaced. It is the white space between print that aids readability. Remember you can use right-margin justification for English, but this is not possible for languages which string together many words.

Further reading

I can recommend *Do's and Taboos of using English around the World* by Roger Axtell (1995).

Appendix 1: Sample 'cultural values' cards

HEADING 1 Cultural values and behaviours that ARE part of my culture	**HEADING 2** Cultural values and behaviours that ARE part of my culture, but are DECREASING
HEADING 3 Cultural values and behaviours that ARE NOT part of my culture, but are INCREASING	**HEADING 4** Cultural values and behaviours that ARE NOT part of my culture
HEADING 5 Cultural values and behaviours that are NOT DISCUSSED openly	**HEADING 6** Don't know
Blank Add or rename your own card	**Blank** Add or rename your own card

A1 **INDIVIDUALISM 'I'** My goals, things, my way of dressing and doing things	A2 **COLLECTIVISM 'WE'** Our goals, things, our way of dressing and doing things
B1 **RESPECT** There are rules of behaviour and protocol	B2 **CASUAL POLITENESS** **Informality**
C1 **HIERARCHY** Many levels in society between the top and bottom	C2 **EQUALITY** Fewer levels, more equal treatment and access
D1 **CONTROL OVER** assertive, competitive people and nature	D2 **HARMONY WITH** cooperative, conflict-avoiding people and nature
E1 **INDIRECT COMMUNICATION** Speech is guarded. You are expected to take in information from whole context, body language, environment etc	E2 **DIRECT COMMUNICATION** Speech is open and to the point Rules, instructions, signs are explained in depth
F1 **KINSHIP SYSTEMS** *not* of major importance	F2 **KINSHIP SYSTEMS** determine marriage choices, place of residence, communication patterns

G1	G2
TASK ORIENTED	**RELATIONSHIP ORIENTED**
Get down to tasks quickly. Efficiency, success, on the move	Maintenance of relationships is more important than achieving goals

G3	G4
BEING ORIENTED	**HAVING ORIENTED**
Content to relax	Materialistic, possessions oriented

H1 TIME: FLEXIBLE	H2 TIME: TIGHT
Deadlines, appointments and punctuality are flexible	Deadlines, appointments and punctuality are important

I1 TIME: PAST ORIENTED	I2 TIME: PRESENT ORIENTED

I3 TIME: FUTURE ORIENTED	I4 TIME: FUTURE CYCLES ORIENTED
Forward thinking, planning, imagining	Seasons, rhythms of life and death

J1 RELIGIOUS/ SPIRITUAL VALUES	J2 SECULAR VALUES
permeate every aspect of society and daily life	Work separated from religion

K1 SHAME People behave well because they do NOT want to bring shame on their family, village and/or country	**K2 GUILT** Individuals' responsibility for wrongs. People behave well so they won't feel guilty inside
L1 **KARMA**	**L2** **FATE**
M1 UNIVERSALISM One way of doing things, ie our way, is transferable to all cultures	**M2 PARTICULARISM** There are many ways of 'doing things' in different cultures
N1 MULTICULTURALISM and rights of minority groups are valued	**N2 MONOCULTURALISM** is valued
O1 MULTILINGUALISM Languages of the main groups of people are valued and in use	**O2 MONOLINGUALISM** The language of the dominant group is valued and in main use
P1 RISK TAKING	**P1 RISK AVOIDING**

Appendix 2: Behaviour cards

There are an infinite number of possible behaviour cards, so they have been clustered into groups which can be used as a focus and stimulus for discussion in specific workshops. They include:

1. Verbal communication.
2. Listening and silence.
3. Writing.
4. Reading/access to information and technology.
5. Body language/space/feelings.
6. Time.
7. Performance/getting things done.
8. Food/drinking/dress/etiquette.
9. Family/gender issues/child rearing.
10. Community.

Space does not allow topics on the following pages to be reproduced as cards. But this is easily achieved using the 'Table' option in Microsoft Word or a similar program.

1 Verbal communication

1a Ideas discussed and decisions often made before meetings	1b Discussion and hearing different ideas valued in meetings
2a It is considered disrespectful to disagree with power holders in meetings and/or public	2b It is OK to disagree with power holders in meetings and/or public
3a It is OK to change decisions made during meetings as things change	3b It is NOT OK to change decisions after meetings
4a It is NOT OK to say 'I don't know'. People will think my family and I are stupid. We all lose face. It is better to make up something.	4b It is OK to say 'I don't know' and 'Let's find out'. Ongoing learning is seen as good.
5a Dialogue is seen as a way to discuss disagreements non-confrontationally	5b Debate is seen as a way of arguing 'for and against' ideas
6a Straight linear expression and sequencing of ideas is valued	6b Circuitous (circular) expression of ideas is valued
7a Asking people in authority questions in public is seen as rude	7b Asking questions of people in authority in public is NOT seen as rude
8a Storytelling as a skill is highly valued	8b Memory of traditional/cultural organizational stories is highly valued and gives a person status
9a Humour is used to manage life and everyday events and even in hardships	9b Humour and jokes are used to make fun of rules and rationality
10a Sexual jokes and innuendo are OK	10b Sexual jokes and innuendo are NOT OK
11a Swearing is tolerated except in very formal situations	11b Swearing is NOT tolerated anywhere

2 Listening and silence

12a Silence is valued as respectful listening (especially to those up the hierarchy)	12b Ability to generate ideas (no matter how crazy) is valued
13a High tolerance of silence during conversations and meetings. It's better to say nothing at times.	13b Low tolerance of silence during conversations and meetings
14a There is silence on some issues that are just not discussed openly, eg between members of the opposite sex and/or with strangers	Blank: Please add a cross-cultural behaviour issue or misunderstanding you would like to discuss

3   Writing

15a Verbal contracts and agreements are enough. People with good relationships don't have to write things down.	15b Written contracts (MOUs, TORs) are valued and seen as a sign of trust and commitment
16a Written plans and decisions are seen as binding. To change plans shows weakness/failure.	16b Written plans and decisions are NOT seen as binding and may be changed as the situation changes
17a Reluctance to put ideas in writing as documents are then seen as binding	17b Push to put ideas in writing, and documents are NOT seen as permanent. They can be added to and/or changed later.
18a Draft reports are NOT read carefully and detailed feedback is NOT given	18b Draft reports are carefully read and detailed feedback is given
19a Use of correct grammar/spelling is highly valued and a sign of respect	19b Use of correct grammar/spelling is not highly valued
20a Formal communication should be transmitted by writing (and possibly e-mail)	20b Formal communication should be conducted face to face

4   Reading

21a Literacy: reading is popular	21b Literacy: reading is unpopular
22a Diverse range of books are available	22b Limited range of books are available
22a Access to technology is easy and fast	22b Access to technology is difficult, slow, expensive
23a Education is highly valued	23b Education is NOT highly valued
24a Literacy includes being able to read the landscape, animal and human tracks	24b Literacy includes being able to read maps

5 Body language/space/feelings

25a It is good to be controlled, centred and calm, NOT loud	25b It is good to show emotions like enthusiasm and speak louder and faster if excited
26a Feelings: emotive reasoning (feelings) and explanations valued	26b Facts/data: rational reasoning (facts) and explanations valued
27a It is NOT OK to show negative emotions	27b It is OK to show negative emotions
28a Direct eye contact is seen as disrespectful to authority figures	28b Direct eye contact is seen as respectful and as a sign of listening
29a Personal privacy is valued. 'I need my own space.'	29b Personal privacy is not important. 'You can walk in any time.'

6 Time

41a Finishing projects by deadlines is NOT seen as important. 'We can renegotiate deadlines.'	41b Finishing projects by deadlines is seen as very important and evidence of good time management
42a Punctuality is important	42b Punctuality is NOT important

7 Performance/getting things done

43a Results need to be shown in the short term and quickly	43b Results are seen as achievements in the long term, perhaps generations
44a We like things to be fixed, unchanging, with clear-cut rules and directions	44b We like things to change. We restructure organizations, move jobs and houses frequently.
45a Astrologers and/or *feng shui* experts sought for advice (on decisions and dates, etc)	45b Astrologers and/or *feng* shui experts are NOT sought for advice (on decisions and dates, etc)
46a Use of small gifts as facilitation payments to get the job done is accepted practice	46b Bribery and small gifts to get the job done is NOT accepted practice
47a People gain power and respect as they get older	47b People lose power and respect as they get older
48a Promotion is through longevity of service	48b Promotion is through performance and demonstration of skills and initiative
49a Promotion is through who you know	49b Promotion is NOT related to who you know

8 Food/drinking/dress and etiquette

50a Locals wearing their national dress is valued/required for official business	50b Locals wearing their national dress IS NOT valued/required for official business
51a Wearing of local national dress by foreigners/outsiders is valued (if they do it right)	51b Wearing of local national dress by foreigners/outsiders is NOT valued
52a Fast departures and leave taking at the end of a meeting or meal are OK	52b Fast departures and leave taking at the end of a meeting or meal are NOT OK
53a Making eating noises and burping is OK	53b Making eating noises and burping is NOT OK
54a Covering the mouth with hands while chewing food is seen as polite	54b Covering the mouth with hands while chewing food is NOT necessary
55a Formal etiquette for greetings and farewells to people in authority	55b Informal etiquette for greetings and farewells to people in authority
56a Drinking alcohol together is used to relax and communicate informally	56b Drinking alcohol is frowned upon for religious or other reasons
57a Food sharing is an important way of getting to know others	57b Food sharing is NOT an important way of getting to know others
58a Respect: showing respect is highly important for parents, elders, people in high positions	58b Respect: all plant and animal life is respected
59a Personal distance from others is important. 'We like to stand/sit at a distance from others.'	59b Personal closeness with others is important. 'We like to stand or sit close to others when we are talking with them.'
60a Ritual dancing according to intricate cultural rules is highly valued	60b Dancing freely in response to music/drumming is highly valued
61a Dancing is performed as a form of worship	61b Dancing is frowned upon

9   Gender/family/child rearing

30a Men have most of the power in the home	30b Women have most power in the home
31a Equal power for men and women in the home	31b Children have little power in the home
32a Women are seen as the teachers/transmitters of cultural values and behaviours	32b Men are seen as the teachers/transmitters of cultural values and behaviours
33a Sex before marriage is frowned upon	33b Sex before marriage is OK
34a Having children outside marriage is frowned upon	34b Having children outside marriage is OK
35a Child rearing: children are allowed a lot of freedom	35b Child rearing involves strict control. They must show respect to elders.
36a Lack of tolerance of homosexual relationships	36b Tolerance of homosexual relationships
37a It's OK between people of the same sex to sit close together, hold hands, link arms, etc	37b It's NOT OK for people of the same sex to sit close together, hold hands, link arms, etc
38a Kissing in public is NOT OK	38b Kissing in public is OK
39a Family members are important	39b Ancestors are important
40a Pregnancy and sexual issues are talked about openly	40b Pregnancy and sexual issues are NOT talked about openly

10   Community

62a It is our duty to help outsiders	62b We do NOT feel responsible for helping outsiders
63a Sport is a major leisure activity (to watch and/or take part)	63b Sport is NOT a major leisure activity (to watch and/or take part)
64a Men have most of the power in community issues and decision making	64b Equal power for men and women in community issues and decision making
65a Women have most of the power in community issues and decision making	65b Women have indirect/unseen power in community issues and decision making
66a Community spirit, joint activities and helping each other are important	66b Community spirit and activities and helping each other are NOT important

References

Abdullah, A (1996) *Going Local: Cultural dimensions in Malaysian management*, Malaysian Institute of Management, Kuala Lumpur, Malaysia

Abdullah, A (2001) *The Influence of Values on Management in Malaysia*, PhD thesis, Universiti Kebangsaan, Bangi, Malaysia

Abdullah, A and Pedersen, P B (2003) *Understanding Multicultural Malaysia: Delights, puzzles and irritations*, Prentice-Hall, Pearson Malaysia, Selangor, Malaysia

Abdullah, A and Shephard, P (2000) *The Cross Cultural Game*, Brain Dominance Technologies, Kuala Lumpur, Malaysia

Adler, N (1997) *International Dimensions of Organisational Behaviour*, 3rd edn, International Thomson Publishing, Cincinnati, USA

Agerbeck, B (2004) *Introduction to Graphic Facilitation* [Online] www.Loosetooth.com [accessed 26 March 2006]

Alia, V (2006) *Names and Nunavut: Culture and Identity in Arctic Canada*, Berghahn Books, New York

Argyris, C and Schön, D (1994) *Theory in Practice: Increasing organizational effectiveness*, Jossey-Bass, San Francisco, USA

Argyris, C, Putnam, R and Smith, D M (1985) *Action Science*, Jossey-Bass, San Francisco, USA

Arnstein, S R (1969) A ladder of citizen participation in the USA, *Journal of the American Planning Association*, 35 (4), pp 216–24

Ashmore, B (2000) *Mapping our World*, Oxfam GB, Oxford, UK

Axtell, R E (1995) *Do's and Taboos of Using English Around the World*, Wiley, New York

Baldwin, S (2002) *The Playful Adult: 500 ways to lighten your spirit and tickle your soul*, In Sights Training and Consulting, Stillwater, USA

Baldwin, S (2005) *Lighten Up And Live Longer: Jokes, anecdotes, and stories guaranteed to tickle your soul*, In Sights Training and Consulting, Stillwater, USA

Barben, M L and Ryter, E (eds) (2005) *Gender Training: Mainstreaming gender quality and the planning, realisation and evaluation of training programmes*, Swiss Agency for Development and Cooperation and Federal Dept of Foreign Affairs Bern, Switzerland [Online] www.deza.ch/resources/deza_product_ en_1519.pdf [accessed 25 August 2005]

Beasley, C and Hogan, C F (2003) *Cultural Dimensions of Australian and Overseas Students*, Edith Cowan University Staff Development Workshop, Perth, Western Australia

Bennett, J M and Bennett, M J (2004) Developing intercultural sensitivity: An integrative approach to global and domestic diversity, in *Handbook of Intercultural Training*, 3rd edn, ed D Landis, M B Janet and M J Bennett, Sage, Thousand Oaks, Calif, USA, pp 147–65

Bhutan Planning Department (2004) *Tshodgu: The people's assembly*, video, Royal Government of Bhutan, Thimphu, Bhutan

Blackman, R (2003) *Project Cycle Management Roots 5*, Tearfund, Teddington, UK [Online] tilz.tearfund.org/webdocs/Tilz/Roots/English/PCM/PCM_E.pdf [accessed 20 September 2005]

Blainey, J, Davis, K and Goodwill, B (1995) *Valuing Diversity: Facilitating cross cultural communication and conflict resolution*, Working Together (Aust), Frenchs Forest, NSW, Australia

Bohm, D, Factor, D and Garrett, P (1995) *Dialogue: A proposal* [Online] World.std.com/~lo/bohm/0001.html [accessed 10 November 2003]

Braden, S and Huong, T (1998) *Video for Development: A casebook from Vietnam*, Oxfam, Oxford, UK

Bradley, S (1994) *How People Use Pictures*, IIED/British Council, London

Brant, L and Harvey, T (2001) *Choosing and Using Music in Training: A guide for trainers and teachers*, Gower, Aldershot, UK

Brenson-Lazán, G (2003) *The Evolution of Conflict and the Facilitation of its Resolution*, Second Chinese Facilitator's Conference, Taipei, Taiwan

Brislin, R W (1981) *Cross-Cultural Encounters, Face-To-Face Interaction*, Pergamon Press, New York

Brislin, R W (2000) *Understanding Culture's Influences on Behaviour*, 2nd edn, Harcourt College Publishers, Fort Worth, USA

Byram, M (1997) *Teaching and Assessing Intercultural Competence*, Multi-cultural Matter, Clevedon, UK

Chakrabarti, S (2005) *Sangam: Inclusive leadership*, Isahar Multicultural Centre for Women's Health, Perth, Western Australia

Chakraborty, S K (ed) (1995) *Human Values for Managers*, Wheeler Publishing, New Delhi, India

Chambers, R (1983) *Rural Development: Putting the last first*, Longman Scientific and Technical, Harlow, UK

Chambers, R (2002) *Participatory Workshops: A sourcebook of 21 sets of ideas and activities*, Earthscan, London

Chambers, R (2005) *Ideas for Development*, Earthscan, London

Chang, S (2002) Cultural dimensions workshop handout, University of Melbourne, Australia

Chase, M, Price, J, Swaby, S and Braden, S (1999) 'Finding a voice through analysis of the everyday experience of poverty,' *PLA Notes*, IIED London (34), pp 31–36

Chasin, R (1986) Exercise on stereotyping, *Public Conversations Project* [Online] www.publicconversations.org/pcp/resources/resources.asp [accessed 12 March 2006]

Choi, C J and Mihaela, K (1995) *Cultural Competencies: Managing co-operatively across cultures*, Dartmouth, Aldershot, UK

Cilliers, F (2004) A person-centered view of diversity in South Africa, *Person-Centered Journal*, 11 (1–2), pp 33–47

Consedine, J (1995) *Restorative Justice: Healing the effects of crime*, Plough-shares, Lyttleton, New Zealand

Cooke, B and Kothari, U (eds) (2001) *Participation: The new tyranny?*, Zed Books, London

Cooney, J and Burtin, K (1986) *Photolanguage Australia: Human values, a manual for facilitators*, Catholic Education Office, Sydney, Australia

Coover, V, Esser, C, Deacon, E and Moore, C (1977) *Resource Manual for a Living Revolution*, New Society Publishers, Philadelphia, USA

Cranny-Francis, A, Waring, W, Stavropoulos, P and Kirby, J (2003) *Gender Studies: Terms and debates*, Palgrave Macmillan, Basingstoke, UK

Dalrymple, W (2005) Celebrate diversity, *Time*, 15–22 August, p 92

Davies, J (1991) The musical mind: how do we perceive music? Do Mahler and Madonna have anything in common? *New Scientist*, 129 (1752)

Davies, R J (1998) *Order and Diversity: Representing and assisting organisational learning in non-government aid organisations*, PhD thesis, University of Wales, Swansea, Wales [Online] www.mande.co.uk/thesis.htm

Davies, R and Dart, J (2005) *The 'Most Significant Change' (MSC) Technique: A guide to its use* [Online] www.mande.co.uk/docs/MSCGuide.htm/ [accessed December 2006]

de Bono, E (1985) *Six Thinking Hats*, Penguin, London

de Bono, E (1987) *The CoRT Thinking Process*, Pergamon Press, London

Deal, R and Jones, M (2005) *Koala Company*, Innovative Resources, Bendigo, Australia

Deal, R and Masman, K (2003) *Stones Have Feelings Too*, card pack, Innovative Resources, Melbourne, Australia

Deal, R and Veeken, J (1997) *The Bears*, St Luke's Innovative Resources, Bendigo, Australia

Dick, B (1984) *Helping Groups to Be Effective: Skills, processes and concepts for group facilitation*, 2nd edn, Interchange, Chapel Hill, Australia

Dick, B and Dalmau, T (1994) *To Tame a Unicorn: Recipes for cultural intervention*, 3rd edn, Interchange, Chapel Hill, Australia

DiStefano, J J and Maznevski, M L (2000) Creating value with diverse teams in global management, *Organisational Dynamics*, 29 (1), pp 45–63

Downs, S (1981) *How Do I Learn?* Further Education and Curriculum Review and Development Unit, London

Downs, S (1995) *Learning at Work: Effective strategies for making learning happen*, Kogan Page, London

Downs, S and Perry, P (1984) *Developing Skilled Learners: Learning to learn in YTS*, Manpower Services Commission and Occupational Research Unit, University of Wales Institute of Science and Technology, Research and Development, No 22

Dresser, N (1996) *Multicultural Manners: New rules of etiquette for a changing society*, Wiley, New York

Dudley, E and Haaland, A (eds) (1993) *Communicating building for safety*, Cambridge Architectural Research Ltd Intermediate Technology Publications [Online] web.mit.edu/urbanupgrading/upgrading/issues-tools/tools/Providing-info.html [accessed 3 January 2006]

Earley, C and Ang, S (2003) *Cultural Intelligence: Individual interactions across cultures*, Stanford, Palo Alto, Calif, USA

Emery, M (1976) *Searching for New Directions, in New Ways, for New Times*, Australian National University, Canberra, Australia

Epstein, S (1999) *A Manual for Culturally Adapted Social Marketing*, Sage, USA

Featherstone, D (1987) *Babakiueria*, video, ABC International Sydney, Australia, 27 minutes [Online] www.abc.net.au

Festinger, L (1957) *A Theory of Cognitive Dissonance*, Stanford University Press, Stanford, Calif, USA

Finlay, M and Hogan, C F (1995) Who will bell the cat? Storytelling techniques for people who work with people in organisations, *Training and Management Development Methods*, 9, pp 6.01–6.18

Fisher, R and Brown, S (1989) *Getting Together: Building relationships as we negotiate*, Penguin, Harmondsworth, UK

Freire, P (1972) *Pedagogy of the Oppressed*, Penguin, Harmondsworth, UK

Freire P (1997) *Pedagogy of Hope: Reliving pedagogy of the oppressed*, Continuum, New York

Fussell, D and Haaland, A (1976) *Communicating with Pictures in Nepal: Report of a study by National Development Service and UNICEF*, UNICEF, Kathmandu, Nepal

Gardenswartz, L, Rowe, A, Dign, P and Bennett, M (2003) *The Global Diversity Desk Reference: Managing an international workforce*, Pfeiffer, San Francisco, USA

Gastil, J and Levine, P (eds) (2005) *Deliberative Democracy Handbook: Strategies for effective civic engagement in the twenty-first century*, Jossey-Bass [Online] www.deliberative-democracy.net/handbook/ [accessed 15 December 2006]

GATT-Fly (1983) *Ah-hah! A new approach to popular education*, Between the lines, Toronto, Canada

Gaver, B, Dunne, T and Pacenti, E (1999) Cultural probes, *Interactions*, Jan–Feb, pp 21–29

Geschka, H, Schaude, G R and Schlicksupp, H (1973) Modern techniques for solving problems, *Chemical Engineering*, 6 (80), pp 91–97

Ginzburg, O (2004) *The Hungry Man*, Hungry Man Books, Bangkok, Thailand [Online] www.hungrymanbooks.com [accessed 3 February 2006]

Ginzburg, O (2005) *There You Go*, Hungry Man Books, Bangkok, Thailand [Online] www.hungrymanbooks.com [accessed 3 February 2006]

Goldberger, N R, Tarule, J M, Clinchy, B M V and Belenky, M F (eds) (1996) *Knowledge, Difference and Power: Essays inspired by women's ways of knowing*, Basic Books, New York

Goleman, D (1996) *Emotional Intelligence*, Bloomsbury, London

Gordon, T (2005) *Global Villages: The globalization of ethnic display*, DVD, 59 mins, Tourist Gaze Productions, New York

Government of Western Australia (2006) *Working Together: Involving community and stakeholders in decision-making*, Department of the Premier and Cabinet, Perth, Western Australia [Online] www. citizenscape.wa.gov.au [accessed 30 December 2006]

Graham, D (1989) *1905 Act*, video, 15 mins, Institute of Applied Aboriginal Studies, Edith Cowan University, Perth, Western Australia

Grove, C and Hallowell, W (2002) *Randōmia Balloon Factory*, Intercultural Press, Yarmouth, Maine, USA

Hall, E T and Hall, M R (1990) *Understanding Cultural Differences*, Intercultural Press, Yarmouth, Maine, USA

Hammond, S A (1996) *The Thin Book of Appreciative Inquiry*, 2nd edn, Thin, Plano, USA

Havet, J (1987), Cartoons, *Development Dialogue*, 2, pp 128–48

Heaney, S (2001) The bridge, in *Electric Light*, Farrar, Straus & Giroux, New York, p 65

Heron, J (1989) *The Facilitator's Handbook*, Kogan Page, London

Heron, J (1993) *Group Facilitation: Theories and models for practice*, Kogan Page, London

Heron, J (1999) *The Complete Facilitator's Handbook*, Kogan Page, London

Heslop, M (2002) *Participatory Research with Older People: A sourcebook*, Help Age International, London [Online] www.helpage.org [accessed 22 September 2005]

Hofstede, G (1980) *Culture's Consequences: International differences in world-related values*, Sage, Beverley Hills, USA

Hofstede, G (1991) *Cultures and Organizations: Software of the mind*, McGraw-Hill, Maidenhead, UK

Hofstede, G H (2001) *Culture's Consequences: Comparing values, behaviours, institutions, and organizations across nations*, Sage, Thousand Oaks, Calif, USA

Hofstede, G J, Pedersen, P B and Hofstede, G (2002) *Exploring Culture: Exercises, stories and synthetic cultures*, Intercultural Press, Yarmouth, Maine, USA

Hogan, C F (1999) *Facilitating Learning: Practical strategies for college and university*, Eruditions, Melbourne, Australia

Hogan, C F (2000) *Facilitating Empowerment: A handbook for facilitators, trainers and individuals*, Kogan Page, London

Hogan, C F (2002) *Understanding Facilitation: Theory and principles*, Kogan Page, London

Hogan, C F (2003) *Practical Facilitation: A toolkit of techniques*, Kogan Page, London

Hogan, C F (2005) *Working Better in Aboriginal and Torres Strait Islander Health: Train the trainer workshop resources*, Aboriginal Health Council of Western Australia, Perth, Western Australia

Holmes, A (1963) *A Study of Understanding of Visual Symbols in Kenya*, OVAC, London

Honey, P and Mumford, A (1986) *Using your Learning Styles*, Peter Honey, Maidenhead, UK

Honey, P and Mumford, A (1992) *The Manual of Learning Styles*, 3rd edn, Peter Honey, Maidenhead, UK

Hooker, J (2003) *Working Across Cultures*, Stanford University Press, Stanford, USA

Hopson, B and Scally, M (1984), *Build Your Own Rainbow: A workbook for career and life management*, Lifeskills Associates, Leeds, UK

Hopson, B and Scally, M (1986) *Lifeskills Teaching Programmes No 3*, Lifeskills Associates, Leeds, UK

Horn, R E (1999) *Visual Language: Global communication for the 21st century*, MacroVU Press, Washington, USA

Howard, S (ed) (2003) *Asian Words of Wisdom*, Talisman, Singapore

Inglehart, R F, Basanez, M and Moreno, A (1998) *Human Values and Beliefs: A cross-cultural sourcebook*, University of Michigan Press, Michigan, USA

Jacobs, C (2005) *Don't Say Sorry*, video, 8 mins, Deadly Yarns Short Film Initiative, Film and TV Institute, Fremantle, Western Australia

James, R (2000) *The Transitional Learning Model: A handbook for training design with special application to cross cultural training*, e.works, Wangara, Australia

Jensen, E (2000) *Music with the Brain in Mind*, Brain Store, San Diego, USA

Kahane, A (2002) *Changing the World by Changing How We Talk and Listen* [Online] www.generonconsulting.com/Publications/Leader%20to %20Leader.pdf [accessed May 2005]

Kahane, A (2004) *Solving Tough Problems: An open way of talking, listening, and creating new realities*, Berrett-Koehler, San Francisco, USA

Kaiser, W L and Wood, D (2001) *Seeing Through Maps: The power of images to shape our world view*, ODT, Amherst, Mass, USA

Kaplan, A (2002) *Development Practitioners and Social Process: Artists of the invisible*, Pluto, London

Kataria, M (1999a) *Laugh for No Reason*, Madhuri International, Mumbai, India

Kataria, M (1999b) *Laugh Your Way to Health: Information guide to hasya yoga (laughter yoga)*, Madhuri International, Mumbai, India

Keating, C (2003) *Facilitation Toolkit: A practical guide for working more effectively with people and groups*, Government of Western Australia, Perth, Western Australia

Kettle, K C and Saul L (eds) (2004) *Guidelines for Managing the Integration of Culture into Development Programmes*, Asean Foundation and Southeast Asian Ministers Education Organisation, Bangkok, Thailand [Online] www.reliefweb.int/rw/rwt.nsf/db900SID/OCHA-6EXCYY/$File/SEAMEO_guidelines.pdf?OpenElement#search=%22%20%22Guidelines%20for%20Managing%20the%20Integration%20of%20Culture%20into%20Development%20Programmes%22%22 [accessed 2 September 2005]

Kettle, K C. and Saul, L (2006) *Guidelines for Managing the Integration of Culture into Development Programmes*, 2nd edn, Asean Foundation and Southeast Asian Ministers Education Organisation, Bangkok, Thailand

Kettle, K C, Hogan, C F, Tossa, W and Tunprawat, P (2005) *Managing the Integration of Culture into Development Workshop*, ASEAN Foundation-SPAFA, Yangon, Myanmar

Kim, H (1999) *Transcultural Customisation of International Training Programs: Problems and opportunities*, Garland, New York

Knowles, M S (1984) *The Adult Learner: The neglected species*, Gulf, Houston, USA

Kohls, L R and Knight, J M (1994) *Developing Intercultural Awareness: A cross-cultural training handbook*, 2nd edn, Intercultural Press, Yarmouth, Maine, USA

Kolb, D A (1984) *Experiential Learning: Experience as the source of learning and development*, Prentice-Hall, Englewood Cliffs, NJ, USA

Kotler, P, Roberto N and Lee N (2002) *Social Marketing: Improving the quality of life*, 2nd edn, Sage Publications, Thousand Oaks, Calif, USA

Kramer, J (2002) *The Other Final*, documentary video (1 hr 18 mins), Robot Communications, Netherlands

Kretzmann, J P and McKnight, J L (1993) *Building Communities from the Inside Out: A path toward finding and mobilizing a community's assets*, Center for Urban Affairs and Policy Research, Northwestern University, Evanston, USA

Landis, D, Bennett, J M and Bennett, M J (2004) *Handbook of Intercultural Training*, 3rd edn, Sage, Thousand Oaks, Calif, USA

Lane, H W, DiStefano, J J and Maznevski, M L (1997) *International Management Behaviour*, 3rd edn, Blackwell, Cambridge, Mass, USA

Lead International (2004) *Training Across Cultures: A handbook for trainers and facilitators working abroad*, Lead International, London

Lesley, E (2005) The hungry man chastises NGO bureaucracy, *Phnom Penh Post*, 10 March

Lewis, S (2006) *Race Against Time*, CBC Massey Lecture Series, House of Anansi Press, Toronto, Canada

Lindner, E G (2006) *Making Enemies, Humiliation and International Conflict: How the dynamics of humiliation are central to conflicts around the globe*, Greenwood, Oxford, UK

Linney, B (1995) *Pictures, People and Power: People-centred visual aids for development*, Macmillan, Basingstoke, UK

Linney, B and Wilson, B (1988) *The Copy Book: Copyright-free illustrations for development*, ITDG, London

Locust, C (2006) *The Talking Stick*, Native American Research and Training Center, Tucson, Ariz, USA [Online] www.acaciart.com/stories/archive6.html [accessed 16 May 2006]

Lonely Planet (2004) *Say What? Talk like a local without putting your foot in it*, Lonely Planet, Footscray, Australia

Luft, J and Ingham, H (1984) *Group Processes: An introduction to group dynamics*, 3rd edn, Mayfield, Palo Alto, Calif, USA

MacDonald, M R and Tossa, W (2004) *Folktales and Story Telling*, Mahasarakham University Storytelling Project, Mahasarakham, Thailand

Margulies, N and Valenza, C (2005) *Visual Thinking: Tools for mapping your ideas*, Crown House, Carmarthen, UK

Martin, M A (2003) *The Nature of the Lived Experience of Co-Facilitation: A phenomenological approach*, PhD thesis, School of Management, Curtin University of Technology, Perth, Western Australia

Maybury-Lewis, D (1992) Introduction, in *Millennium: Tribal wisdom and the modern world*, Viking, New York, p 7

McKeen, N, Salas, M and Tillmann, H (eds) (1998) *Games and Exercises: A manual for facilitators and trainers involved in participatory group events*, Visualisation in participatory programmes UNICEF-ESAPO, New York [Online] www.unssc.org/web1/services/downloads/Games%20&%20Exercises%20VIPP%20UNICEF.pdf [accessed 22 December 2005]

McLaren, J and Brown, H (eds) (1993) *The Raging Grannies Songbook*, New Society, Gabriola Island, USA

Meier, D (2000) *The Accelerated Learning Handbook: A creative guide to designing and delivering fast, more effective training programs*, McGraw-Hill, New York

Melamed, S (2005) Comedy of errors, *Cambodia Daily*, April

Merali, Z (2005) Are you seeing what I'm seeing? *New Scientist* (27), August, p 12

Milgram, S (1963) Behavioural study of obedience, *Journal of Abnormal and Social Psychology*, pp 371–78

Millbower, L (2000) *Training with a Beat: The teaching power of music*, Kogan Page, London

Miner, H (1956) Body ritual among the Nacirema, *American Anthropologist*, 58 (3) [Online] www.msu.edu/~jdowell/miner.html [accessed 1 May 2005]

Morgan, J (2003) *Long Life: Positive HIV stories of the Bambanani Women's Group*, Double Storey Press, Cape Town, South Africa

Morgan, S (1988) *My Place*, Fremantle Arts Centre Press, Fremantle, Australia

Mumford, A (1999) *How to Choose the Right Development Method*, Peter Honey, Maidenhead, UK

Nass, L (1998) *Facilitating Participation: Training materials for development workers*, ISODEC: Participatory methods training and information facility, Accra, Ghana

Nipporica Associates and Saphiere, D H (1997) *Ecotonos: A multicultural problem-solving simulation*, 2nd edn, Intercultural Press, Yarmouth, Maine, USA

Nolan, J (2005) *Interpretation: Techniques and exercises*, Multilingual Matters, Clevedon, UK

Nsitmane, R (2005) Memory boxes and Zulu culture, in *Never Too Small to Remember: Memory work and resilience in times of AIDS*, ed P Denis, Cluster Publications, Pietermaritzburg, South Africa

O'Hara-Deveraux, M and Johansen, R (1994) *Globalwork: Bridging distance, culture and time*, Jossey-Bass, San Francisco, USA

Office of Regional Advisor for Culture in Asia and the Pacific (2005) *Cultural Diversity Programming Lens Toolkit*, UNESCO, Bangkok, Thailand [Online] www.unescobkk.org/fileadmin/userupload/culture/Culturallens/CDPLToolkitAugustWorkshop.pdf [accessed 20 January 2005]

Owen, H (1992) *Open Space Technology: A user's guide*, Abbott, Potomac, USA

Owen, H (ed) (1995) *Tales from Open Space*, Abbott, Cabin John, Md, USA

Owen, H (1997) *Expanding Our Now: The story of open space technology*, Berrett-Koehler, San Francisco, USA

Owen, H and Stadler, A (1999) *Open Space Technology*, Berrett-Koehler, San Francisco, USA

Pasmore, W and Woodman, R (eds) (1987) *Research in Organisational Change and Development*, Vol 1, Jai Press, Conn, USA

Peavey, F (1994) Strategic questioning, in *Insight and Action: How to discover and support a life of integrity and commitment to change*, ed T Green, P Woodrow and F Peavey, New Society, Philadelphia, USA

Pretorius, M (2004) *An exploration of South African diversity dynamics*. Unpublished Master's dissertation, University of South Africa, Pretoria, South Africa

Radloff, A and Murphy, E (eds) (1992) *Teaching at University*, Department of Education Employment and Training, National Priority (Reserve) Fund Project, Perth, Western Australia

Reese, R (1997) *A Proactive-Interactive Approach to Bridging Cultural Differences* [Online] www.csupomona.edu/~rreese/MULTICULTURALhtml [accessed 6 November 2001]

Reese, R (2001) Building cultural bridges in schools: the colorful flags model, *Race, Ethnicity and Education*, 4 (3), pp 181–207

Reuvid, J (ed) (2006) *Working Abroad: The complete guide to overseas employment*, 26th edn, Kogan Page, London

Revans, R (1982) *The Origins and Growth of Action Learning*, Chartwell Bratt, Bromley, UK

Rifkin, W D (1999) A mime is a terrible thing to waste, *Training and Management Development Methods*, 13, pp 7.45–7.60

Roberts-Smith, L, Frey, R and Bessell-Browne, S (eds) (1990) *Working with Interpreters in Law, Health and Social Work*, National Accreditation Authority for Translators and Interpreters (NAATI), Perth, Western Australia

Rocha, E M (1997) A ladder of empowerment, *Journal of Planning, Education and Research* (17), pp 31–44

Röhr-Rouendaal, P (2006) *Where There Is No Artist: Development drawings and how to use them*, 2nd edn, Intermediate Technology, London, UK

Samovar, L A and Porter, R E (2004) *Communication Between Cultures*, 5th edn, Thomson Wadsworth, Belmont, Calif, USA

Sarkissian, W C A and Walsh, K (2000) *Community Participation in Practice: Workshop checklist*, 2nd edn, Institute for Sustainability and Technology Policy, Murdoch University, Murdoch, Perth, Western Australia

Satir, V (1983) *Conjoint Family Therapy*, Science and Behavior Books, Palo Alto, Calif, USA

Scharmer, C O (2001) Self-transcending knowledge: organizing around emerging realities, in *Managing Industrial Knowledge: Creation, transfer, and utilization*, ed D Teece, Sage, Thousand Oaks, Calif, USA

Scharmer, C O (in press) *Theory U: Leading profound innovation by presencing emerging futures* [Online] www.dialogonleadership.org/Theory%20U. pdf [accessed 30 December 2006]

Schein, E H (1987) *Process Consultation: Vol 2, Lessons for managers and consultants*, Addison-Wesley, Reading, Mass, USA

Schön, D A (1983) *The Reflective Practitioner: How professionals think in action*, Basic Books, New York

Schuman, S (2000) *The Meaning of Wilderness* [Online] www.storiesatwork. com [accessed 16 May 2005]

Schuman, S (ed) (2005) *International Association of Facilitators Group Facilitation Handbook*, Jossey-Bass, San Francisco, USA

Schwarz, R M (2002) *The Skilled Facilitator: A comprehensive resource for consultants, facilitators, managers, trainers and coaches*, new and rev edn, Jossey-Bass, San Francisco, USA

Scott Peck, M (1990) *The Different Drum: Community-making and peace*, Arrow, London

Sen, A (2005) *The Argumentative Indian: Writings on Indian history, culture and identity*, Penguin, London

Senge, P M (1990) *The Fifth Discipline: The art and practice of the learning organisation*, Doubleday, New York

Sher, B (1979) *Wishcraft: How to get what you really want*, Ballantine, New York

Shiny Bum Singers (1999) *The Tiny Shiny Bum Songbook: Work songs of the public service*, Boris Books, Canberra, Australia

Shiny Bum Singers (2000) *It's Been a Long Year: The second Shiny Bum song book*, Boris Books, Canberra, Australia

Shiny Bum Singers (2001) *They'll Go Ape at Our Procedures: The third Shiny Bum songbook*, Boris Books, Canberra, Australia

Shiny Bum Singers (2002) *Have You Been Told Lately?* Boris Books, Canberra, Australia

Shirts, G R (1975) *BaFá BaFá: A cross culture simulation*, Simulation Training Systems, San Diego, USA

Slovo, G (2002) *Red Dust*, W W Norton, New York

Sonneman, M R (1997) *Beyond Words: A guide to drawing out ideas*, Ten Speed Press, Berkeley, USA

Spencer, L (1989) *Winning Through Participation*, Kendall Hunt, Iowa, USA

Stanfield, R (ed) (1997) *The Art of Focussed Conversation: 100 ways to access wisdom in the workplace*, Canadian Institute of Cultural Affairs, Toronto, Canada

Strachan, D (2006) *Making Questions Work: A guide to what and how to ask for facilitators, consultants, managers, coaches, and educators*, Jossey Bass/ Wiley, San Francisco, USA

Strang, H and Braithwaite, J (eds) (2001) *Restorative Justice and Civil Society*, Cambridge University Press, Cambridge, UK

Stringer, D M and Cassidy, P A (2003) *Fifty-two Activities for Exploring Values Differences*, Intercultural Press, Yarmouth, Maine, USA

Teaching, and Learning Committee (1999) *Teaching with Diversity Checklist*, University of Western Australia [Online] www.acs.uwa.edu.au/csdtl/ 99TDChecklist.htm [accessed 11 November 2003]

Templeton, R and Jackson, S (2004) *Tell Me Why*, Magabala Books, Broome, Australia

Thiagarajan, S and Thiagarajan, R (1990) *Barnga: A simulation game on cultural clashes*, Intercultural Press, Yarmouth, Maine, USA

Thissen, J (2005) Creating cross-cultural effectiveness, *Monthly e newsletter*, 5, Nov

Tony, K (2005) Frameworks and use of frameworks in community development, talk, Department of Health and Community Services, Perth, Western Australia

Trompenaars, F (1993) *Riding the Waves of Culture: Understanding cultural diversity in business*, Economist Books, London

Trompenaars, F and Hampden-Turner, C (1997) *Riding the Waves of Culture: Understanding cultural diversity in business*, 2nd edn, Nicholas Brealey, London

Trompenaars, F and Hampden-Turner, C (2000) *Building Cross-Cultural Competence*, Wiley, Chichester, UK

Trudgill, P (2003) *A Glossary of Sociolinguistics*, Edinburgh University Press, Edinburgh, Scotland

Vecchio, R P, Hearn, G and Southey, G (1992) *Organisational Behaviour: Life and work in Australia*, Harcourt Brace Jovanovich, Marrickville, Australia

Verghese, T (2003) Facilitating successfully with culturally diverse groups, workshop handout, Sixth Regional Facilitators Conference, Kuala Lumpur, Malaysia

Waisbord, S (2001) *Family Tree of Theories, Methodologies and Strategies in Development Communication: Convergences and differences*, Rockefeller Foundation [Online] www.comminit.com/strategicthinking/stsil viocomm/sld-1783.html [accessed 22 March 2006]

Watson, L (1995) Quoted in *Forest Trees and People Newsletter*, 26/27, April

Wehrli, U (2003) *Tidying up Art*, Prestel Munich, Germany

Wendt, J (1984) DIE: A way to improve communication, *Communication Education*, 33, pp 397–401

Westcott, J and Landau, J H (1997) *A Picture's Worth 1,000 Words: A workbook for visual communications*, Jossey-Bass, San Francisco, USA

Williams, R (2002) *Working in a Culturally Safe Environment: Introduction* [Online] www.flinders.edu.au/kokotinna/SECT04/OVERVW.HTM [accessed 5 January 2005]

Wilson, J (1961) *Authority and Leadership in a New Style Aboriginal Community: Pindan, Western Australia*, MA thesis, Department of Anthropology, University of Western Australia

Wong, T (2005) When does silence occur in counselling? 8th Annual IAF Asia Facilitator Conference, Kuala Lumpur, Malaysia

Index

Name Index